A Calm Place in the Storm

Buddhist Teachings on Finding Wisdom and Compassion

KARMA THINLEY RINPOCHE

Edited by Lama Jampa Thaye
and Karma Naljorma

© Norbu Publications

A CALM PLACE IN THE STORM
Buddhist Teachings on Finding Wisdom and Compassion
Karma Thinley Rinpoche

Published by
The Sumeru Press Inc. for Norbu Publications
PO Box 75, Manotick Main Post Office,
Manotick, ON, Canada K4M 1A2

Copyright © 2025 by Norbu Publications, the publishing name of
Kampo Gangra Drubgyudling, Toronto, Canada.

ISBN 978-1-998248-08-7 paperback / ISBN 978-1-998248-09-4 hardcover

Edited by Lama Jampa Thaye and Karma Naljorma
Illustrations and book cover © by Namkha Tashi (Christopher Banigan)
Illustrations © by Karma Thinley Rinpoche, pages 16, 80, 98, 112, 128
Front cover photo by Kirsty Chakravarty
Back cover and page 10 photos courtesy of Kampo Gangra Drubgyudling
Book design by Karma Yonten Gyatso

All rights reserved. No part of this book may be reproduced, stored in a retrieval system, or transcribed in any form or by any means—electronic, mechanical, photocopying, recording, or otherwise—without the prior written permission of the publisher.

LIBRARY AND ARCHIVES CANADA CATALOGUING IN PUBLICATION

Title: A calm place in the storm : Buddhist teachings on finding wisdom and compassion / Karma Thinley Rinpoche ; edited by Lama Jampa Thaye and Karma Naljorma.
Names: Karma Thinley, Rinpoche, 1931- author | Thaye, Jampa, 1952 - editor | Naljorma, Karma - editor.
Description: Includes bibliographical references.
Identifiers: Canadiana 20240524519 | ISBN 9781998248094 (hardcover) | ISBN 9781998248087 (softcover)
Subjects: LCSH: Tantric Buddhism—Doctrines.
Classification: LCC BQ8915.4 .K37 2024 | DDC 294.3/925—dc23

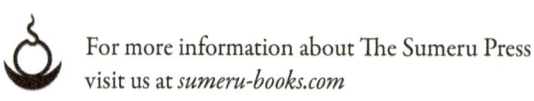

For more information about The Sumeru Press
visit us at *sumeru-books.com*

CONTENTS

Foreword 5
Editor's Preface 7
A Brief Biography of Karma Thinley Rinpoche 11

Introduction 17
1. Non-Sectarianism 21
2. Milarepa 25
3. Refuge 29
4. General Points 47
5. Bodhichitta 57
6. Loving-Kindness 61
7. Mahayana 65
8. Meat Eating 71
9. Lojong 81
10. The Four Limitless Thoughts 89
11. A Calm Mind 99
12. Shamatha 103
13. Vipashyana 113
14. Emptiness 121
15. The Spiritual Friend 125
16. Devotion 129
17. Vajrayana 133
18. The Three Yanas 143
19. Karma 169
20. Mandala Offering 173
21. Pilgrimage 189

Notes 207
Glossary 221
Editors' Biographies 227
Acknowledgments 229
Dedication 231

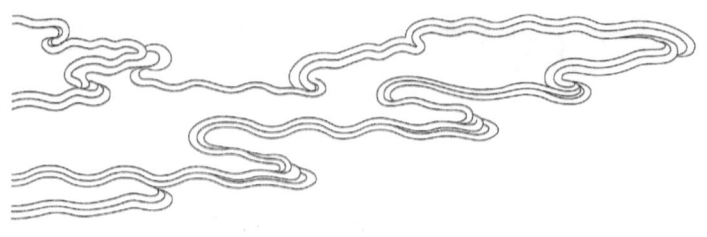

FOREWORD

This foreword was prepared for an edition planned at an earlier time, and is still relevant now as Rinpoche's book is finally published.

THE MARKET PLACE FOR BOOKS ON BUDDHISM is rather full these days but every so often one comes along which speaks right to the heart. Karma Thinley Rinpoche's *A Calm Place in the Storm* is one such work. This book will serve as both a crystal-clear introduction to Buddhist practice and as a friend that sustains us on the spiritual path. It is written out of the timeless wisdom of the Tibetan Buddhist tradition yet cuts to the bone of the contemporary situation. The central theme of *A Calm Place in the Storm* is the journey through the 'Three Vehicles' (Yanas) of Buddhism – a journey which takes us from the level of a beginner right up to the level of complete awakening. With dazzling mastery Rinpoche shows us the interdependence of the Shravakayana, Mahayana and Vajrayana and in particular how this last vehicle, the tantric vehicle, is the crowning glory of all Buddhist practice. Karma Thinley Rinpoche is well known in Tibetan circles as a leading scholar but in this work he presents the teaching in an easy and open manner making it accessible to all. In fact, the contents of this book have been gathered from dharma talks and other informal presentations made by Rinpoche in English for his students in Toronto and then edited in such a way as to preserve the essential flavour of Rinpoche's voice. Nevertheless, careful readers will notice how the work reflects Rinpoche's own contemplative and philosophical background, being replete as it is with references to such seminal works as the *Suhrlekha*, *Bodhisattvacharyavatara*, *Uttaratantrashastra*, and the *Kunzang Lame Zhallung*.

Lama Jampa Thaye
July 10th, 1994

EDITOR'S PREFACE

Up until the 1970's very few books about Buddhism had been published for the western reader, and exceptionally few on Tibetan Buddhism. However, as more lamas began to teach and reside in the West, interest increased, and many more books began to be published. Karma Thinley Rinpoche's first book in English, *The History of the Sixteen Karmapas of Tibet*, was published in 1980. A few years later, Rinpoche decided to start on this book of his own teachings, and asked me to assist. Apart from a few years' experience scribing and improving the fluency of his teachings for Kampo Gangra Drubgyudling's newsletters, my only credentials were a good educational background in the UK, and a wish to help. About ten years on from taking refuge I still knew precious little about the Buddhist path. As it turned out, and entirely due to the great kindness of the guru, this experience was to provide a foundation of Buddhist education that was all I could ever have hoped for.

Karma Thinley Rinpoche always taught directly in English to his western students, with no translator. For the most part, *A Calm Place in the Storm* was scribed verbatim, while sitting at Rinpoche's feet and occasionally asking for clarification. Two of the chapters were scribed by Ani Tsultrim Zangmo, who also helped with grammar. For the Refuge chapter, Rinpoche orally translated a completed part of a work he himself had started writing at an earlier time, and sections of the chapters on Shamata, Vipashyana and Mandala Offering take a more formal structure interspersed with oral commentary. Rendering everything into standard English and editing were an organic process similar to the branches of a tree spreading out as it grows. While listening back, or in response to a question, Rinpoche might suddenly and spontaneously add several new pages, or edit out whole passages. Always his astuteness and fluidity of mind amazed, picking up so precisely on any word or nuance that did not render the meaning completely or where there lay any possibility of confusion. A great master, and as all his students know, Rinpoche is able to convey his true meaning straight to the heart. The chapters are in the order Rinpoche chose, many accompanied by a specific illustration at his request. Throughout, we have tried to remain true to his charming, yet incisive, style of delivery.

Lama Jampa Thaye, with his extensive scholastic study and deep understanding of Tibetan Buddhism, wrote the Foreword, and kindly checked and edited the content to correct any unintentional errors and provide most of the end notes. We are also indebted to Namkha Tashi (Christopher Banigan) for his generosity and fine artistry in creating the lovely illustrations and cover design. A few of Rinpoche's own poems and drawings are also included.

A few more chapters were added in the years that followed completion of the original manuscript, as fine tuning and corrections continued. We are all so happy that this collection of precious teachings is now published and available to everyone.

I deeply apologise to Rinpoche for any mistakes in this presentation of his teachings.

Karma Naljorma
January 29th, 2025

A BRIEF BIOGRAPHY OF KARMA THINLEY RINPOCHE

Garchen Choje Lama Karma Thinley Rinpoche was born into the noble ruling family of Bongsar of the Gong Lha Bu Clan in Nangchen, Kham, in eastern Tibet in 1931. His family line includes many great Buddhist masters. Amongst these, the Nyingmapa terton (revealer of hidden dharma treasure) Urgyen Chogyur Dechen Shikpo Lingpa, the first Chogyur Lingpa (1829–1870), was Karma Thinley Rinpoche's great, great, great uncle; and the following incarnation, Neten Chogyur Lingpa, was his great, great uncle. The fourth Choling Tulku Rinpoche, His Eminence Dewe Dorje (1953–2020), was Rinpoche's cousin.

At the age of one month, Rinpoche first received refuge with the 'hair-cutting ceremony' and a long life blessing from the young Gyalwang Karmapa Rangjung Rigpe Dorje (1924–1981). When Rinpoche was two-and-a-half years old, His Holiness the 39th Sakya Trizin,[1] Dakshul Trinley Rinchen (1871–1936) from Dolma Phodrang, recognized him as the incarnation of the Sakya Lam Dre master Beru Sharyak Lama Kunrik. A terton himself, Lama Kunrik Rinpoche had found several sa ter ('earth treasure') at Rakchen Dag Nag ('Sacred Black Rock of Rakchen', known as Rahula's mountain) and at Palkha Jowo Min Dzo ('Lord of Medicinal Herb Treasure Mountain of Palkha'). He had also built several Hevajra retreat centres and began the construction of his main seat, Sharyak Dorje Ling Monastery. Jamyang Tenphel (1860–1921), the great ascetic meditation master, declared that Lama Kunrik was the incarnation of Lotsawa Vairotsana, a student of Padma Sambhava. Jamyang Tenphel had told him, "You are a higher tulku than I am, but because I have worked hard I have reached a more profound level of enlightenment."

Thus, in 1934, Rinpoche was given an official letter of recognition and the name Wangdud Norbu Nyingpo, a name borne by many members of the Sakya Khon family. His Holiness the 41st Sakya Trizin [Ngawang Kunga Rinpoche] (1945–) later officially confirmed Rinpoche's letter of Sakya tulku recognition.

Rinpoche went on to receive teachings from many masters of the four schools. During his younger years Rinpoche's teachers included his uncle, Lama Jigje, a great yogi and terton who discovered the special treasure of Chu Nag Gogu, a nine-headed garuda deity. This terma cycle included drubtap (Skt. sadhana) and lhetsok (observances for various functions and benefits). Rinpoche received these teachings, as well as the Dzokchen Ngondro and others, from Lama Jigje. Two of his maternal uncles, Hutuktu Yanggon Phakchok Rinpoche and Shabtrung Rinpoche, who together headed Riwoche Taklung Kagyu Monastery, gave Rinpoche some initiations and much good advice. He received ordination and many initiations and teachings from the Sakya Ngor Khangsar Khenpo, Ngawang Yonten Gyatso. In addition, the Sakya mahasiddha, Ngawang Tashi Chopel, gave Rinpoche the initiations and transmissions of Chod, Vajrayogini Naro Khechari and other teachings.

As a teenager, Rinpoche studied medicine under the great yogi-physician Taksar Tengchok, who was a famous doctor in the lineage of Mipham Rinpoche, and personal family physician to the ruler of Nangchen. He also studied astrology, poetry, art, grammar and Buddhist doctrine, with various abbots. During this period, he completed many retreats. With his noble uncles, the Chod master Namkha Dorje and Trakpa Namgyal, he built a large Nyungnye Lhakhang (temple) for the fasting ritual of Chenrezig. The main shrine room housed many statues: a two-storey-high Thousand-Armed Chenrezig; one-storey-high Guru Rinpoche, Amitayus, and Four-Arm Chenrezig statues; and many life-sized statues including that of terton Chogyur Lingpa. They also constructed a sixty-foot-high chorten (Skt. stupa) and several smaller ones. Rinpoche directed the education of three hundred monks while his own education progressed in a variety of subjects with various teachers.

The Sixteenth Gyalwang Karmapa advised Rinpoche's uncles to construct great monasteries, and gave them the name Karma Drubgyud Dargyeling Monastery. Rinpoche and his uncles had also built a Rime three-year retreat centre that was later changed to a three-year retreat centre for *The Six Yogas of Naropa*. The retreat master, Drupon Lama Bongsar Dorje Rinpoche, guided Rinpoche step by step through the Mahamudra preliminaries and guru yogas, and gave him all the requisite retreat initiations and teachings. Older monks remember Rinpoche in his teens memorizing texts more quickly than other lamas and young monks. Younger relatives recall him constantly surrounded by an adoring group of children with whom he would spend endless hours, enchanting them with spontaneous tales and hiking in the hills gathering medicinal herbs. During his teens he also wrote several sadhanas, fables and legendary histories. Two of these were *The Owl and Sun Conflict* and *Bear and Mouse in the Court of the Mountain Gods*, both about Kagyu-Sakya debating contests. He also wrote guru yogas devoted to Tashi Chopel and Jamyang Tenphel, and an introduction to meditation for his mother.

In the 1950s Rinpoche received full monastic ordination in Tsurphu, principal monastery of His Holiness Gyalwa Karmapa, and, subsequently, the Very Venerable Drupon Tenzin Rinpoche bestowed upon him the following: detailed teachings on the long, mid-length, and concise versions of the three principal Mahamudra texts of the ninth Karmapa; *The Jewel Ornament of Liberation*, *The Six Yogas of Naropa* (Tib. *Dutsi Nying khu*) with Drupon Rinpoche's own explanation, and Domsum texts (explaining the three vows); transmissions of Karmapa Rangjung Dorje's *Zabmo Nangdon* (*The Profound Inner Meaning*), the *Two-Part Hevajra Tantra* and the *Uttaratantrashastra* (Tib. *Gyud lama*), in addition to the initiation and teaching of the Chetsun Nyingtik, and many other transmissions.

His Holiness Kyabje Dilgo Khyentse Rinpoche (1910–1991) gave him many initiations, transmissions and teachings. Particularly special among these was the *Gyud Sangwei Nyingpo*, (Skt. *Guhyagarbha Tantra*) the root-tantra of the Maha Yoga system of the Nyingma school. While he received this teaching Rinpoche wrote everything down, thereby recording a book-length commentary on the text. During this time Rinpoche, together with Tobga Rinpoche, the then Vajra Master of Tsurphu monastery, and Ato Rinpoche, built two stupas at holy sites to the east and west of Tsurphu monastery. When they had finished, the Gyalwang Karmapa said of one of the stupas that by circumambulating sixteen times one would accumulate such great merit that the kindness of one's mother would be completely repaid. Later on, the Gyalwang Karmapa gave Rinpoche the title of the Fourth Karma Thinleypa.

In 1959, Rinpoche left Tibet with the entourage of the Gyalwang Karmapa and the consort of the Fifteenth Karmapa, Khandro Chenmo Rinpoche. During the journey Khandro Rinpoche very kindly offered him shelter. He received the *Tunshi Lama Naljor* (*Guru Yoga of the Four Sessions*) and Mahamudra transmission from her. In 1960, Sister Palmo (Freda Bedi (1911–1977), who worked for the Indian Ministry of Welfare, founded the Young Lamas' Home School for the four great sects of Tibetan Buddhism at Hauz Khas, in New Delhi, and the Gyalwang Karmapa appointed Rinpoche as its abbot. While there, Rinpoche taught Shantideva's *Bodhisattvacharyavatara* and Atisha's *Lamp of the Path of Enlightenment* (Tib. *Jangchub Lamdon*). At that time Chogyam Trungpa was the principal of the school, and Rinpoche received Rigzin Jigme Lingpa's *Yeshe Lama* from him – a profound Nyingma teaching. Later, in New Delhi, he also received the initiation and transmission for a hidden treasure of Karma Pakshi and Dorje Drollo from Trungpa, who had revealed it a month earlier while in retreat in Guru Rinpoche's 'Tiger's Nest' in Bhutan.

At Sarnath, Rinpoche's uncle Namkha Dorje requested and sponsored Karma Kagyu initiations, transmissions and teachings, including *The Six Yogas of Naropa* and Mahamudra, from His Eminence Kyabje Kalu Rinpoche (1905–1989) in order to establish a Three-Year Retreat Centre at the Mainpat Refugee Camp in central India. Rinpoche also received these teachings. In 1962, His Holiness Karmapa ordered Sister Palmo to move the Home School to Dalhousie, in Himachal Pradesh, and also asked Rinpoche to establish, and act as head lama of, the Karma Drubgyud Thargye Ling Mahayana Buddhist Nunnery also to be established there. Rinpoche and Sister Palmo invited Kyabje Kalu Rinpoche on two occasions. On his first visit, they received the *Dam Ngak Dzod*, the initiations and transmissions of all eight teaching lineages as collected by Jamgon Kongtrul Lodro Thaye (1813–1899). The second time, Kalu

Rinpoche stayed for one month in the nunnery and gave the complete collections of Shangpa Kagyu and Karma Kagyu initiations, transmissions and teachings including *The Six Yogas of Naropa* and Mahamudra, and established a three-year retreat centre. Besides these activities, they also invited groups of Sakya and Gelukpa nuns with the intention of opening further nunneries.

During these years Rinpoche received many teachings from the great Geluk master, His Holiness Ling Rinpoche (1903–1983). These included Tsong Khapa's *Lam Rim Chenmo* that explains the whole path of the Mahayana, and the initiation of the great deity Yamantaka, together with teachings and transmission. He also received Lojong, many other initiations, and Bodhisattva vows. From Khunu Rinpoche Tenzin Gyaltsen (1884–1976), the great Buddhist saint and scholar, Rinpoche received a very special transmission and teaching of the *Bodhicharyavatara* from the Patrul Rinpoche lineage, and the *Changchub Semkye Topa (Praising Bodhichitta)* written by Khunu Rinpoche himself. Khunu Rinpoche trained in Lojong and bodhichitta for many decades and, greatly inspired, had compiled this text by writing a verse each day for an entire year. Khunu Rinpoche explained two shastras, and also gave Rinpoche both Patrul Rinpoche's commentary on the *Three Statements of Garab Dorje* and Mahayana vows several times.

In 1967 Rinpoche received the Tsog Shay transmission of the *Lamdre (Path and its Fruit)*, the chief practice cycle of the Sakya tradition, from His Holiness the 41st Sakya Trizin, in Varanasi. Two other major cycles that Rinpoche would obtain later were the *Precious Treasury of Revealed Teachings* from Dilgo Khyentse Rinpoche in 1978 and the fourteen volumes of *The Collection of Sadhanas* from Chobjay Trichen Rinpoche in 1983.

In 1968, the Gyalwang Karmapa told Rinpoche and Sister Palmo to relocate the Kagyupa nunnery to Tilokpur. Karmapa told Sister Palmo that since this was the site where Naropa had encountered Tilopa eating fish and was purified of all his doubts, he was concerned about having a Kagyupa presence to take care of this holy cave. The site had been considered as an exclusively Hindu holy place up to that time, cared for by Hindu priests. Another reason for the move was that the Indian government was relocating the various Tibetan monasteries and their lay followers to settlements in different parts of India, such as Mysore and Delhi.

Soon after that, the great dharma master Chogyam Trungpa Rinpoche invited Rinpoche to stay and teach at Samye Ling in Scotland. However, as a divination by His Holiness Karmapa was not positive, Rinpoche did not go there immediately. When, a few years later, a conflict at Samye Ling proved impossible to resolve, Trungpa Rinpoche moved to the USA with a few of his chief students. In 1971, Karma Thinley Rinpoche came to Canada in accordance with the predictions of Kyabje Sakya Trizin Rinpoche and the Gyalwang Karmapa. In April 1973 he founded Kampo Gangra Drubgyud Ling in Toronto and subsequently established Marpa Gompa, a Calgary meditation centre under Susan Hutchison, Rigdzin Khandro. Later that year he was invited to Edinburgh University to assist in some anthropological research done by Dr. Barbara Aziz, and stayed there for a while. He visited Akong Rinpoche and stayed at Samye Ling where he taught a Tibetan language course and gave refuge to several people. Here, he met his regent David Stott (Jampa Thaye). This was a period during which he received many omens and wrote many poems.

When visiting Toronto in 1974, the Gyalwang Karmapa reiterated, for western students, Rinpoche's title of Garchen Choje Lama. That year Rinpoche also founded a centre in New Zealand and named it Karma Rime Thegsum Choling. Together with his regent Lama Jampa Thaye, Rinpoche founded several centres in England. These include Sakya Trinley Rinchen Ling and other Sakya centres, and Kagyu Ling, Kagyu Dechen Dzong and other Kagyu centres. A Sakya retreat in France was also founded, and was named Chang Lo Chen by His Eminence the Very Venerable Chobjay Trichen Rinpoche. Rinpoche was invited by Vidyadhara Trungpa Rinpoche to teach at the Naropa Institute in Colorado on two occasions. In 1988, Rinpoche founded Tekchen Lekshay Ling Monastery near Boudhanath, in Nepal, the holy land of Lord Buddha's birth and Guru Rinpoche's full enlightenment.

In 1982, Rinpoche visited Nangchen. He built a twenty-five-foot-high stupa at Sangjong, a sacred place near the old site of the Chogyur Lingpa monastery and the 'treasure-source' mountain. He also visited the Jamyang Tenphel retreat centre, Garuda Nest, and made some repairs. On a second visit in 1993, Rinpoche began planning a temple to be built on a small piece of land with a beautiful view of the nearby town. With this in mind he provided one thousand brass Buddha statues and various other religious articles and books. In 1997, Rinpoche again visited Nangchen and started building the temple. Also, his disciple and assistant, Kirsty, a great British meditator, started building a school for local Tibetan children. Subsequently, Rinpoche constructed a retreat centre in the holy location of Pharping, a place sacred to Padma Sambhava that is close to Kathmandu.

In addition to being an accomplished poet and artist, Rinpoche is a renowned historian, having written an authoritative history of Nangchen and, in English, the *History of the Sixteen Karmapas* (1980). He has continued to be a prolific author and in more recent times has written *The Telescope of Wisdom*, *The Lamp Dispelling Darkness*, *Dispelling the Darkness of Suffering*, *Sweet Drops of the Nectar of Bliss*, and a sadhana of Buddha Shakyamuni entitled *Cloudbanks of Merit*. Over the years, Rinpoche has taught extensively in Canada, the U.S., New Zealand, and the U.K.

For further information, see Rinpoche's website at karmathinleyrinpoche.com

The young crystal moon in the sky
Casts its reflection into the clear pond.
This illusion is the unity of form and emptiness
Dancing in the sphere of natural mind.

INTRODUCTION

A LL THE RELIGIONS OF THE WORLD have teachings that are true and helpful. Buddhism, in particular, places its emphasis on inner practice. Lord Buddha stressed this because he realized that inner training and discipline reveal true, natural, and beneficial mind itself. Buddha nature, this true and natural mind, is like a diamond found in rock, because once the dirt and dust are cleaned away one finds the purest of clear gems inside. Natural enlightenment dwells in sentient beings in a similar manner since all sentient beings possess mind, and mind in its pure state is buddha nature – enlightenment itself. The nature of mind can be compared to a medicinal herb that, while merely a plant if not used, becomes beneficial medicine when used properly.

The three Buddhist systems of Shravakayana,[1] Mahayana and Vajrayana employ different methods of spiritual practice. The Shravakayana tradition places great emphasis on the teaching of the Four Noble Truths[2] and the Eightfold Noble Path,[3] and therefore views samsara[4] (the cycle of birth and death) as suffering. Even though everything in samsara is impermanent, one cognizes what seem to be pure, positive and pleasurable sensations due to the influence of ego-consciousness. However, there is nothing that has permanent existence. Everything is changing all the time; whatever appears changes in time into something else. The tendency to think of everything as permanent and unchanging is a creation of the ego's attitude towards time. From yesterday to today things appear to remain constant, likewise the cycle of the four seasons appears to repeat itself. This apparent similarity over time gives the illusion of permanence. Boulders on a mountainside are all different shapes and sizes. If one is dislodged and falls it may break into a new number of rocks, each a different size and shape. Eventually a rock may be worn down into many grains of sand, and so, again, different numbers, shapes, and colours result. Nothing escapes change. Every single thing is in the process of changing and becoming different.

In samsaric existence primordial mind and ignorance arise together. Ignorance carries along with it the various inner structures of sentient beings and their external world. This is due to karma (action)[5] and the elements, both of which are constantly changing and producing endless waves of suffering, pain, pleasure, etc. Thus, samsaric happiness is always changing into suffering, and everything is really the very opposite of pleasurable. For example, upon feeling very hungry one may then enjoy the pleasure of eating, only to become hungry again later on, while overeating may bring sickness or even death. If one looks carefully, one will see that there is no true pleasure to be found in samsara because everything is bound to suffering. One cannot feel youthful once one is old, wrinkled, and grey-haired. Therefore, hidden beneath the pleasure of youth is this suffering of slowly and unknowingly becoming old or unhealthy. Nobody escapes birth, sickness, old age, and death.

There is no such thing in existence as an 'I', but the habitual tendency to ignorance creates the illusory existence of this self to which one clings for security. If one analyzes one's body and mind, one cannot find that such a thing as this 'I' truly exists. However, under the influence of unawareness one cognizes phenomena as good, bad or neutral in relation to this illusory self, and this categorization produces various mental states. Yet when this process and the inherent lack of self is clearly understood and meditated upon, one achieves the sorrowless stage of the arhat.[6]

According to the Mahayana teachings, everything included within the realm of sentient beings is to be understood as delusory and space-like. In whichever direction one looks there is an infinity of space containing all of the different shapes, forms, sense organs, and other delusory appearances that bind sentient beings. This delusion locks all sentient beings, not only oneself, into suffering and the causes of suffering. The bodhisattva (practitioner of Mahayana) begins by meditating on his or her mother, who is understood to be kind in many ways. Having recognized the mother's kindness, he or she goes on to meditate on all sentient beings as mothers from previous lives, and in gratitude for their kindness resolves to remove their suffering. Thus, the bodhisattva meditates on boundless love and boundless compassion, on boundless rejoicing for those who achieve happiness, and on boundless equanimity – not distinguishing between higher or lower realms, or between friend and enemy, since he or she wants to remove the suffering of all beings equally.

When one looks for the cause of the suffering of sentient beings one can see that it is all produced by self-clinging and dualistic attitudes.[7] Consequently, Mahayana practice involves two approaches, or methods. One of these, known as relative bodhichitta, involves working in the conventional sense to remove the existence of suffering. The other method takes the ultimate bodhichitta perspective where everything is seen as groundless and empty of inherent existence – just like a magic display where nothing really happens even though a great variety of appearances manifest. In this way one cuts the very root of delusion and achieves buddhahood – the fully awakened state.

There are three seeds of bodhisattva motivation (bodhichitta): firstly, the compassionate wish to free all countless sentient beings from suffering and to protect them from future suffering; secondly, the realization of the most profound pure emptiness (Skt. shunyata) free from duality and the two extremes of existence and non-existence; and thirdly, the wish to lead all sentient beings into full and complete enlightenment (buddhahood). As said in the prayers that start all Vajrayana deity sadhanas: "… therefore, I myself will attain Buddhahood."

INTRODUCTION

The Mahayana understands suffering to be a form of 'wrong contact'. Touching a lighted stove by mistake would burn one's fingers – this is physical suffering. Suffering exists as a relationship between external and inner, between self and the environment. Mental suffering is caused by an habitual tendency to form negative conceptions – this habitual tendency arises from dualistic obscuration.

The Vajrayana, however, understands that primordial enlightenment is self-arising, just as a clear crystal becomes dark when placed in the dark, or light when placed in the light. It describes the two kayas: the rupakaya (form body) which is the manifestation of enlightened qualities arising from enlightenment itself, and the dharmakaya (formless body) which is the true nature of the emptiness of all phenomena. The red and the white drops (bindu) and subtle winds (prana) of ordinary human beings, produce the vajra body, speech, and mind. These are the five elements of enlightenment that are the basis of the enlightened form of the Buddha. At the same time these are presently obscured by delusion, and thus the practitioner needs to practice the yogas and Mahamudra. Mind itself possesses the inherent potential of the four kayas[8] and so, through practice, all obscurations are transformed into these four different aspects of buddhahood.

The six senses cause the six objects of the senses to manifest, thus creating the appearance of the phenomena of the obscured states (of samsara). Due to this, one's pure nature and its four inherent qualities of enlightenment are not realized. Therefore, the Vajrayana uses a method of practice focusing upon the intrinsic enlightened nature. Techniques related to the four initiations are used to purify the four samsaric states of human experience, which are the waking state, sleep with dreaming, dreamless sleep, and male-female union. So, the practitioner first takes the four initiations, in which the skandhas (the aggregates of form, feeling, perception, formations and consciousness) are ripened. Subsequently, the practices of the visualisation development and completion stages of meditation deriving from this initiation correspond to the illusory-form kaya and the luminosity of the enlightened mind of the buddha (formless dharmakaya). Just as in legend the peacock is said to have developed the beauty of its feathers by eating poison, so samsaric energy itself is used as a condition for enlightenment, the achievement of the four kayas.

Whereas in the other two yanas it is not considered possible to achieve enlightenment in the span of just one lifetime, it is said that Vajrayana practice can lead even very ordinary and sinful human beings to enlightenment within this very life – even beings in whom the force of samsaric energies (such as desire, anger, jealousy, pride, and ignorance) are tremendously strong. Through Vajrayana practice these samsaric energies can be transformed into the innate wisdom of the four kayas. Delusion, time, and space are destroyed by the vajra method. This is also known as the method that 'takes the fruit as the path.'

1
NON-SECTARIANISM

Aʟʟ Bᴜᴅᴅʜɪsᴛ ᴛᴇᴀᴄʜɪɴɢs originate from Lord Buddha Shakyamuni, and fall into the three main divisions of Shravakayana, Mahayana and Vajrayana. While these teachings provide a variety of methods to suit the different dispositions of students, the fundamental principles and purpose of all the teachings are identical.

This identity can be seen, firstly, in their shared view that everything is impermanent and arises in a sequence of cause and effect. It is in this way that phenomena, time, space, and ideologies come into being. Everything exists in dependence upon everything else, and therefore different combinations cause different phenomena to come into existence. All these phenomena are controlled by time, which is itself impermanent and an illusion. Thinking of everything as permanent and unchanging is simply a misconception. For example, if one looks at a river it seems to be the same all the time, morning and evening, while in reality it is changing every instant as different atoms pass by. Therefore, it is important to see that everything is impermanent, and to meditate on this.

Secondly, common to all the teachings is the recognition that the nature of samsara is suffering. The very existence of sentient beings is suffering because their existence is impermanent. For example, birth is suffering because it leads to death: youth changing to old age is suffering, old age leading to frailty and sickness is suffering, and sickness leading to death is suffering. Impermanence happens naturally but because no one accepts it, it is experienced as suffering. This is illustrated by the fact that beings will try anything they think will provide an antidote to impermanence. However, nothing brings permanent happiness. All of life is like swimming in an ocean of suffering, whether one is human or any other kind of sentient being. The Buddha said this is the truth of things. Suffering hooks us and we cannot get free from it. Even if one has every imaginable comfort some kind of suffering, maybe mental, or involving one's family or friends, can still arise. This existence is never one hundred percent perfect. Even when science is used to try to relieve suffering it seems to bring new sufferings in its wake.

Thirdly, all three vehicles teach that all the phenomena of the outer universe and of our inner being are naturally egoless (devoid of permanent essence). Phenomena are just delusory samsaric conceptions that only evolve through cause and effect. For example, when stone, wood, and metal are put together they could become a large apartment building, or alternatively, a single house. Different effects occur as the five elements of the earth change in their interdependent balance; therefore, it is not possible for any singular, permanent thing to exist. This lack of intrinsic existence is clearly explained by Nagarjuna.[1] Nothing has any real basis; this is the meaning of emptiness. Phenomena occur because of time, and cause and effect. This means that houses, cities, and so on, are really just so many different combinations and, in fact, this is also the nature of all names and ideas. Therefore, everything is empty and egoless.

Thus, as is said in the *Heart Sutra*:

> Form is emptiness, emptiness is form, emptiness is none other than form, and form is none other than emptiness.[2]

A good analogy for this is provided by the example of the moon's reflection in a pond. It is not possible to find the moon in the pond. It is neither at the bottom, nor at the surface, nor in any of the ten directions of the pond, yet it is very clear. If someone were to try to catch the moon because it appeared to have fallen into a lake, he would find nothing, no matter how hard he worked at it.

The fourth shared fundamental view is that nirvana is sorrowless. Because mind is the basis of all delusion, the only way for a person to find an antidote to samsara is through mental practice, and nirvana is the state in which one's mind is free from defilement. Through study and practice delusion slowly loses its power, just as icebergs on the ocean slowly melt, until one's mind realizes the true view. At this point the roots of suffering no longer exist; there is no suffering, delusion, or sorrow, and one benefits sentient beings automatically. This is like the sun that is always in the sky benefitting the growth of gardens and forests and whose clear light is seen by everyone; all of this benefit it does quite spontaneously.

After Buddhism came to Tibet, different sects developed, but they are all essentially the same in following these four points, or as they are often known, 'Four Seals,' so it is better not to become sectarian. If we look at any of the religions in the world, we can find examples of fanatical religious views and see how these only bring about an increase in suffering. When one holds such views, it is as though the mind is locked in an iron cage from which it cannot escape to freedom. Fanaticism brings only suffering because it results in more division in society, more unhappiness, and ever mounting jealousy – jealousy that can lead to fatal conflict. This has happened so often in the history of the world that we can easily see that fanaticism is a mistake. It can spread and infect others, just as if one has a contagious sickness like tuberculosis and does not try to cure oneself. Even gentle and peaceful people can catch such a disease. Historically, fanatics have produced much useless suffering and many human lives have been needlessly sacrificed. We can now see how useless this is, and how it only serves to create even more suffering.

Non-Sectarianism

All Buddhist paths rely on the Triple Gem (the Buddha, the Dharma, and the Sangha), therefore if one becomes sectarian in view towards other Buddhist traditions one is breaking one's vows of refuge. For this reason, please try not to be sectarian or negative towards another tradition. All paths resemble many birds flying, or many fish swimming, in the same direction. At the same time, it is important to follow the teachings of one's own tradition properly.

2
MILAREPA

The great Kagyu yogin and poet, Milarepa (1040–1123), completely attained the state of Vajradhara[1] in one lifetime due to the power of his correct practice of Vajrayana meditation in accordance with the instructions of his guru, Marpa Lotsawa (1012–1097).

Milarepa had experienced a great deal of suffering in his life and this was the cause of his striving to reach the goal of the most profound happiness. In the first part of his life, he engaged in negative activities but the results of this led him, in his middle years, to develop a very strong renunciation of all negative action, resulting in his subsequent practice of dharma. His renunciation was so strong that, upon entering his cave to meditate, he vowed to remain there until he became enlightened. This change to virtuous activity resulted in the attainment of full enlightenment.[2] Finally, in old age, he stated that he was beyond all positive and negative action, had transcended both hope and fear, pain and pleasure, and had attained realization of the true nature of phenomena which is baseless delusion.

One winter, Milarepa went to practice in solitude on Mount Everest. It was a very long winter and he had only a little food. Since no one could penetrate the snows to reach him, his disciples and their families began to worry about him. Thinking that he must be dead, they performed a ganachakra puja (tsok feast ceremony) for his holy spirit and made many offerings, praying to Milarepa as though he had passed on. Once the snows had melted in the spring and the path was opened, they met Milarepa again. He asked what they had done in that particular month as he had felt all his students around him and had experienced a full stomach for days and weeks. They told him about the ganachakra offering and he said that that it was a very wonderful thing. Even though they had not seen each other and no food had actually been brought to him, his hunger had been satisfied through the spiritual connection. Incidentally, this illustrates why one can also benefit beings in the intermediate state between death and rebirth by making offerings.

As Milarepa said:

> When worldly men make charitable offerings
> It is surely helpful to their bardo state

However, it is still better and more useful to realize
The bardo of here and now.³

Ganachakra puja is both a way to accumulate merit and the most powerful method of purification. When those who have received Vajrayana empowerment feel that they have broken samaya⁴ (pledges) this is the best means of purification. It is very difficult for ordinary yogins and yoginis to keep Vajrayana samaya perfectly. Guru Padma Sambhava⁵ said that there are one hundred thousand samaya vows.

Performing a ganachakra puja provides a swift means for receiving the blessings of the guru and the deities. Furthermore, during this ceremony each cell of our bodies and our nervous system is blessed and visualized as the mandala of deities, as originally occurred during initiation. In this way the ganachakra is also a feast offering to them. Therefore, during the puja, the body is like a field of merit, and this is an inner mandala offering. Since Milarepa said that whoever hears his name will not take rebirth in the three lower realms during their next seven lifetimes, we now recite his name, and hold ganachakra ceremonies – which are even more beneficial than simply hearing his name. These ceremonies are of importance for both groups and individual practitioners who have received Vajrayana empowerment.

As a guide leading sentient beings to enlightenment, Milarepa is the most powerful. Kagyupas call him 'The Father of the Ocean of Mahasiddhas' in recognition of the fact that he himself worked so hard and led his followers to do likewise. During his lifetime, many of his followers attained enlightenment, as have many others since that time. In fact, one could consider Milarepa as the father of all the Kagyupas. Late in life, Marpa Lotsawa said that although he himself was now an old man, his life had been successful because Milarepa had become his disciple and meditation lineage holder. He predicted that Milarepa's lineage would continually improve and grow stronger like the cub of a lion, or the chick of the garuda. Marpa Lotsawa also had a dream in which he saw a vulture with one chick on a rocky mountain and the surrounding sky completely filled with birds. He said that this vulture symbolized Milarepa, and the chick, Gampopa, while the birds represented the extensive number of students. Gampopa (1079–1153) was a Kadampa when he first met Milarepa and became his main lineage-holder. In doing so, he united the two lineages of Kadampa and Mahamudra and thus created the Kagyupas – an event known as 'two streams becoming one'.

The Kagyu sect had twelve branches. The four main ones were the Phagmo Drupa Kagyu, the Karma Kagyu, the Baram Kagyu and the Tsalpa Kagyu. The Phagmo Drupa branched out to produce the Taklung Kagyu, Drukpa Kagyu, Drigung Kagyu, Trophu Kagyu, Yamzang Kagyu, Shugseb Kagyu, Martshang Kagyu and Yelpa Kagyu. Later, the Karma Kagyu had several other branches, such as the Surmang Kagyu, which was founded by Trungmase Rinpoche, student of the Fifth Gyalwang Karmapa, and the

Nendo Kagyu, founded by Karma Chagme, student of the Ninth and Tenth Gyalwang Karmapas.

Each Kagyu branch has a long lineage, and in each generation many followers have achieved enlightenment. For example, in the Karma Kagyu, the first Karmapa Dusum Khyenpa (1110–1193) founded the Karma Khamtsang and reached complete enlightenment. The name 'Karma' originates in Dusum Khyenpa's vision in which all the dakinis[6] of the ten directions appeared to him and said that he was the activity (karma) of all the Tathagatas.[7] 'Khamtsang' refers to Kham – the original home where Dusum Khyenpa and his disciple Drogon Rechen[8] first founded the Karma Khamtsang in Kampo Nenang, at Kampo Gangra. Secondly, it was said of the Drukpa Kagyu that "half the population of Jambuling continent[9] is Drukpa Kagyu, half the Drukpa Kagyu are poor, esoteric practitioners, half of these are enlightened, and that these mahasiddhas are spread over an area of country as great as that covered by a vulture flying continuously for eighteen days." Finally, concerning the Drigung Kagyu – Jigten Sumgon (1143–1217) and his disciples are said to have led one hundred and eighty thousand followers to enlightenment. These are only three of many possible examples concerning the branches of the Kagyu tradition.

It is because of this great success of the tradition derived from him that Milarepa is regarded as a great benefactor of sentient beings, fully and completely saving them by leading them across the ocean of suffering of samsara to enlightenment. As all the power of the Kagyu lineages has its source in Milarepa, when one has devotion to him it is the same as having devotion to all the Kagyu lineages.

Furthermore, Milarepa did not die in an ordinary manner. The day his body was cremated, many people met him on their way to his funeral in quite different locations. When two villages in different districts fought over who should keep the body, Milarepa's body miraculously appeared in each village. Also, when his body was cremated, it would not catch fire until Mila's student Rechungpa arrived, at which time Milarepa rose up, pushing all the flames aside, and sat on the fire singing in conversation with Rechungpa in front of all his disciples. When the fire died away, there were no bones or ashes. Only one single egg-shaped relic remained, and the dakinis carried this away to Akshobya Buddha's realm.

3
REFUGE

REFUGE IS THE PATH TO ENLIGHTENMENT, giving one full authority to practice Lord Buddha's teachings. At the beginning when one goes for refuge, one needs to know what the objects of refuge are, how to actually take refuge, what constitutes the complete taking of refuge, which precepts accompany the taking of refuge, the results of breaking one's refuge vows, and the benefits of taking refuge. I will briefly discuss the objects of refuge because refuge is the fundamental basis for all the three principal vows of Buddhism, which are the seven types of precepts of the Shravakayana vow, the two streams (lineages) of bodhisattva vows of the Mahayana vow, and the different levels of pledges and initiations of the Vajrayana vow. Of course, taking refuge in the Triple Gem is also of immense importance since it is the point of differentiation between the Buddhist and the non-Buddhist.

In describing the objects of refuge there are four topics to consider:
- A. The seed or cause of taking refuge,
- B. The number of objects of refuge,
- C. The permanent nature of this refuge,
- D. The qualities of Buddha that endow him with the ability to give protection and refuge.

A. THE CAUSE OF TAKING REFUGE

From the student's point of view there are three essential causes of taking refuge:
1. fear of the dangers of samsara,
2. faith,
3. compassion.

These three can be likened to the three processes involved in building a house, which are, firstly, looking for a suitable location, secondly, digging the foundation, and thirdly, pouring the concrete.

1. The first cause: fearing samsara

The cause constituted by fearing samsara falls into the two categories of temporary and permanent. 'Temporary cause' refers to fear of the threat of sufferings in the present life only. 'Permanent cause' refers to the belief that in the future one will endlessly be led into different existences in the six realms[1] of suffering and therefore great protection is needed. The unvarying sufferings experienced in the human realm of samsara are sickness, hindrances caused by negative spirits, bad reputation, ungrounded gossip or slander, harm caused by the four elements, starvation, poverty, disappointment, unhappiness, and undesirable events. Some of these are caused by the ripening of karma (action, cause and effect), while others are accidental.

In the face of danger, one seeks protection. For example, if one were starving, one would ask a friend for help. Seeking refuge is natural. If one were walking along a steep, narrow mountain trail with a sheer drop to the side, one would immediately be careful of one's step and want to hold on with one's hands. This is analogous to standing on the edge of samsara, in danger of falling into the suffering of negative emotions, negative thoughts, and so on, which would be no different from falling prey to fierce wild animals such as tigers or bears. At such times it is logical to look for refuge.

However, if the protector is not yet free from fear himself then he cannot protect others, just as the blind cannot safely guide others because they might lead them into danger. It may be possible to obtain a small degree of temporary protection from worldly gods, or other spirits such as yakshas, rakshas, nagas, or even demons, but even these are themselves really formless manifestations of one's own deluded mind. If they are happy, they can be of some benefit; if they are not, they can spread sickness and many hindrances. A person in authority, such as a king or a general, could also benefit one a little, but ultimately, they too are bound by karma and delusion.

When one goes for refuge in the Triple Gem (Tib. Konchog sum) one is recognizing that these other forms of refuge offer only temporary protection and are not really reliable. The safest protector is Lord Buddha because he offers profound, permanent protection. Buddha showed us many manifestations of himself, such as Amitayus and White Tara for those seeking long life, the Healing Buddha for those threatened by sickness, or the many different wealth deities for those leading difficult lives under poor conditions. Buddha offers manifestations of different deities, forms, and mantras as individual antidotes for each form of suffering. In this way he offers much more protection than any temporary refuge offered by worldly protectors. Some local people in the Himalayas, out of misunderstanding, would seek protection for family happiness, harvests, and health from the many different sacred mountains of the region. It is a great mistake to take refuge in gods of the mountains, or in water, fire, or animals in this way because they offer only some limited protection; for example, fire can provide protection from cold, water can alleviate thirst, or a mountain can provide the shelter of a cave. Buddha taught different methods and manifestations in the sutras and tantras to provide for people's need for an answer to their problems.

Even though one might seek only the common result from these practices, such as long life, health, wealth, or removal of hindrances, as long as one keeps one's vows and proper meditation, different dream-like experiences will arise. Whatever the kind of experience, if one cuts through it with awareness and does not conceptualize, one progresses quickly to realization. As one can be sure of these blessings there is no need to seek refuge in any worldly protectors. The *Nirvana Sutra* says:

> Whoever takes refuge in the Triple Gem receives every protection, need have no fear of cyclic transmigration, and is gradually liberated from samsaric suffering and the danger of falling back into cyclic existence.

Also, Arya Asanga[2] states:

> To take refuge in the Triple Gem is the most profound path. The Mahayana form of refuge is the most profound as it gives protection from all hindrances, the suffering of rebirth in the lower realms, and from mistaken dharmas.

All the sufferings of samsara are created by negative actions and the five negative emotions.[3] These are a tremendous threat as they are the natural cause of suffering and, if not purified, will lead one into deep and lasting suffering of all kinds in the future. If one is without bodhichitta and possesses a strong belief in duality, then even though the practice of prostrations, generosity, and moral discipline may lead one into happy realms of existence, one can still fall again into suffering when good karma (action, cause and effect) is exhausted. Thus, permanent freedom is not achieved. There are also so many other sufferings: birth as the beginning of death, old age, failing health and youth, sickness, loss of strength and power, and death itself – the end of life and breath. All countless sentient beings are involved in suffering in this way. If one investigates this carefully in one's mind, it is very frightening. Therefore, one needs some protection from this permanent threat.

2. The second cause: faith

The second cause, faith, actually constitutes the first step in taking refuge. As Guru Padma Sambhava says in the *Seven Chapter Prayer*:

> I have no doubt that complete faith and confidence brings complete realization.

How can one develop faith? One should first know about the temporary and permanent sufferings of samsara as just detailed. The Triple Gem has the characteristics of being unaffected by these sufferings, of having the power to give this protection to others, and also of compassionately wanting to protect beings. The first Jewel, the Buddha himself, realized the truth of suffering, the truth of how it is caused by negative mental actions, the truth of the antidotes that constitute the path of enlightenment, and the truth of the achievement of sorrowless nirvana.

Buddha subsequently taught these 'Four Noble Truths' and they comprise the second Jewel, that of the Dharma. These teachings prove that he is omniscient and the most profound source of protection. The antidote to suffering is developing the wisdom of the path of Buddha Dharma. Complete freedom from suffering is the perfect realization of nirvana, complete enlightenment. These two, the path and the result, both come from practice and meditation and therefore the Dharma is the second source of profound protection.

The third Jewel is the Sangha, which consists of the holy spiritual friends who have developed great understanding and wisdom, and are very skillful. They are therefore the third source of profound protection. When one develops faith one realizes that these Three Jewels are the most profound refuges, and that nothing equal to this profound protection is to be found anywhere in the universe. This faith of clear understanding becomes one's motivation, and leads one to develop the three faiths of wanting to become enlightened oneself, complete confidence, and unswerving faith. These four faiths are extremely important in making a strong foundation for practice.

3. The third cause: compassion

The third cause of taking refuge is compassion. The teachings of the Kadam[4] tradition say that if one takes refuge to free oneself alone from the lower realms of samsara, then one is an inferior type of practitioner. Of the three paths that a practitioner might follow this one is known as the path of 'the inferior person'. If this is one's aim, it is a mistake. The practitioner who is known as 'the mediocre person' is motivated to take refuge to free himself completely from samsara and not just from its lower realms. However, even this is not the profound path. The profound path is that of 'the great person' who practises the Mahayana, or 'Great Vehicle', since he or she believes that it is not enough to seek freedom from suffering and attainment of nirvana for oneself alone.

In his *Song of Parting from the Four Attachments*, the great Vajrayana master Sakya Drakpa Gyaltsen[5] said:

> To leave behind sentient beings who are our mothers in the suffering of samsara, while seeking happiness ourselves, is hard-hearted indeed.

All sentient beings, our mothers in previous lives, completely fill all of space and endure limitless sufferings. They are continually threatened by starvation, sickness, disagreements, and weapons. Thinking about this gives rise to the wish to protect them through great compassion and this becomes one's motivation in taking refuge. This is the most profound and the greatest vehicle, and is taken by the student of superior strength.

Dignaga[6] said:

> Samsara is deep and limitless. All sentient beings sink in this ocean, in danger of being consumed by the crocodiles of negative emotions. We must immediately seek protection by taking refuge.

One sutra says:

> Taking refuge is of great benefit as by this limitlessly profound quality one progresses, because great limitless compassion for all sentient beings increases, and the incomparable quality of enlightenment is achieved.

B. THE NUMBER OF REFUGES

It seems that the number of objects of refuge varies in different Buddhist traditions. However, according to my gurus, they can be enumerated as follows:
1. three outer,
2. three inner,
3. three secret, and
4. 'thatness'.

1. The Three Outer Refuges

The Triple Gem, or Three Jewels, have already been established as the source of refuge. Equally, one could say that the Three Jewels are the source and refuge is the fruit. The term 'Konchog' means most rare and perfect (i.e., jewel). It is like the wish-fulfilling gem of ancient mythology, a very rare gem that was in the care of the naginis during the spiritual era of the world. It is said that if one holds this gem all one's prayers are fulfilled.

Maitreya[7] described the six qualities of the Triple Gem as follows:

> They are called rare and perfect because they are profound and free from defilement, with great power, ornament of the world, and most perfect, and unchanging.[8]

It is because the Three Jewels have these six qualities similar to the wish-fulfilling gem that they are called 'unchanging' or 'the rare ones.' There are three reasons for refuge being three-fold. Firstly, Lord Buddha was the first in our time period to become completely free from duality and delusion, to cut off ignorance completely, and to realize the four kayas and five wisdoms, thereby reaching Buddhahood. Secondly, the only way to achieve Buddhahood is to follow the path of the Dharma. Thirdly, the only companions on this path of practice are the Sangha. Since people can be grouped into the three capacities mentioned above, they hold three corresponding views of the Triple Gem and, consequently, take refuge in three different ways: 'worldly', Shravakayana and Mahayana:

a. The first is to take refuge in the Buddha in front of either a painting or a statue, in the Dharma as the three 'baskets' of scripture (vinaya, sutra and abhidharma), and in the Sangha as those holding monastic ordination whether or not they are 'noble ones'. One might ask whether a non-Buddhist who follows the morality of giving up negative actions, but does not take refuge in the Triple Gem, would be reborn into one of the three higher realms. He would, because his religion has an equally strong morality. Both Milarepa and the *Vinaya Sutra* say that the most profound cause of rebirth in the higher realms is morality. Thus, if one gives up negative actions the automatic result, for Buddhist or non-Buddhist alike, is the achievement of rebirth in the higher realms.

b. The second way is to take refuge in Buddha as the symbol of the complete achievement of the sorrowless wisdom of nirvana, in the Dharma as the route to this enlightenment, and in the Sangha as those who have achieved the four 'noble' levels that culminate in enlightenment. These levels are 'having entered the stream to enlightenment', 'once returner' (to samsara), 'never returner' and 'arhat'. When taking refuge in this manner, Buddha is viewed as the teacher, Dharma as the path, and the Sangha as friends who give one the right example.

c. The Mahayana way of taking refuge differs in its understanding of the Triple Gem and in its motivation. Lord Buddha dedicated himself to the benefit of sentient beings. He was the first to take bodhisattva vows and then to practice the ten perfections[9] over many aeons until finally becoming fully and completely enlightened. Also, for as long as sentient beings exist, Buddha will continue to appear in nirmanakaya form as different spontaneous emanations. Taking refuge in the Dharma is twofold. Firstly, one is taking refuge in the doctrine of the Mahayana scriptures, such as the *One Hundred Thousand Verses of the Prajnaparamita*, the *Diamond Sutra*, the *Heart Sutra*, the *White Lotus Sutra* or the *Avatamsaka Sutra*. Secondly, one is taking refuge in the realization of the dharma of the bodhisattva path. This is the realization of 'The Thirty-seven Qualities of Enlightened Mind', which are the qualities of the bodhisattva's journey through the five paths and ten bhumis,[10] culminating in Buddhahood, the supreme, or eleventh bhumi.

The Sangha here, in the Mahayana, refers to the bodhisattvas who have achieved the first to the tenth levels of realization, termed 'bhumis' (stages). The outer refuges are the same in both the Shravakayana and the Mahayana; the Mahayana differs only in its view of the Triple Gem and in its motivation.

2. The Three Inner Refuges

The three inner refuges, or 'Three Roots' (Tib. Tsawa sum), are specific to the Vajrayana view. The first is the root guru (Tib. Tsawai lama) who bestows the blessings of the four empowerments, as well as other blessings and siddhis.[11] This Vajrayana doctrine is clarified in the *Hevajra Tantra*:

> Bow down to the Guru, precious form,
> How great his kindness,
> Great bliss, suddenly illuminated.

The second root or inner refuge is the deity (Tib. Yidam). Mahamudra (The Great Seal),[12] Maha Sandhi (The Great Perfection)[13] and other high realizations, as well as the eight ordinary siddhis, all have their source in the practice and meditation of the deities. Therefore, deities are the source or root of siddhis and blessings and are the second refuge. The dakinis and dharmapalas, the third inner refuge, are the root of the four beneficial activities of pacifying, progressing, magnetizing, and wrathful activity. In this way the guru, the yidam and the dakini are the three inner Vajrayana refuges. The guru is the source of blessing, the yidam is the source of siddhis and the dakini is the source of the four activities. The method of taking refuge is to request the protection of the guru, follow the path of deity practice, and rely on the dakinis as one's spiritual friends.

3. The Three Secret Refuges

The three secret refuges also belong to Vajrayana. The Vajrayana is unlike the Shravakayana and Mahayana, both of which take many aeons to lead one to enlightenment. It is a very special method that leads one to enlightenment in one lifetime, or in a very short period of time. Only this method practices the purification of the inner chakras and results in the achievement of the union of the four kayas and five wisdoms. This is known as the secret refuge. It is automatically secret because the common vehicles cannot incorporate these three concepts into their view. By this method, the nadis (channels) are purified into Nirmanakaya, which is the Sangha, the pranas (winds) are purified into Sambhogakaya which is the Dharma, and the tilaka (drops) are transformed into Dharmakaya which is the Buddha.

Actually, all these outer, inner and secret methods of taking refuge are included in taking refuge in the root guru. One who takes Vajrayana refuge in this way realizes that the Three Jewels and Three Roots are all inseparable from the body, speech and mind of the guru. It is with this understanding that one takes refuge in the root guru. For example, if one were to make a pilgrimage to Bodhgaya in India one would have to choose a means of getting there. Travelling by plane would be the fastest and most comfortable way to reach one's destination. One does not take refuge in the root guru as an ordinary person as he is really Buddha Vajradhara. One takes refuge in him because Vajradhara is the embodiment of all the wisdom of the Buddhas and is therefore the finest form of refuge.

4. Thatness as refuge

'Thatness', (Skt. Tathata; Tib. Dezhin nyid) the natural state of one's mind, is the ultimate refuge. One's own intrinsic mind is beyond words – it is primordial wisdom (Skt. jnana; Tib. yeshe). Whoever realizes this is completely enlightened but, as long as this is not realized, one is continuously circling in samsara.

Saraha[14] stated:

> Mind is the one seed of everything,
> both samsara and nirvana spring from it.
> To this mind, which like a Wish-fulfilling Gem
> grants all things, I bow down.[15]

As it is the source of samsara and nirvana, one should train one's mind. Whoever realizes the mind of the four kayas has reached the final stage of realization. The wisdom of natural emptiness is Dharmakaya. Naturally radiant mind is Sambhogakaya. The activity form of all-pervading loving compassion is Nirmanakaya. The nature of the three kayas as being the same in essence is the Svabhavikakaya. Those who realize this take refuge in mind itself – thatness. There is nothing to reject, nothing to accept, there is no distinguishing, there is only purity contemplating purity.

Mahabodhisattva Maitreya said:

> Nothing whatsoever to remove from, not the slightest thing to add,

properly seeing the true nature. When it is truly seen this is complete liberation.[16]

What is meant by 'taking refuge in non-dual mind'? Mahayana teaches that whoever realizes that all phenomena are without any basis in reality but are primordially pure, realizes the Buddha. Buddha is neither form, nor name, nor characteristic, nor phenomenon. Buddha is dharmakaya. This is taking refuge in the Buddha. Seeing all dharmas (phenomena) as depending on the sphere of 'thatness' or the dharmadhatu (Tib. cho ying) is taking refuge in the Dharma. The dharmadhatu is the true nature, or ground, of all phenomena – all of samsara and enlightenment. Seeing no difference between composite phenomena and that which is non-composite is taking refuge in the Sangha.

Buddha is the only refuge in ultimate truth, because Buddha is synonymous with dharmakaya itself. Therefore, the final and greatest refuge is the Buddha. The other two refuges are like the road that leads one there. Dharma as refuge includes the dharma of scriptural study and the dharma of realization. The study of Dharma is no longer needed once one achieves complete realization. This is similar to no longer needing the boat once one has crossed the ocean. Those who are fully enlightened no longer need to practice the path that leads there.

The dharma of experience is the gradual accomplishment of the stages on the way to enlightenment. At the first stage the qualities that are acquired are small and increase as each successive stage is reached. Each stage also includes those that precede it. The qualities of an arhat do not compare with the much greater and more profound qualities of a bodhisattva, in the same way that water caught in a hoof-print does not compare with the water contained in an ocean. A further point is that bodhisattvas who are just starting out on the path are not yet free from the duality of samsara. Therefore, the Dharma and the Sangha are not ultimate refuges and are to be transcended, since the qualities of enlightenment are not complete within them.

Mahabodhisattva Maitreya said:

> Because it can be relinquished, because it is deceptive, because it is nothing whatsoever, and because they are not free from fear – the two dharmas (of scripture and experience) and the sangha are not ultimate refuges. The ultimate refuge is only buddha.[17]

Why is Buddha the ultimate refuge? Dignaga says:

> Whoever experiences ultimate truth is generating benefit for sentient beings, is turning the Wheel of the Dharma, has gone beyond and is an ultimate refuge.

C. THE PERMANENT NATURE OF THIS REFUGE

Buddha protects sentient beings from suffering. This is not said in order to trick people – it is a correct and dependable truth. Buddha's teachings provide us with a method for ending the suffering of sentient beings, and as this method actually works it is indeed true to say that Buddha protects sentient beings from suffering. Whereas Hindus describe Shiva, the supreme God, as self-generated and eternally existent, Lord Buddha was a human being. His initial wish to protect sentient beings from suffering and his subsequent development of compassion led him to enlightenment, the complete realization of egolessness. This combination of method and wisdom together cleansed away all negativity, just like cleaning a crystal mirror. Once cleansed in this way, mind can never again become sullied by the negativity of samsara. The root cause has been completely severed because, once ignorance has been removed, samsara cannot return. This complete rejection of negativity is the same as burning a dirty cloth in the fire. The cause of negative karma (action) and suffering is thereby completely eliminated.

Selfishness and the tendency toward negative actions and emotions represent the very opposite of bestowing protection upon sentient beings. In eliminating them, Buddha became like the sun sailing free from the clouds. His activity became permanent and spontaneous just as the sun spontaneously and constantly radiates energy and removes darkness. Therefore, it is in this way that Buddha has the nature of a permanent refuge.

One might ask whether it is true that Buddha's methods of giving protection from suffering are completely free from error. The answer to this is, "Yes," because by logical deduction one can look at the results of using these methods and discern the omniscience of the source, in the same way that sighting water birds in flight indicates close proximity to water.

In *The Jewel Ornament of Liberation*, Gampopa says:

> Because he has completely awakened from the sleep of ignorance and has acquired the two kinds of deep understanding, He is Buddha.[18]

Dharmakirti said Buddha is omniscient. We would not use this word to describe a person who, for example, simply has the ability to number a great multitude of insects, or to see a great distance. If one takes refuge in someone who has knowledge only of such material things, one may just as well be taking refuge in a vulture that can also see a tremendous distance, or in an animal that is able to see the tremendous numbers of tiny insects. As this kind of knowledge is not beneficial for enlightenment, we would not address one who possesses it as 'Omniscient One.' Instead, this title is reserved for one who has complete knowledge of how to liberate sentient beings from suffering. There is no mistake in the Four Noble Truths that teach both what is to be rejected and what is to be attained through practice. There is no mistake or confusion in any stage of the path taught by Buddha, from the very beginning, through all the gradual stages to full enlightenment. Following this path is like climbing to the top of a mountain one step at a time. The expanse of knowledge demonstrated in the formulation of this teaching is what we mean by true omniscience. Buddha's knowledge about liberating the mind is the best for guiding beings to enlightenment. It is the most beneficial. Therefore, he is called omniscient or all-knowing. As he is truly the omniscient one, we can have confidence in him. As applied to Buddha, the term 'omniscient' encompasses three characteristics:

1. he knows 'thatness', which is beyond all duality,
2. his knowledge is stable and unchanging, and
3. he completely understands the Four Noble Truths of cause and effect, two of which belong to the cycle of transmigration, and two to the enlightened level.

In this way Buddha provides complete benefit for others, and the source of this great benefit is his realization of great compassion, love, and egoless wisdom. These are the seeds of omniscience. The quality of bringing complete benefit to others arises from the removal of the three hindrances of negative emotions and dualistic and habitual tendencies. The realization of egoless wisdom, great compassion, and love, all grew from the original seed of compassion that had been established in a much earlier lifetime when Buddha was an ordinary man.

D. THE QUALITIES ENABLING THE BUDDHA TO GIVE REFUGE TO OTHERS

The Tibetan title for Buddha is 'Sangyay', which means 'completely free from the threat of samsara'. Firstly, Buddha is as fearless as the greatest of heroes and is thus able to protect others from suffering. On one occasion while staying in a cave he was giving a discourse on the dharma when a frightened pigeon fleeing from a hawk landed in the lap of Arhat Shariputra, where it rested. It remained frightened until it moved onto Lord Buddha's lap, where it became very tranquil and relaxed.

Secondly, Buddha is very skillful in guiding his followers to enlightenment and provided different teachings according to individual needs. For those with a certain way of understanding things he gave the Shravakayana discourses, for others with a different way of understanding he gave the Mahayana teachings, and for those who were so suited, he gave the Vajrayana teachings. He never made a mistake in giving any of these teachings. He never tried to teach something to a follower who was unqualified to receive and understand it. He invariably gave each person the teaching that was correct for him or her, and no one received unsuitable teachings from him. Some people who lacked discipline became immediately disciplined upon seeing or talking with him, those who were spiritually inclined but as yet unripened, he ripened completely like fruit in the sun, those who were already endowed with great spiritual qualities he led to complete enlightenment. Therefore, during Buddha's time many people advanced quickly to the level of an arhat, and then continued to progress towards complete enlightenment, becoming great bodhisattvas and siddhas.

Thirdly, Buddha treated everyone equally, both friend and enemy. For example, even though Buddha's cousin, Devadatta, was driven by jealousy to try to hinder him, Lord Buddha treated him in just the same way as he treated others, even his own son Rahula, giving compassion, love, and teaching to all.

> Some teachers say that one should not teach religion to the lower castes, but Buddha taught even the most sinful butchers or fishermen. To all people, as to kings, he gave great compassion. His teaching was available for whoever was ready to receive it, each being taught in the method best suited to his or her qualities. Buddha made no discrimination whatsoever on the basis of caste or condition, just as a shower of rain falls everywhere indiscriminately, upon the high mountain peaks or in the deepest valleys.
> (from *The Shastra Praising the Superiority of Buddha*)

Fourthly, Buddha was not interested in material and worldly matters. It was the same to him whether someone gave him offerings or not. Offerings did nothing to bring a student closer to, or further from him, and Buddha did not dispense teachings according to the offerings made to him.

Buddha therefore possesses the complete and most profound qualities of enlightenment. He is the most honourable and reliable of teachers and the source of the two great accumulations, the accumulation of merit and the accumulation of wisdom. Merit can be either ordinary or profound. Ordinary merit is associated more with speech and physical activity, such as generosity to sentient beings, building temples, or giving medicine. Profound merit is associated more with mental activity, such as faith, devotion, or bodhisattva wishing prayers. This is illustrated by an event that took place when Buddha was once walking along a road begging for alms and food. On this occasion he encountered two young Brahmin boys who were very excited to see him approaching. As they had nothing to offer, they gathered handfuls of sand, and since they could not reach his alms bowl, one of the boys climbed up onto the shoulders of the other to put the sand into the bowl as if it were food. Lord Buddha told Ananda (his disciple and attendant) that this sand was very important and should be brought back to the monastery. Once there, Buddha mixed the sand with water and cow dung and asked all the five hundred arhats to keep some in their meditation cabins. Everyone wondered what the significance of this could be. Buddha said that the two boys who made this offering had accumulated great merit and that one century after he had died and passed from the world, one of these boys would become the universal emperor[19] known as Ashoka, while the other who had helped his friend would become Ashoka's minister. King Ashoka would then conquer all of India and would build as many stupas as the grains of sand he had offered that day, each of which would house a single hair or strand of cloth of Buddha himself. King Ashoka did build more than one million stupas in his day. Similar great benefits are received by all who bow down to Buddha, or to an image or picture of him, and recite mantras. This is especially true if one's motivation is to contact the 'heart' of Buddha, to stay in meditation and give rise to bodhichitta.

As I mentioned previously, the true nature of each individual sentient being's mind is Buddha: natural and primordial purity. The radiant clarity of mind is the Dharma – transcending duality, beginningless, unchanging, and unceasing. The manifestations that appear in order to lead sentient beings to the goal of primordial happiness are the Sangha. When we realize this inner Triple Gem, then the two streams of outer and inner become one, and lead to the realization of a new Triple Gem which is the full realization of the true nature of bodhichitta, otherwise known as Tathagatagarba, or Buddha nature. Thus, outer and inner Triple Gem unite, and in that moment, one becomes a protector for sentient beings oneself, able to protect others from suffering and lead them into enlightenment.

Until this realization is reached, the two Triple Gems, conventional (relative) and ultimate, function like the two wings that the swan needs to fly through the sky. One needs both of these if one is to continue the journey towards enlightenment for the purpose of saving sentient beings. The external refuge is like the handle of a sword, the inner Triple Gem is like the blade itself, and the person holding the sword is the power of faith, respect, and compassion. Fighting with these weapons one will be victorious on the battlefield of negativity and suffering.

One who continuously strives to become a dharma hero is a true hero, like Buddha. One who can accumulate merit and overcome and remove the two darknesses of negative emotions and the basic ignorance of the nature of reality is a true warrior. Compared to this, one who is able to overcome and kill enemies in the conventional sense is merely a failure. Even if one is illiterate and does not know prayers and rituals, recitation of the refuge prayer alone is sufficient practice, as it is the best source of blessings and wish-fulfilment.

In fact, many other great world religions concentrate mainly on practice of strong devotion and worship, on developing very strong confidence and love, and on making many offerings. Through this, many people following these systems receive blessings and healing. Some people weep with trembling bodies and almost lose consciousness, feeling that they actually touch their god. Analogously here in Buddhism, taking refuge is a powerful means of making a connection between the Triple Gem and oneself.

However, if one does not have confidence when engaged in prayer and worship, then even though one were to practice many different rituals there would be very little result.

When Atisha[20] went to Tibet, he constantly gave teachings on going for refuge in the Triple Gem. Even though he was the greatest scholar and practitioner of Vajrayana and Sutrayana he encouraged everyone wherever he went to recite hundreds of thousands of refuge prayers. He is sometimes known in Tibetan as 'the Refuge-Teaching Scholar.' Many people feel that taking refuge is relatively unimportant as if it is just something with which to begin one's practice, while really it is the main prayer because it is a means of direct contact with Buddha. The different deities and rituals are another method of invoking the blessing of the Buddha, as all deities are manifestations of him. If one is always reciting the refuge prayer and thinking of the Triple Gem then whatever activity one is engaged in, the four daily activities of walking, moving, sitting, and sleeping, prayers at the beginning of the day, or actions throughout the day, will automatically be free from mistakes. In this way one will avoid taking an evil or mistaken path leading to bad results.

However, if one does not take refuge, or has no refuge, then even being able to memorize much of the Tripitaka, or all the Shastras, or know Sanskrit or Pali, is meaningless. This is no different from a tape recorder playing back what has been recorded, or a mynah bird repeating 'Om Mani Padme Hum', which it mimics without having any faith in the Buddha, in Dharma practice, in following the Sangha, or in the Bodhisattva attitude. Someone who has given up refuge and does not respect the Triple Gem but still continues to practice many mantras and different daily practices, is building a beautiful house on a foundation of ice. On the other hand, someone who does not give up refuge journeys automatically towards enlightenment and the benefit of sentient beings. It is by taking refuge in the Triple Gem that one is, by definition, a Buddhist. Without this refuge one could belong to any of the other religions, such as Christianity or Islam. Therefore, the initial act of taking refuge followed by continued worship of the Triple Gem represents the beginning, duration, and end of a lifetime's practice of Buddhism.

There are many stories of the benefits that accrue to those who take refuge. If one takes refuge with deep confidence, from the bottom of one's heart, one receives protection from evil and many other different threats. It also brings success, many blessings, and the achievement of one's wishes. One will never suffer results such as those of the man described in dharma history who recited one hundred million Hevajra[21] mantras, only to be reborn in a demonic form due to practicing with the wrong motivation. This happened because he was only interested in acquiring worldly power and siddhis from his practice and did not focus first upon taking refuge. He really did not understand the teaching of Lord Buddha and his followers, the sangha. It was due to the inherent energy of Vajrayana meditation that his mistaken path finally led him to this form. Therefore, one must practice the refuge prayer sincerely to avoid such an outcome.

Each sect recites this prayer according to its particular lineage. The short form is:

> Buddham sha ra nam ga cha mi
> Dharmam sha ra nam ga cha mi
> Sangham sha ra nam ga cha mi

One can also simply repeat the Tibetan form, 'Sangyay la chab su chio' many times. An old friend of mine in Surmang Gaden Gompa, a Gelukpa geshe, was always reciting the following form, which you might also find convenient:

> 'Sangyay la chab su chio I take refuge in the Buddha
> Cho la chab su chio   I take refuge in the Dharma
> Gendun la chab su chio' I take refuge in the Sangha

If very busy, one can say:

> 'Konchog sum la chab su chio' – I take refuge in the Triple Gem

While others might look with contempt on someone who only practices the refuge prayer, actually such a practitioner is acting out of faith and confidence in the Triple Gem just like the great Atisha himself. It would be incorrect to conclude that this person is doing very little, because taking refuge is the greatest source of blessing. It is like a victory banner, and whoever holds this practice is ultimately victorious.

If one wishes to make a more detailed study of the qualities of Buddha one should study the *Uttaratantra Shastra*, the *Prajnaparamita Sutra*, and the *Abhisamayalankara Shastra*, as well as various other Mahayana sutras. The more one studies, the more understanding and wisdom accrues. Doubts and confusion are reduced while faith and confidence are increased. One finds that the qualities of Buddha are mentioned a great deal in the sutras; however, this is not praise for only Shakyamuni. In fact, the reason for such praise is that it causes one to discover how great one's own natural qualities are, because each one of us is capable of fully understanding the dharmakaya, true natural primordial emptiness.

The guru does for his student what Buddha Vajradhara does for his followers in the sambhogakaya realm who are close to the fullest enlightenment. He directly introduces the student who is qualified for Vajrayana practice by virtue of possessing the sharpest intelligence, to the state of enlightenment. By this initiation and transmission, the guru authorizes the student to practice the Vajrayana method that can lead to the complete realization of enlightenment in one lifetime, or in a short period of time. Without the guru there is no Vajrayana transmission and no blessing, just as without a magnifying glass one cannot start a fire from the sun's rays no matter how hot a day it is. Therefore, the guru is most important.

Some special students who are ready due to having keen faculties may actually become enlightened in the moment of receiving initiation, as in the cases of Guru Rinpoche and Indrabhuti. Such a practitioner who has been opened to the enlightened state in this way instantly escapes the cognition of illusory reality and manifests the four kayas. Ordinary delusion and impurity, the ocean of samsara, are all in one moment transformed into the energy of the four-kaya nature. The student is immediately freed from the conception of the duality of samsara and nirvana, from both positive and negative paths. For other students of moderate or lesser intelligence, an initiation plants the seed for the cultivation of enlightenment. The seed will grow and its fruit ripen later, through meditation and practice. In this case one needs to apply right conduct, samaya, more discipline, correct view and understanding, and patient and diligent practice.

The Vajrayana is the primordial teaching. It is precious and rare. It is transmitted mind to mind, by symbols and by oral teachings. It is there from the beginning, but appears before one moment by moment. It is transmitted to us through the guru and the lineage. For example, it is difficult for us right now to understand the concept of the smallest atom being equal to the universe. However, for the enlightened mind there is no dualistic discrimination; the space of one atom equals universal energy, universal time and space. Another way of putting this is that the whole universe is completely 'zero', empty, in the same way that an atom is empty. The expanse of the universe, and the space occupied by the tip of one hair, do not contradict each other. They are both 'zero'. There, you find enlightenment. There, is the primordial true nature, beyond time and space. Where this 'zero' contacts relativity, our ordinary reality emerges, and limits are created (perhaps analogous to what science terms the 'big bang'). Buddha said that the tip of a hair equals the expanse of a buddhafield, and that the elements of the world equal the elements of a buddhafield. In the space of the tip of one hair are countless buddhas of the three times and their buddhafields, but it is not crowded. Whether in the buddhafield or in the world of time and space, the nature of elements remains unchanged: 'zero.'

Therefore, what we might read as a praise of some external being such as Shakyamuni – is actually a method through which one also gains more respect for oneself. The doctrines of the Mahayana sutras and shastras are a form of self-examination. As one recites, understands and learns from these teachings, the ignorance and duality of viewing oneself or other sentient beings as very low or insignificant (in comparison to something else which has great qualities) disappears. So, it would be good whether one studies Buddhist doctrines extensively and becomes a very learned scholar, or whether one just understands the refuge prayer and practices the essence of Buddhism with strong faith and determination. Both kinds of practitioner are very important. Being a scholar is just the same as having good eyesight so when journeying through a dangerous place one will not step into danger or take the wrong road, even though one is without a guide.

On this point, the most important emanation of Manjushri, the great saint and scholar Sakya Pandita,[22] said:

> However much the wise are lacking in resources,
> they will not go the way that fools have taken[23]

Therefore, it is very beneficial to study. In this respect the great nineteenth century Nyingma[24] master Patrul Rinpoche declared that people should study the teachings of 'the three great Manjushri lamas'. He was referring to the great master Sakya Pandita Kunga Gyaltsen (1182–1251), the great Nyingma master Longchen Rabjampa (1308–1364), and the founder of the Gelug[25] sect, Je Tsong Khapa Lobsang Drakpa (1357–1419). The various Kagyu sects have also had famous scholars, for example, the Eighth Karmapa Mikyo Dorje of the Karma Kagyu, Padma Karpo of the Drukpa Kagyu, Drigung Chokyi Dakpa of the Drigung Kagyu, and Ngawang Namgyal of the Taklung Kagyu.

Studying the work of these great scholars brings real understanding of Buddha's teachings, and more importantly, removes any sectarian views one might hold. Removing sectarian views is the best activity; holding them is the worst. During debate the various philosophical tenets of the different sects are challenged or criticized. However, this is just like sharpening a pair of scissors in preparation for use, because the views held by each sect come to be better understood as all the different levels of conflict are cut away.

4
GENERAL POINTS

MANY PEOPLE ASK ME ABOUT THE PRACTICE OF BUDDHISM but I really see no separation between Buddhist practice and daily life. It is unlike practices in which an outside authority dictates the rules that you are to live by. In human life all activity takes the three different forms of thought, speech, and physical action. When these three forms of activity do not spring from the correct motivation they result in the creation of problems and suffering. Lord Buddha's teachings are all antidotes to this suffering and its causes. I remember what my gurus taught. The first priority is to knock down the ego. To ascertain the benefit of one's activity one should consider the following: if there is little benefit to others but great damage to self then one should refrain from that course of action; if there is tremendous benefit to others and great damage to self then one should proceed, if there is great benefit to others and little damage to self then one should proceed, and finally, if there is little benefit to others and little damage to self one should choose to proceed. This is the skillful means of the Mahayana practitioner. At the very least, always avoid hurting others in order to benefit oneself. These are difficult truths but we have to know them. Sakya Pandita said that those with good eyesight will not step over the edge of a cliff; however, for someone without sight even a small misstep of half an inch could result in a fall.

Firstly, the actions of the mind are very important. From the moment one gets up in the morning, and through all the minutes and hours until going to bed at night, one needs to concentrate very precisely on right thinking – one's motivation for doing things. One should consider this from the standpoint of what is beneficial for oneself, one's family, and all others. Right thinking is the bodhisattva's principal motivation of benefitting others where all virtuous thinking that arises, such as egolessness in dedicating oneself for others, wanting to prevent the suffering of one's family and all other beings, practicing the Buddhist path, or taking ordination, is dedicated in loving compassion to others. Whatever success one achieves in holding this attitude through the course of the day should be rejoiced in. Also, if family members or other people enjoy some spiritual or worldly success, or become free from problems or mental suffering, it is also reason to rejoice.

One should investigate to see how to create more benefit through the practice of the ten perfections (Skt. paramita). Milarepa said that to have no covetousness is transcendental generosity, to have no mental clinging is transcendental morality, to have no hatred in the mind is transcendental patience, to have no forgetfulness is transcendental diligence, and so on. Therefore, there are two approaches. Milarepa's bodhisattva way is one of freedom from worldly actions, speech, and thought. The other is that of worldly virtue, where the bodhisattva works in the material world with material goods. One can choose either the solitude of esoteric practice as a homeless bodhisattva, or to be a bodhisattva in the world. If one has the material means, one can give; if one has nothing, one can simply meditate. One should always choose the course of action that is the most beneficial for others, whether in business, spiritual, political, or everyday situations. This is the source of happiness.

Consider how much the great bodhisattvas of the past and present have cherished and continue to cherish others. Try to emulate their bodhisattva attitude by bringing benefit to both others and oneself, and rejecting whatever is wrong or harmful. This can be compared to climbing to the top of a snow mountain. In order to do this, one copies those who have already made a safe and successful trip, such as Sherpa Tenzing,[1] using similar good equipment and the same safe and direct route. Maintaining correct motivation and right thinking is the best source of benefit for everyone. In order to develop this, one needs to learn from the two best teachers, which are past mistakes and past successes. Mind is the basic creator of happiness and suffering. When one's motivation is pure, good, and correct, it is like the raw silk thread that the master weaver uses to create the most beautiful silk cloth with many different hues and patterns – cloth so fine it could be used for the hats and crowns of royalty. On the other hand, if the mind is involved with jealousy, anger, hatred, mistrust or selfishness it is no different from concealing a bomb, because this can lead to great suffering for oneself and others. If one touches a bomb by mistake, or unknowingly puts it in a fire, it will explode and be capable of destroying many beautiful buildings and flowering parklands; and young girls as lovely as peacocks and gentle, old and wise people who happen to be in the vicinity would be killed. It is better to meditate on the danger of these emotions and to try to reduce or conquer them, or transform them into wisdom.

Therefore, one's first plan for a day, month or year, and one's first thought each day, are very important, as one is thereby choosing to follow a positive or negative path. This is a very profound teaching of Buddha that comes from the Eightfold Noble Path of the Shravakayana, where it is known as 'right view'. Even if one should wish to become the prime minister of a country, this initial seed of motivation is very important. According to the Mahayana teachings, if one does not have the correct view the seed of bodhichitta cannot be established. It is for this reason that the Mahayana makes no distinction between lay and ordained practitioners. Correct view is the same as honey, which is delicious to all who taste it whether they are poor, royal, or crazy. In the Vajrayana also, one's initial thought or plan is very important since, if correct, it quickly leads to enlightenment. Therefore, Buddhism places great emphasis on the individual's motivation.

Sometimes non-Buddhists visit a monastery, and even though they consider it a lowly place, they ask the Triple Gem for a blessing to take them to paradise. This is a mistake, for as long as a person's mind is unclean no one can lead him or her to a high goal. This would be like throwing a stone into the air – it can only fall back down again and might even hit your head or hurt someone else. Also, some poor people visit holy beings and ask for blessings to bring wealth and success, but this too is impossible because it is like asking someone to do the job of an elected prime minister when they do not have the power to do so. However, with right motivation one can plan a good way to avoid poverty and improve one's life situation, and then as long as one has also accumulated merit, a holy being does have the power to give a blessing for success. One can also use effective practices such as Tara, Dzambala, Vaishravana, and Ganesha. This kind of blessing for great worldly success was created by Buddha and is part of his energy. Therefore, in everything one does it is important to use right thinking and planning, and to have good accumulation of merit. This is like having two feet for walking. Also, if one is able to correct one's actions and accumulate good karma in daily life, one can then request the Triple Gem to lead one to the pure realm of Sukhavati at the time of death.

Buddhism is called the 'Middle Way', transcending extremes. Many people have told me that those who become Buddhist should give up all worldly success, should see worldly business as impermanent, useless, and full of suffering, and choose to live in poverty. I think this view is mistaken. Although thinking that everything is in essence only suffering and impermanence and giving up all property is very, very important, such practice is only for those bodhisattvas who become ordained sangha and lead a monastic life, or for practitioners such as Milarepa, who stay in solitude. This kind of ascetic bodhisattva practice, that uses the four dharma thoughts[2] as a generator and keeps one's journey solely on the path of enlightenment, is wonderful. This is the path of the Shravaka and bodhisattva sanghas.

Milarepa thought of nothing other than reaching enlightenment in one lifetime. However, amongst ordinary lay people who become Buddhists not everyone is ready for such ascetic practice. This is why those who say that even lay people should give up everything are mistaken. Lay people can continue a practice where daily life is inseparable from the Buddha Dharma (Lord Buddha's teaching). The ascetic approach is good for the monastic sangha but bad for the laity, and it is a mistake to think this should apply to all Buddhists. Adherents of this mistaken view see Buddhism as something very separate from daily life; however, this is not the Buddhist view. There are many lazy and somewhat ignorant people quite lacking in any merit who live in poverty, so merely being poor does not mean one can call oneself a Buddhist. The Mahayana puts great emphasis on the relief of the mental and physical suffering of others. Suffering is the lack of good conditions for the body and mind, such as the lack of medicine, nutritious food, adequate living conditions, houses, position, money, and so on. Lack of these leads to tremendous physical suffering, and in turn to mental suffering as people become desperate and act in unrestrained and wicked ways. This suffering is precisely what Mahayana is designed to stop, and one method of achieving this is through practicing generosity, the first of the six perfections (paramitas).

A person who is rich and comfortable is usually deeply involved in samsaric life. If attachment to riches and power is very strong it results in another kind of suffering, one that leads people to destroy each other. This comes about through the creation of pride, jealousy and hatred. Discrimination is also created by this kind of attachment to samsara, making some people seem stupid and ugly while others seem intelligent and attractive. The source of this discrimination lies in attachment. It is not created by God or some primordial being such as Samantabhadra Buddha, but by individual hatred, jealousy and pride. In fact, the name 'Samantabhadra Buddha' refers to 'the never deluded initial purity', usually called buddha nature or enlightenment, that is the hidden nature of each individual sentient being. Samantabhadra Buddha radiated the sambhogakaya and nirmanakaya for the benefit of sentient beings in each of the twenty-six directions.

Secondly, having checked that one's mental actions are positive, the next most important concern in Buddhist teaching is one's daily use of speech. This is highly emphasised as one part of the Eightfold Noble Path proclaimed in Buddha's very first teaching in the Deer Park in Sarnath, India. In Mahayana teachings, gentleness of speech is considered very important. Even if one's speech is very wrathful it should be so only for the benefit of others. The basic source of speech is one's daily breath. This same breath is also used to create Lojong[3] – where on breathing out one sends goodness and happiness to all sentient beings, and on breathing in one takes in all their sufferings.[4]

Breath creates sound, and speech is a combination of sound and breath that creates words and sentences. Speech can be likened to the sound of a running car. When the sound changes, one knows that the car may need oil or some other kind of attention. One's mind is like the driver of the car. If one's speech causes others to be angry or upset, it indicates that an incorrect attitude is affecting one's speech. However, if one's initial thoughts are correctly motivated, they will lead to correct speech. Most mental suffering is created through speech because this is our main form of communication with others. Speech is important for both worldly and spiritual success. One's reason for speaking and the manner of one's speech can have a positive or negative effect, creating either happiness or suffering. If one's first words on meeting others are good, such as, "Are you well?" or, "Did you have a good journey?", the ensuing conversation will continue to follow your initial good motivation and thoughts. This is the same as the naturally beautiful sound created by blowing the bagpipes by which the piper plays different notes and rhythms. Even though it eventually ends, this music can bring relaxation and ease anger or tears with a little happiness. One of the qualities of Lord Buddha's enlightenment is that his wisdom precedes his speech, rests with his speech, and continues with his speech until it finishes. This means that in order to use words correctly one must always connect good motivation with one's speech. To speak correctly, truthfully and beneficially each day is what Buddha taught. Some people think that in order to practice one must refrain from speech, or that Buddhist practitioners do not talk much, but these ideas are wrong.

Speech can create tremendous happiness and can remove many different sources of suffering. In worldly life, if a politician is eloquent, it will help him or her appear more interesting. Lord Buddha could not have transmitted his realization of great loving compassion were it not for his speech. People who think that speaking creates trouble and that it is better to stay as silent as possible are greatly reducing the bodhisattva's capacity for action. If a partner, best friend or parent is sad or crying, one's sweet speech may immediately bring a smile. On the other hand, speech can also be a hindrance, because useless talk can upset one's routine and encourage laziness. Therefore, it is very important for the Buddhist practitioner to speak less when engaged in intensive practice. Speech can also be very dangerous, for example it can lead to actions such as killing. For this reason, the Vajrayana method always uses mantra, thus turning speech into a source of tremendous accumulation of merit that brings purification and leads to enlightenment. So never talk about the faults of another or be unpleasant, even if he or she is a friend or a member of your family. Always be polite and use pleasant words to try to create happiness. Speech can make people happy in many ways, such as recounting jokes, stories, legends, history or myths, or by singing songs. These are very good worldly ways of creating happiness in society and preventing many unpleasant mental sufferings. Therefore, one's first words when speaking should always be good ones, such as, "How are you?" For the spiritual practitioner the first speech of the day is prayer and the morning puja is very important. So, this second form of activity, the world of speech, is inseparable from the Buddha dharma. Speech in Buddha dharma does not mean only chanting and prayer, or someone sitting on a throne teaching the sutras. These activities are very good as a method for accumulating merit and blessing, but the Buddha dharma is really the correct use of one's own speech.

Thirdly, good motivation and good thinking lead to good physical action, which is very important. Pure action is also part of the Eightfold Noble Path taught by Lord Buddha. Following the path of pure action in daily life affects what one does in business, serving others, and preventing the suffering of oneself and others. Kind mind and gentle speech cannot achieve much without physical action. A dilapidated old car with broken wheels, doors, and windows cannot go very far even though the driver might be highly qualified and the road very good. Daily actions are therefore very important. If one has good motivation but one's actions are negative or careless, suffering follows, just as if one leaves fine milk in a hot place, it turns sour and cannot be used. Therefore, always try to be sure that your first action in the morning is very good. For example, good spiritual behaviour would be to sit properly in meditation each morning, or to bow to the shrine. One should start with this spiritual activity and then mentally promise never to indulge in any bad physical activities from that hour, through all the days, weeks, months, years, and lifetimes until full enlightenment is reached. If you are a bodhisattva living a family life, remember that loving kindness begins in the home. For example, do not be rude to your family in the morning, smile at your partner with eyes of loving kindness, joke together happily. Sweetly wish your children a happy time at school with gentle and good behaviour, and to return home gently and happily. Do not speak harshly to them or fight in front of them and do not be grouchy, but at the same time show them correct discipline. This gives them direction for their future and for leading a good life both generally and at school. If you can, offer your wife or husband some pleasant and helpful advice for the day. If this is not possible then keep a positive attitude, forgetting problems, irritating habits, and resentments. If your situation is half bad and half good, remember the good half. This advice applies to normal situations. However, if the situation is always negative it is better to separate. Dampe Sangye said, "A relationship between loving, sweet, always positive friends is Dewachen[5] (heaven), and divorce in an unhappy family is Dewachen." Stop all actions that are bad for self and others. Stop them in the mind, and never engage in them physically. Try to do this all the time. This is the same as a shepherd constantly watching each individual sheep so it will not wander away and get lost.

Always endeavour to generate a bodhisattva attitude of generosity and morality, and always try, according to one's individual capacity, to make this permeate one's physical activity. One worldly wish is to become wealthy. To achieve this one should work hard physically, first looking for a suitable and good job and then doing it correctly and well without thinking solely of one's income. This helps to bring enough comfort to one's home and family, and allows one to be generous towards spiritual and worldly causes that bring benefit to others. If one wishes to have good living conditions, one also needs to engage in correct physical action and work, either one's own or directing another to work correctly. Physical action is therefore very important and one's daily correct physical actions are not separate from the Buddha Dharma, Lord Buddha's teaching.

As daily human life is never separate from Buddha's teachings everyone should try to become a good Buddhist. Some Buddhist people say that others are very sectarian; but if one truly understands daily life in Buddhism what remains of sectarian concerns? Everyone is a child of Buddha following the same path with the same fruit; the only difference is the interpretation of the various lineages where, if one looks carefully, there is actually no essential difference. So, whatever one's karmic connection with Buddhist practice, one should practice with confidence and faith. All good motivation, speech, and action is Buddha Dharma. A holder of Buddhism who practices this main teaching is a most profound son or daughter of the Buddha. If one looks carefully, all sentient beings come from the same source and are equally of one family, so there is no reason for discrimination or sectarianism. A divisive attitude is only created when someone turns his or her religion into some kind of property and then becomes frightened or threatened by views that are not the same. Buddha told bhikshus and bhikshunis that they should never keep extra clothes and should even dye and resew discarded clothing to make what they need. Such humble clothing signifies that goodness cannot be measured by outward appearance, but only by the degree to which the mind holds correct view and inner discipline and is purified by bodhichitta. Buddha provided monastic rules for those suited to a more humble path, and who need the discipline and relative solitude of monastic life.

On the other hand, Buddha also said one could wear the best quality robes woven with one hundred ounces of gold, or wear rags from the charnel grounds as did the most disciplined of ascetics. The earliest Buddhist statues from Gandhara dating from the first century BCE, portray bodhisattvas such as Avalokiteshvara and Manjushri wearing jewels and rich clothing. This signifies that Mahayana teaching does not solely encourage one to give up worldly life. The statues show that because the minds of these great bodhisattvas are fully developed in the two bodhichittas of absolute and relative truth, they can either wear wealthy costumes or dress as monks in saffron robes and hold alms bowls. The royal quality of the bodhisattva's costume represents the royalty of the inner strengths of generosity, morality, patience, and diligence. A bodhisattva could give his clothing away without any attachment if someone were in need, whereas a mind of greed and attachment can never be free. When not disciplined by bodhichitta, even if wearing rags, one would not be able to give away one's clothing without attachment. When one has the strength of bodhichitta, one's inner clothing is that of Manjushri even if one's outer garments are rags. Thus, this rich costume is a source of merit and does not interfere with bodhisattva activity. It does not bring greed, selfishness, or the desire for wealthy conditions. Therefore, for a good Mahayana practitioner, daily life is always very important.

The holders of the Buddha Dharma fall into the two groups of monastic and lay practitioners. Living a monastic life is a source of merit. Bodhisattvas who follow this kind of practice wear saffron robes, shave off their hair, and lead a homeless life, thereby attaining benefit for self and others. The sangha is one of the three objects of refuge. Buddha said that those of his disciples who live the monastic life, no matter how weak they might be, are spiritually superior to lay people. Therefore, lay people should always respect the sangha. This is true because even if a member of the ordained sangha engaged in many negative actions of mind, speech and body, there still remains the possibility that he or she could retain many positive actions and precepts. This is not so for lay people, who, if they do not practice or maintain correct mindfulness, cannot achieve very much at all. This is a hindrance to the bodhisattva way of life and creates a great deal of suffering. It is actually opposite to Lord Buddha's teachings through which all of one's life becomes the Buddha Dharma. However, if, as a householder, one turns one's home into a Buddhist temple and always sees one's environment, elements and inner organs as a shrine, then whatever one does there is no cause for worry, even if one is not successful. If one tries to follow the path of goodness, then worries, sadness, or disappointment over lack of success will disappear.

The essence of daily life in Buddhism is the mindfulness that comes from the practice of shamatha and vipashyana[6] and the Vajrayana views of Mahamudra, and Maha Sandhi (Tib. Dzog Chen – literally 'Great Perfection') which derives from the meditation tradition of the great Nyingmapa sect that was founded by Guru Rinpoche Padma Sambhava and Vimalamitra. When great Vajrayana practitioners achieve enlightenment, the body turns into that of the deity and the mind to luminosity, and thus the practice and the deity become inseparably united. Buddhist deities are different manifestations of enlightenment, and as the practice of the deity meditation gradually improves, daily life itself becomes buddha-mind. It does not matter whether one holds to monastic life as a bhikshu or bhikshuni, or remains a member of the laity – one now holds enlightenment in the palms of one's hands.

Thus, in the thirteenth and fourteenth centuries the Nangchen region of Tibet was known as Gomde Nangchen, which means 'Meditation Country'. It was given this name because its people put great emphasis on the learning and practice of meditation, thereby attaining enlightenment. An expression which has come down in legend from that time says, "The ladies spinning wool are enlightened, the men wearing bows and arrows are enlightened and the children at play are enlightened." I hope that this will also happen here in the West. Perhaps a country such as Canada can become known as 'Gomde Jang' (Northern Meditation Country) or 'Gomde Nub' (Western Meditation Country).

The previous advice about body, speech and mind in daily life, and the good qualities I mentioned, are all 'conventional truth' (relative truth) teachings. These are like a boat or ship for those wishing to cross the ocean. The last points regarding meditation practice refer to 'ultimate truth' teaching, which is like the captain of the boat. However, all depends upon the individual practitioner. If one cannot do all these practices, it should not be a cause for worry – simply carry on steadily with what one can do. Instructions for the ultimate truth aspect of Buddhist life are included in the sections on meditation. One should continuously share the merit of whatever good actions of mind, speech and body one accomplishes, both great and small, with all sentient beings.

I think that for the East and now for the West, Lord Buddha was most compassionate because he came intentionally offering equal protection for all sentient beings, from humans to the smallest ant. His teaching of bodhichitta (loving, compassionate mind), called the Mahayana or 'Great Vehicle', is expounded in the *Prajnaparamita* (*The Perfection of Wisdom*). This sutra is also named *The Great Mother of Enlightenment* as it includes all the Shravakayana and Mahayana training for transcending duality and realizing shunyata. The long, medium and short *Prajnaparamita* texts are, *The Prajnaparamita in One Hundred Thousand Verses* (Tib. *Bum*), ... *in Twenty Thousand Verses* (Tib. *Nyitri*), and ... *in Eight Thousand Verses* (Tib. *Gyay Tongpa*), which fill many volumes. Shortest of all is the single syllable, AH. The essence of the *Prajnaparamita* is the *Heart Sutra*, which we should study and contemplate. This sutra is short, concise, and easy to memorize. Initially its meaning appears simple, however, the more one studies it the deeper it becomes, for the knowledge it contains is infinite. This means that until one achieves enlightenment it is not possible to completely plumb the profound depths of this teaching, no matter how scholarly one might be.

Indeed, the *Heart Sutra* contains all the five paths and ten bhumis that culminate in buddhahood. The first, the Path of Accumulation, is that of the ordinary beginner who has some capacity for understanding the *Heart Sutra*. This is the path on which the practitioner works to stabilize his or her experience. On the second, the Path of Application, the understanding of shunyata taught in the sutra becomes much deeper and vaster. These two paths are those of the worldly level bodhisattva, while the next two are those of the bodhisattva who has progressed beyond the worldly level. The third path, the Path of Perfect Seeing, is the stage at which the complete meaning of the *Heart Sutra*, the Sixteen Emptinesses[7] (shunyata), is realized. Here the first bhumi ('Joyful One') is reached, where the depth of understanding is much greater than on the previous paths. The fourth path is the Path of Meditation, where one cultivates or deepens one's understanding and, during which, one ascends from the second to the tenth bhumis. The final path is that of Buddhahood itself, which is known as the Path of Fulfillment.

Compassion is the strong wish for all sentient beings to be free from all suffering. The development of compassion moves through three stages. At first one's compassion is based merely upon one's awareness of the sufferings of sentient beings, then one's compassion ripens as one learns the Buddha doctrine, until eventually one realizes the lack of true existence and non-conceptual compassion arises. On the first two paths (Accumulation and Application) the worldly concept of compassion disappears; in this way compassion is strengthened and refined, becoming more subtle. Before reaching the first bhumi, shunyata was like the flower and loving compassion was like its honey (Tib. tongnyi nyingjay nyingpo chan). At the first bhumi, shunyata and compassion are just one. United and inseparable, they are like honey and sweetness (Tib. tongdang nyingjay zungjug).

On the Path of Accumulation, one may feel that one knows all the Buddhist teachings, but one's understanding is still very simple compared to one who is on the second path. This is true even if one holds a high scholarly degree such as: 'Geshe', equivalent to a western doctorate (Ph.D.); 'Khenpo', degree of abbot; 'Rabjampa', master of all the five Buddhist sciences; 'Kazhipa', master of four subjects; or 'Kachupa', master of ten subjects. These titles come from the ancient Buddhist scholastic institutes, or shedras.

It is said that truly profound knowledge begins only with the attainment of the first bhumi. So, if someone says they know everything there is to know in Buddhism I would think that this could not be true. It is better to keep quiet and simply teach what one knows. At the present time everyone is on the path of the accumulation of merit through listening, investigation, and meditation. As I am now answering questions put to me about Buddhism, which is limitless, then what I say in reply is just my point of view. I will tell you only what I have heard and what I know. However, I am sure that I make mistakes all the time in explaining the doctrine of Lord Buddha, so I apologize for this to the dharmapalas.

5
BODHICHITTA

EVERY DAY ONE SHOULD MEDITATE ON and think about the Prajnaparamita for a short time. It reveals the nature of bodhichitta and how to give rise to it. Bodhichitta (literally 'enlightenment thought') means to 'wake oneself up', in the sense that we are asleep and merely playing in our dreams. In this dream situation we are not really sure how to act; sometimes we are right and sometimes wrong. While we experience confusion, sadness, happiness, and joy, all of these are really just states of delusion. Between birth and death is a constant dream. Understanding this gives rise to bodhichitta.

Whatever happens in this dream of delusion yields no fruit, as its basic characteristic is suffering. When it is cold in Canada, for example, one may wish to be in a warmer place like India. However, if one went there, one would find that although the Indian winter may be pleasant, the summer is so unbearable that even one's clothes become burning hot. If one should attempt to avoid the heat by staying in a cool house, showering continually, lying on the ground or drinking as much cool water as possible, the only result would be discomfort. At this point one may well wish to go somewhere cooler, and the attachment to warm places disappears. Next, one may wish to be in a more temperate climate, but eventually this would become so boring that, once again, one would wish to change one's surroundings. Viewing things in this manner reveals the continually dissatisfying nature of everything.

As a further example, when a handsome young man meets a beautiful woman, he may think she is like an angel and they may greatly enjoy each other's company. After staying together for a while, their mutual enjoyment fades and is forgotten, the relationship deteriorates, they part, and finally they cannot even bear to think of one another again. No lasting satisfaction is achieved. The problem is caused by their losing interest in loving each other, and then, internally and externally, many conflicts begin to arise and create disturbances. Therefore, in this kind of situation, each person needs continual mindfulness. Each one needs to try hard to hold loving-kindness and sharing toward the other, as well as openly declaring problems and trying to solve them. When people wander in a world of illusory dreams, interactions with one another are similar to rubbing a stone against a piece of iron; the result is fire and both partners have a feeling of dissatisfaction.

In life, whatever one does does not last. However, when one acts with bodhichitta

the results are longer lasting. Relationships between people who are 'awake' are similar to healers working together. If problems are experienced it is first necessary to realize what is happening and to reflect on the nature of the problem. Then one must endeavour to be more gentle and patient and learn to subdue the 'self'. If the situation cannot be resolved by means of patience and bodhichitta then it is better for each to go their own way, rather than to stay together unhappily. Hence the Tibetan expression that if people stay together in friendship and joy it is Dewachen, but if people are staying together in an unfriendly manner, then separation is Dewachen. We are living on this earth as human beings for such a short time that it is best to be as relaxed and comfortable, and to have as much happiness and enjoyment as possible through the hours, days, months, and years.

How does one become awakened? Firstly, one needs to develop conventional bodhichitta, and secondly, one must attain ultimate bodhichitta. These are the two feet needed to walk. To go about this, one must first realize that each sentient being possesses the causes of suffering. Negative emotions and thoughts can lead to negative actions. If one engages in such actions, one is planting the seeds of one's own future suffering, and these will inevitably ripen. For example, if you habitually lie, eventually no one will believe you anymore, you will become known as a liar, and people will gossip about you. Thus, you will have created suffering for yourself. There are many karmas that ripen in the same lifetime, but there are also many that will ripen in future lives. Once one can see how beings cause their own suffering, the wish arises to protect sentient beings and remove their suffering – this is compassion. At this point one needs to sit and meditate upon all aspects of suffering. This is like a doctor who cannot give medicine to a patient until learning about the nature of sickness. Suffering is caused by the five negative emotions, which are desire, pride, envy, aggression, and ignorance. If one resides in this web of emotions and pays them too much attention, the result is mostly suffering. It is best to wake up to the realization that these are one's real enemies, and will continue to be as long as one does not employ the correct antidotes to subdue them.

The Shravakayana, Mahayana, and Vajrayana systems present many methods to subdue and cut off negative emotions. The Shravakayana attitude is to regard the five negative emotions as enemies that must be subdued by developing discipline, as the Buddha said that one must subdue one's own mind. This means subduing the negative emotions through the daily activity of disciplining the mind by training in how to speak, think, and act. Some people find it very easy to practice this discipline and are able to live a family life. Others find it much more difficult and need the opportunities provided by monastic ordination. They cut their hair, an act which represents negative thoughts falling away, and hold a begging bowl that represents maintaining conscientiousness. It is for this reason that there are the two separate classes of ordained and lay practitioners. Lord Buddha handed down many rules, known collectively as the

Vinaya, all of which serve the purpose of disciplining the mind. However, if one finds the Shravakayana methods of disciplining the mind too austere, then perhaps one can try the Mahayana methods, especially the practice of Lojong, or different Vajrayana techniques.

6
LOVING-KINDNESS

IF YOU READ THE LIFE STORIES of the founders of religious discipline and morality you see that Buddha and Christ were very gentle and did not use weapons and armies. They both taught loving-kindness, and through this they were victorious and religions were established in their names. I myself do not know of others like this, maybe the histories of all founders of religions are similar to these; however, I have used these two particular examples. I have heard that in the Middle Ages some Christians were quite zealous, but since then the influence has been more gentle and this has resulted in the establishment of good social services in the West today. Maybe it is for this reason that in the West there is a basically very good way of life.

Without loving-kindness for everyone, religion becomes wild. For example, I heard about an ancient Central American religion where the priests wore golden gauntlets to tear out the hearts of living human beings as sacrifice to their gods. Although I consider sacrifice to be nothing more than superstition, hundreds of thousands of beings have died in sacrificial rites. This kind of religion is very much the opposite of Lord Buddha's doctrine, and Buddhists would never accept that this method of practice could lead to any good results. One can easily see from either a Buddhist or scientific point of view that the sacrifice of living beings does nothing to achieve the intended aims, such as stopping sickness or bringing rain. Buddha said that if you kill or cause harm to others, then this life and subsequent lives will be short and full of sickness. It would be more effective to try to cut off the hope for external assistance that led to using this method of seeking happiness.

If one gave rise to the four limitless thoughts[1] of bodhisattva training and meditation there would be no need to sacrifice life, or waste family necessities. Legend recounts the tale of a very selfish king who lived in the Kham region of Tibet. In front of his castle a high rocky mountain blocked the morning sun, so the king ordered his subjects to cut the top off the mountain. After they had endured the toil of this labour for two years, an ordinary and very wise old man, who realized that the task was impossible, saw that the same effect would be achieved by cutting off the head of the king. Finding many others approved of this idea he led them to the castle, where they beheaded the king. There was then no need to continue the fruitless labour of removing the top of the mountain. Apparently, the scar that was left on the mountain can still be seen today.

As a further example, Shantideva[2] says in the *Bodhisattvacharyavatara*:

> Where would I possibly find enough leather
> with which to cover the surface of the earth?
> But leather just on the soles of my shoes
> is equivalent to covering the earth with it.
> Likewise, it is not possible for me
> to restrain the external course of things,
> But should I restrain this mind
> what would be the need to restrain all else?[3]

Therefore, one should cut through negative emotions and wrong ideas about harming sentient beings, and instead practice discipline and loving-kindness. 'Beheading the king' is an apt metaphor, because there is then no longer any need to hope for some external change while continuing to develop internal ignorance. The inner development of ignorance and the outer hope for a different situation both lead to activities such as making sacrifices. So, one should try to cut ignorance. Where there is no ignorance, there is the end of the creation of suffering.

It is very important for those who are in positions of power to have compassion and to practice the training of loving-kindness, because they are able to achieve so much more than thousands of ordinary people. In this nuclear age especially, there is need for a great, compassionate leader. Mahatma Gandhi, for example, served all the people of India equally for a long time through his compassion and selflessness. He did not rely on bodyguards and could shake hands with, and stay among, the people. In this way he served everyone equally for many years and was of great benefit to the nation. A dictatorial leader may have much power to conquer but he cannot visit his own people in the street because they would immediately threaten him. This would indicate that he is not really serving his people with kindness.

Of course, Gandhi himself was eventually murdered and I have heard that this was due to religious bigotry. The man who killed him gave no thought to the Mahatma's good bodhisattva way of life and his beneficial influence, which was such that one might have wished for his life to be extended for a further hundred years. The assassin also gave no thought for the needs of the people of the country or for their future, but only considered his own extremist point of view. I think that this kind of person is totally caught up by his religion and has a very narrow view. I also have a quite strong belief in my own religion, which could be termed a kind of sectarianism. However, when I look carefully at the reason for this, I find that it is not simply a strong attachment to my religion such that I would die for it, or that I must convert others to it. Instead, I feel that the principle of Lord Buddha's teaching is to help all universal sentient beings equally through bodhichitta, whether they are my close friends, my enemies, or those towards whom I feel neutral. I see that the Mahayana is much stronger than other teachings. Even though the Buddhist system of logic and debate has a kind of sectarian view in that it tries to invalidate other views and establish its own philosophical points, it is in essence seeking to find the true path by which to cherish all beings and lead them to liberation.

Genuine Buddhists do not believe in discriminating against any sentient being, each of whom has mind, feelings, hope, and fear, because all need to be saved from suffering and to have loving-kindness for each other. Buddhist deities themselves are the highest bodhisattvas. We therefore believe that they would not accept the idea of having any sentient being sacrificed to them in exchange for bestowing happiness. Bodhichitta is therefore very important. This shows that everyone, regardless of status, whether a wealthy businessman or an ascetic leading a humble life, needs to practice bodhichitta training.

It is very easy to talk about this training but it is very difficult to actually practice it. It can make one very happy to hear Mahayana teachings, more so than those of the Shravakayana or Vajrayana, but to really gain experience through practice is a much harder to achieve. Out of a hundred practitioners of the other yanas there would probably be only a few who have achieved true experience of bodhichitta. Therefore, in one of his first acts as a perfectly enlightened Buddha, Shakyamuni turned the Wheel of Dharma of the Four Noble Truths, the Eightfold Noble Path and the Vinaya, because most people needed to practice this kind of discipline. Many people followed these teachings and achieved the state of an arhat – 'one who has subdued all his own evil tendencies'. Mahayana practice was, by comparison, very rare indeed.

7

MAHAYANA

As we have made clear, Mahayana is a very important teaching of Lord Buddha. Concerning this point, it is often said that Buddha has three sons. This refers to his physical son, Prince Rahula, the 'sons of his speech' who are those who follow the Shravakayana, and, finally, his 'heart sons', the bodhisattvas who practice the Mahayana teachings. These are called 'heart sons' because their path is really the Buddha's own path to enlightenment. The sutras relate how as an ordinary person, long ago, Buddha experienced the arising of loving-kindness in his mind. He then took the bodhisattva vow from Mahamuni, the Buddha of the previous world, to help sentient beings and relinquish self-cherishing.

This arising of loving-compassion was the seed of his enlightenment. Thereafter, over countless aeons, he practiced the ten perfections of generosity, morality, patience, diligence, meditation, wisdom, skillful means, prayer, power, and primordial wisdom, until he achieved the final result of full enlightenment, beyond the two extremes. Buddha is beyond the extreme of remaining in nirvana (the state of sorrowlessness that is the dharmakaya) because he also manifests in sambhogakaya mandalas and nirmanakaya forms in order to help all suffering beings as long as they exist in space. Buddha also transcends the extreme of worldliness (the state in which one can never achieve enlightenment nor liberate any being, even one's self) because he is completely free from ignorance. 'Returning to help all suffering sentient beings', means to turn the 'Wheel of Dharma' for them, thereby showering teachings like rain. Buddha's enlightenment and compassion are infinite, like sunshine radiating to fill all universes. 'Buddha activity' is the spontaneous fulfilling of all of his bodhisattva wishing prayers, continuing for as long as beings remain in samsara. This activity includes accomplishing temporary benefits and temporary relief of suffering for all beings through such good things as the light of the sun, moon and stars which dispel darkness, beautiful mountains, flowers, gemstones, and beneficial medicines, as well as eventually leading all beings to enlightenment and infinite happiness. Therefore, one can see clearly that Mahayana is the path of Lord Buddha's heart.

I am not presenting a sectarian view with respect to Shravakayana and Mahayana. If one studies Mahayana doctrine one will fully understand that it is the most profound means of achieving enlightenment for the benefit of sentient beings, and is the doctrine of Buddha himself. In ancient times there was much sectarianism between the

Shravakayana and Mahayana schools, as evidenced by arguments presented in such ancient texts as the *Bodhisattvacharyavatara*. The Shravakayana criticised the Mahayana as not being a direct teaching of Buddha. However, I feel that this is just normal conflict between people following the religion of their own sect, and does not mean that the Mahayana was not established as early as the Shravakayana. If one compares the two schools, one finds that they are basically the same, except that the Mahayana has much stronger teaching on loving-kindness and the ten perfections. They share many similar views. For example, Shravakayana also includes the Four Limitless Thoughts and compassion, and the Mahayana also teaches the Four Noble Truths and the Eightfold Noble Path. So essentially, they are the same and there are only a few differences. One cannot declare that one is the truth while the other is not. Generally, I believe that Mahayana is Shravakayana, and Shravakayana is Mahayana. For example, the teaching of emptiness involves the same notion of egolessness in both traditions, however, the philosophical explanation of emptiness is more profound in the Mahayana. Similarly, both traditions teach meditation on compassion, while the Mahayana teaching and practice of the six perfections extends this further.

Nowadays, some Western scholars also claim that Mahayana teachings were not in existence in Lord Buddha's time. I do not think this is true because many Mahayana sutras have survived, and sutras are direct teachings of Buddha. From just after his enlightenment at the age of thirty-five until his parinirvana at age eighty-two, a period of forty-seven years, Buddha only taught spiritual Dharma. No one knows exactly what he taught each day, month, or year. This cannot be established because it was not recorded at the time. In his first sermon, Buddha taught the Four Noble Truths. He then gradually established monastic rules for the ordained sangha. He gave the Shravakayana teachings of the Eightfold Noble Path, and the Three Vessels of the doctrine and their essence – the three trainings. These three, moral discipline (Skt. silashiksa), concentration (Skt. samadhishiksa) and prajna (Skt. prajnashiksa), comprise the three vessels of the Abhidharma, the Vinaya, and the Sutras upon which the Shravaka school is founded, and which spread all over Asia.

However, in general Mahayana practice, especially in the tradition of Nagarjuna, it is not necessary to take monastic vows, only bodhisattva vows are vital. The bodhisattva vow requires one to cherish sentient beings. The Bodhicharyavatara teaches that sentient beings are as precious to the practitioner as the Buddha himself. This is because while Buddha shows the path of enlightenment, sentient beings are the cause of the opportunity to practice compassion, loving kindness, bodhichitta, the ten paramitas, and all the practices of the path. Monastic vows prohibit much that a bodhisattva can do selflessly for others. For example, it is not always necessary for bodhisattvas to entirely give up worldly desire as there are some situations in which desire is not a hindrance. The bodhisattva Chakravartin kings participated in the worldly realm, attached to and working for sentient beings just as a mother is attached to her children, and they needed princes to continue their work. Bodhisattva activity therefore tended to be maintained by kings, queens, merchants, both the wealthy and the poor, and both lay men and lay women. It is likely that bodhisattvas such as Avalokiteshvara, Manjushri and Tara, wore the costumes of Indian princes, princesses, or ordinary people, rather than monastic robes.

It is possible that monks and nuns could have found it difficult to accept the dress and precepts of such family-oriented teachings. Also, the monastic institutions may not have accepted this teaching and lifestyle, perceiving it as a potential threat that might lead to the gradual decline of the monastic sangha. If this was indeed the case, they would have tried to discourage Mahayana practice and prevent it from progressing. Later, when the Shravakayana split into eighteen sects and became weaker, the Mahayana could have found enough freedom to restore itself and increase its influence, establishing many Mahayana schools and monasteries. Nalanda University was a Mahayana monastery and was the biggest educational institution in that part of ancient Asia. Furthermore, while the Shravakayana stressed the importance of shaving one's head and wearing saffron-coloured robes, the Mahayana did not find monastic vows as important. Therefore, it is possible that the Mahayana may not have been readily accepted at a time when everyone worshipped the sangha and built monasteries everywhere. In this way the Mahayana teachings would automatically have become rare and would have been rendered almost invisible.

Some scholars say that there are no old Mahayana sutras dating back to the time of Lord Buddha. However, I feel that for several reasons these could well have been very hard to preserve in India at that time. The hot climate and prevalence of insects in India can, even today, destroy cloth and whole books in one summer unless they are preserved carefully, with mothballs or some similar protection. Also, there were no woodblocks for printing in those days and books had to be copied by hand. By contrast, it is likely that Shravaka texts were extensively copied and carefully preserved in the monasteries of the day. Furthermore, at Nalanda University, one of the largest repositories of literature and especially of Mahayana texts, the libraries were destroyed by fire three times.

Another point concerning the seeming lack of dissemination of the Mahayana sutras is shown in the example, in Tibet, of the seventh Karmapa's two-volume commentary on logic and epistemology. This text had never been seen, and maybe never even heard of, in the monastic institutions of other sects, even though this was written about five hundred years ago. It has now been published, and the scholars from many different schools who have seen it have expressed their praise and respect. If a text could have become so obscure in a sparsely populated country like Tibet, it seems much more likely to have happened in a country as populous as India. The proponents of Shravakayana teachings were very influential and did not accept the Mahayana view. For these reasons the Mahayana sutras would have remained almost hidden because only a few bodhisattvas were practicing and preserving them.

Many Mahayana doctrines came from non-human sources. For example, it is said that Nagarjuna received the long, one hundred thousand verse form of the *Prajnaparamita Sutra* from the nagas.[1] This is either literally true, or it was a statement made with a specific intention at the time. However, even if it came to us from the naga realm this does not mean that it was not taught by the Buddha. Basically, whoever believes in deities or God, or in demons or ghosts, should accept the existence of nagas as well. If there is one kind of non-human spiritual being, then why not two, or three kinds? For example, when the Buddha turned the wheel of his teaching many gods and goddesses gathered to listen – the Shravakayana teachings also state this. Even Jesus said that he met angels and demons that tempted him during his forty-day fast in the wilderness. Examples like this may be found in all religions and provide proof of the existence of invisible beings. So, I believe the nagas preserved the *Prajnaparamita Sutra* and later passed it to Nagarjuna; I do not think that this is wrong. I also believe that some bodhisattva nagas have the ability to preserve the Buddha's teachings. Many other Mahayana sutras have similar stories and no one can prove these texts did not exist in India in Lord Buddha's time. Maybe if someone had stayed alive for two thousand five hundred years, he might remember. Therefore, if one says that this is untrue, one is discriminating, and furthermore, if one is incorrect in making such a statement it creates very bad karma. Faith and confidence are very important. Arya Asanga said that, in the end, it does not matter who gave the teaching because the teaching itself can purify the negative karma and negative emotions of the three worlds (the desire realm, the form realm, and the formless realm), and also teach us the method for attaining enlightenment, perfect buddhahood. We have to accept that this is the doctrine of Lord Buddha and treat it as such.

Mahayana practice is very difficult for ordinary people. In such practice, external monastic rules are not important because it is more an inner practice of right motivation. The principal aim is to completely lead sentient beings to enlightenment, with the bodhisattva himself or herself last of all. He or she is not frightened by either the duration or the vastness of the universe, and wants to stay as long as sentient beings exist in order to carry their sufferings. Secondly, the bodhisattva is not deterred by the limitless number of sentient beings in the universe, nor by taking responsibility for carrying and dealing with the sufferings of each one, and is also not afraid of the very difficult sacrifice of his or her self for sentient beings. It is said that even in going to hell to save sentient beings, the bodhisattva is like a swan diving joyfully into a lotus lake. He or she is unafraid to give property, organs, or flesh to sentient beings if necessary, or to practice the six perfections of the bodhisattva. Very few people can practice this difficult path but it is really the heart teaching of the Buddha. The goodness of the bodhisattva can be seen when one considers just how difficult it is to carry even one's own mental and physical suffering, and how happy and grateful one feels if someone tries to help you even in tiny matters such as giving one medicine for a bad headache, or kindly and gently giving directions if one is lost. The bodhisattva wants to completely carry all the sufferings of others and to stop all the suffering of the universe through extremely powerful loving-compassion. So, one can see that very few people can follow the true bodhisattva path. Whoever is a naturally qualified bodhisattva is joyful and happy to act in this way. Even if they needed to give their flesh, then through their great compassion they would give it with great joy and happiness, and it would not cause them any pain or suffering. Chandrakirti[2] said that should a qualified bodhisattva give his own flesh it would be the same for him as sharing a delicious soup.

Chandrakirti also said of the bodhisattva:

> His devotion to giving even his own flesh
> is reason for inferring the unimaginable.[3]

and:

> If some person, angry without reason, cut from his body ounces of flesh and bone for a long time, his patience towards his torturer would only increase.[4]

All those who are born with the bodhisattva characteristics of love and compassion do not find it difficult to act in this way. Some people, who do not show strong bodhisattva characteristics at birth, initially find this kind of bodhisattva activity difficult. However, as one practices step by step, one eventually becomes able to do everything joyfully. So, there is no need to discriminate between who is and who is not qualified.

The Mahayana is a very important and beneficial teaching given to us by Lord Shakyamuni. Even though we cannot truly and strongly follow the practice ourselves we should rejoice in the practice of the bodhisattvas. If merit had form, then the merit of rejoicing in this way for even one moment would fill the whole sky. It is also the best purification practice. Since one cannot achieve the level of the true bodhisattva immediately, one must begin gradually and continue practicing until one achieves it. At first, even though it is only a tiny effort by comparison, one should try to keep loving-kindness all the time and meditate on shunyata for brief sessions. At the same time, it is very important to study the Mahayana doctrines. A beginner cannot automatically develop into a bodhisattva. This happens little by little through knowledge, education, and practice. So, this humble way comes first.

How can one remove negative hindrances that obscure realization of emptiness? I have already briefly mentioned the Shravakayana approach to the five negative emotions. The Mahayana approach is to accept them and the suffering they create, and use them for the creation of loving-kindness and compassion. This is just the same as Khampa farmers using human waste that had been stored for one year to fertilize their fields, where it provides nutrients for a beautiful harvest of barley and fruit. Even though you may want to benefit and help sentient beings, you must first understand the self and develop bodhichitta. Our negative emotions are just like a teacher or a mirror. One cannot see oneself without a mirror, but one can see the whole of one's face with one. One can then practice Lojong.

8
MEAT EATING

It is very important to make an offering to the Triple Gem before eating food, because making such an offering connects us with the ceremony that we participated in when taking Refuge. There is an offering included in sadhanas which one can use, but a simpler way to practice it is to make a short prayer at each daily meal. In monasteries, each tradition uses its own particular prayers that are always said before the morning meal, lunch, and so on, and also at the conclusion of each meal. Ordinary people can use the following prayer before eating:

> I make this offering to the precious Buddha, unsurpassable teacher,
> To the precious Dharma, unsurpassable refuge,
> To the precious Sangha, unsurpassable guide,
> To the Three Jewels, the sources of refuge.

If the meal includes meat, one should recite the one hundred syllable mantra of Vajrasattva as well as those of Akshobya and Vairochana Buddha. Alternatively, one can use the short, six syllable mantra of Avalokitesvara,

> OM MANI PADME HUNG

or the short mantra of Vajrasattva,

> OM BENZA SATTVA HUNG

One particularly special mantra is:

> OM AH BHIRA HUNG KHETSARA MAM SWAHA

Other mantras can be learned from one's own Vajrayana tradition. Mantras continue to help the animal that has died, because the flesh of one lifetime is only one bead in a whole mala of lifetimes. The continuum that passes through each rebirth is the string joining the beads. So, the breath and sound of mantra brings the benefit of purification to the next rebirth. As Vajrayana Buddhism is quite popular at the present time, these mantras can be found quite easily; however, if one wants to use them, one should contact Buddhist teachers for transmission and correct pronunciation. By using mantra, one is recognizing the need to bring benefit to the animals whose flesh one is living off, and therefore one prays for them. The last mantra mentioned has especially great primordial power to benefit both the practitioner and the animal. The eater is purified of the bad karma of eating the flesh of another sentient being, and the animal also receives benefit.

In ancient times Tibetan lamas used the expression, "Those who eat meat should have compassion and those who drink alcohol should have samaya." This means that one has to recognize that the flesh belonged to a sentient animal and eat it with a compassionate mind, remembering where the meat has come from. A dharma practitioner who has taken no precepts forbidding the drinking of alcohol and who wants to drink, should still not do so to get drunk, but instead should view drinking as representative of energy and strength for the vajra body. This teaching is a very important one for all Buddhists who eat meat, as well as for lay Vajrayana practitioners who drink alcohol. Generally speaking, eating meat and drinking are harmful physical and mental activities that create negative karma for the Buddhist practitioner; therefore, it is better to stop consuming them. Whoever refrains from eating meat for reasons of compassion is truly following Buddhist activity, otherwise there is only a little positive karma gained. Compassionate motivation for not wanting to eat meat because it is the flesh of a sentient being that was once one's mother in a previous life, is very good indeed. This is especially true after one receives Mahayana precepts not to harm others, and thereby becomes a Mahayana practitioner. Many Buddhist people do not eat meat and one must rejoice in this very great activity. If one cannot break one's own habit of eating meat, then one should pray to be able to do so in the future.

Some people ask what difference there is between the many Tibetan lamas and monks who eat meat, and someone who actually kills an animal for their own consumption. There is a big difference. Many lamas compassionately refrain from eating meat because it is the flesh of sentient beings. Most do eat meat, but as I described earlier, recite mantras that have the power to benefit the animal. Also, these lamas could be high bodhisattva incarnations or other highly realized beings with very great compassion; upon tasting this flesh they remember where it comes from and are able to bring such great benefit to the mind of the animal as to either liberate it, or lead it to a better rebirth.

In the Shravakayana tradition, the Vinaya does not prohibit the eating of meat as long as the action is free from the 'three causes of hindrance'. These are firstly, oneself or a close friend seeing the animal being killed, secondly, hearing that the animal was killed for oneself or the spiritual community to eat, or thirdly, feeling that the animal may have been killed especially for oneself to eat. One is prohibited from eating the meat in any of these three circumstances. The Vinaya says that if one simply goes into a shop and buys meat one can eat it. Meat itself has nothing sinful about it, but killing does.

Killing involves four causes that completely mature the bad karma (action, cause and effect). These four causes apply to those who are in a normal state of mind, free from intoxication, mental illness, or being forced to kill by a more powerful person, and are as follows:

> One realizes that an animal that has good flesh for eating is actually a living being,
> One wants to kill the animal,
> One arms oneself with the equipment needed to kill the animal, such as a knife or gun,
> One kills the animal and feels satisfied upon seeing it dead.

Together these four conditions complete the bad karma (activity) of killing, which the individual then carries. If one of these four is missing then the bad karma is not complete. Generally speaking, when meat is bought in a shop these four causes are missing and the only negative mentality involved is that of wanting to eat meat in the first place.

Meat itself has no bad or good karma attached to it and it actually provides many important proteins that help nourish the body. For example, Milarepa spent nine years in ascetic retreat, during which he ate no nutritious food. One time he ate some venison that was offered to him by a hunter and as a result all his meditation improved. This is because the protein strengthened the weakened nervous system and chakras of his vajra body. The chakras of the vajra body are the same as a palace and the mind is the same as a king, they are interdependent. If a king were to live in a freezing-cold palace that was only a fraction larger than his body, he would be unable to accomplish much even if he was capable of great victories. However, if his palace was large and warm with more space and dignity, and many offices, he could achieve much more. It is the same with the mind and the chakras. The improvement experienced by Milarepa was not caused by the animal he ate, but by the protein in the meat. It is for this reason that the samaya, or precepts, of a Vajrayana practitioner always include keeping oneself healthy, and never using the body for ascetic practice where it is allowed to become hungry, starved, or consume unhealthy food. I think that beer contains much nourishment and can also increase one's strength, but it is not the alcoholic portion of it that has this quality. In ancient stories, while some ordained lamas described drinking as a harmful activity and breaking vows, other highly realized yogins said that limited drinking is somewhat beneficial as it brings some joy and positive feeling. Accordingly, beer or wine can be consumed as a samaya substance. Milarepa said that one should drink no more than the amount that would fill one skullcup, because one must be mindful when using this substance.

In the Mahayana tradition, killing also has different degrees of seriousness. The worst of these is to kill out of anger because this is the opposite of compassion. Without anger there is less bad karma (action) involved. Therefore, in the Mahayana, killing is permitted if it is done compassionately for the purpose of saving other lives. In both the Mahayana and the Vajrayana, one's motivation is of principal importance. Inner motivation of the mind is much more important than discipline that is imposed from the outside. Nagarjuna described four types of practitioners by comparing them to mangoes:

> Persons should be understood to be like mango fruits which are unripened, ones that seem ripe, ripened ones that seem unripe, unripened ones that do appear unripe, or ripened ones that do appear ripe.[1]

This means that the top priority is the quality of one's inner motivation. It is the mind's conduct that produces good or bad karma because the actions of body and speech only follow the mind's intentions. In this way the mind is like a king, and the speech and the body are his followers. If one can discipline one's speech and physical actions so well that even though the mind is swirling with the five poisons, they do not find expression in action, it is very good. This is more the way taught in the Vinaya, because if one is very disciplined externally this can slowly discipline and subdue the five poisons of the mind. The Mahayana approach is a much stronger form of mental discipline, because if in one's mind itself morality is very strong and correct, bad karma of speech and body cannot be created. Milarepa was an example of this.

It would be better if there were fewer meat eaters because then the number of animals killed for food would be reduced. In North America where there is such a variety of foods and alternative sources of protein available, it would not pose a problem to give up eating meat. In general, it is true to say that eating meat lowers the level of one's compassion for sentient beings because it reinforces one's conception of other beings as food. In ganachakra ceremonies, meat and alcohol must be offered. This meat should not have come from an animal that was killed to provide food, rather, it should be from an animal that has died from a natural or accidental cause. Gampopa said that if one puts meat from an animal that had been purposely killed onto the shrine, all the Buddhas and bodhisattvas become extremely upset, feeling the kind of shock that would cause one to lose consciousness. After first establishing the seed of compassion, Lord Buddha Shakyamuni practiced loving compassion towards all sentient beings for countless lifetimes, as though each was his own mother. This practice reached its highest level in his final rebirth as Siddhartha, who achieved full enlightenment. To include the meat of a purposely killed animal as an offering to such a being is thus very disrespectful.

The wrathful Vajrayana deities are none other than enlightened forms in whom the peaceful manifestations of compassion are replaced with wrathful ones. These deities are shown holding weapons and skull cups full of blood, and wearing garlands of skulls. These objects symbolize two things. Firstly, because angry activity results in using weapons and drawing blood, these possessions are used to symbolize cutting through anger. Anger is symbolized by the blood, and compassion by the skull cup. Their weapons symbolize the great compassion and wisdom by which anger is destroyed. The garlands of skulls, clothing of skin, and corpses, represent all forms of anger being completely destroyed; because once one's anger no longer exists, it is like the corpse, skin or skull, that remain after death. No matter how wrathful a deity may seem, it is really no different from full enlightenment that can only be reached through training in love and compassion. Therefore, it would also be wrong to make an offering of purposely killed animal meat to these deities. Furthermore, in Buddhism all wrathful Vajrayana deities wear these symbolic decorations because in order to protect sentient beings from harm they have subdued such things as maras[2] and demons that supposedly live in cemeteries and really use such weapons and costumes.

This is just the same as a humble, cave-dwelling, warrior-hermit killing his enemy who is also a warrior. This enemy lives in a great castle with his wife, wears very rich clothing, decorates his palace with the heads of his enemies, strings their fingers into necklaces, and drinks their blood. After killing this terrible enemy, the warrior-hermit then displays these same possessions as symbols of his victory and strength. It does not mean that the warrior-hermit becomes like the dead warrior in thought and behaviour or engages in his terrible activities. Therefore, even though the wrathful Vajrayana deities wear costumes similar to that of Maharudra, they themselves are no different from the love, wisdom, and power of full enlightenment. The costume of each specific deity is also significant because it symbolizes a particular aspect of enlightenment.

Wrathful deities are fully Buddhas, and so to make an offering of killed animal meat to them would be just as disrespectful as offering it to the Buddha himself. In fact, making such a mistaken offering will never bring any blessing from these deities, but instead may attract negative influences such as local demons or evils that desire to eat flesh and drink blood. These could all gather around instead of the Vajrayana deities, and bring with them such harm as sickness, bad weather, increasing anger, and wars. Such offerings may bring temporary success, but gradually one's own good karma and loving compassion will be destroyed, and disappointment will arise. These negative influences can also affect the mind by undermining one's renunciation of samsara and one's pure vision, as well as all patience and diligence for practice. They can eventually destroy one's faith completely, and once this has happened even seeing Buddha miraculously flying in the sky would arouse neither interest nor faith. Once one's compassion has been destroyed in this way, then even if seeing beings walking along with their bellies ripped open and their intestines trailing on the ground behind them, one would never feel any compassion or sympathy for their suffering. One's character would have become constantly rude and wrathful, and pride would increase. After death, one would go either to the lower realms, or may be reborn as a follower of some evil demon and so create further harm for sentient beings.

In Tibet during the time of the dharma king Trisong Detsen, everyone followed the unmodified old Bon[3] religion. When people were sick or dying, they would make many animal sacrifices and offer the blood and meat to their gods. Guru Rinpoche Padma Sambhava was very unhappy to see this. "This is not bodhisattva activity," he asserted, and was so upset that he could not eat. He succeeded in completely stopping all sacrificial rituals in Tibet, and anyone who refused to give this up was removed to the Himalayan border regions. It is said that this old Bonpo sect still practices sacrifice. For example, in Sikkim, sacrificial killing was still taking place in the valley by Rumtek monastery until the Sixteenth Gyalwang Karmapa intervened. One time when people were sick, he wrote a special prayer for the local spirits, and substituted the smoke of burning barley as an offering to their protectors, in place of the blood of chickens, goats and cows. Many lives were saved by those who followed this new ritual. As a result, they then stopped seeking help for their families through the use of the traditional sacrificial offerings.

Patrul Rinpoche said that followers of Buddha and Guru Rinpoche Padma Sambhava who offer killed animal meat to the shrine are not bodhisattvas or Mahayana practitioners. He said this is exactly the same as killing a man's mother, and then offering her organs, flesh, and blood to her loving son for a celebration. The son would never accept such a thing. Shakyamuni and his followers begged for alms once a day in order to eat and accepted whatever was offered, whether bad or good. There are different accounts presented in the sutras regarding whether Buddha and his followers ate meat or were vegetarians. The Mahayana view is that Buddha and his followers and arhats never ate meat. However, for those of his followers who could not stop eating meat he gave the three principal rules for deciding whether or not it should be eaten. (These are the 'three causes of hindrance' mentioned earlier.)

In the *Lankavatara Sutra*, Buddha says that whoever becomes a bodhisattva should not eat the flesh or blood of other sentient beings. Once one has taken bodhisattva vows and become a Mahayana practitioner it is best if one avoids eating meat altogether. If this is not possible then, as I mentioned earlier, one should pray and recite mantras out of compassion to help the dead animals. The instantaneous delivery of great blessing and purification by the mantras shows the effectiveness of the Vajrayana. Nowadays, Mahayana followers and practitioners often do eat meat; therefore, because the Buddha and many holy lamas have given these teachings, whoever becomes a Mahayana practitioner must maintain this awareness at all times.

In the Vajrayana, meat is always used for ganachakra pujas where it is a substitute for samaya. Meat that has not come from a killed animal is best, but if this cannot be found one can simply buy some from a shop because then the meat has passed through many hands. Meat is special because it provides energy for the body. During the ganachakra puja it is not referred to as 'meat' as even the name itself is not peaceful and compassionate. I myself eat meat and so I am unable to criticize meat eaters, but as

I am discussing the pure Mahayana view, I am very happy to be saying these things. It makes me feel a little like a tiger or wolf when I eat meat, but it is my habit.

If one starts each day with Mahayana motivation by reciting the prayers of refuge and the four limitless meditations early in the morning, this attitude will become a normal part of one's energy throughout the day. Thus, when one eats meat, the prayer for the being whose flesh one is eating has already been said. In this way one does not lose one's bodhisattva vows and the animal is not left outside the sphere of one's love and compassion. This is better than just eating meat in an ordinary fashion. However, to practice properly it is best to stop eating meat. Failing that, it is best to say all the prayers and mantras properly before eating the meat. There is much more negative karma (action, cause and effect) if one eats food such as shrimp where many animals die to provide one meal, compared to beef, which comes from only one animal. One needs to recognize this, and to pray and meditate more on compassion.

Many people say that we are continuously killing bacteria and germs because they are everywhere. As in Jainism, Lord Buddha said that even our breathing leaves many beings dead, and that although one cannot see them there are countless beings even in an area the size of the palm of one hand. However, he said that since they are invisible to the naked eye one should not worry about this, but just have compassion for them. So even though one cannot help but destroy them, one must have compassion and pray for these sentient beings.

Those who have taken bodhisattva vows and later kill insects, worms, germs, or even the tiniest of creatures that can be seen by the naked eye, must take compassionate responsibility for them, by promising never to forget these beings and to liberate them before all others once one has reached enlightenment. In this way the bad karma is purified, and one benefits all those who have been connected to oneself in this way. It is also important to use the technique of giving benefit and taking the suffering of others onto oneself, which is integral to Lojong practice. One should think, "May I completely take their bad karma onto myself." This is because it is their bad karma that has led them to be living as cockroaches, ants, germs, or bacteria. This is a method of purification.

Nowadays it is very difficult for Mahayana practitioners to completely avoid harming others. This is especially true because our powerful modern technology magnifies good and bad karma (activity) – consider the powerful potential of chemical warfare, the atomic bomb, mass media such as television and radio, and the Internet and social media. However, if one keeps a compassionate bodhisattva attitude one avoids creating as much negative karma. Even vegetarians have to be concerned because, although one may think there is no bad karma associated with eating rice, barley or fruit and that it is a good activity to eat such food, even more sentient beings have actually died to supply one single grain of rice than have died to supply a portion of meat. This is the result of having to farm the land, as both digging and cultivating the soil kills many beings. Also, birds follow the plough and eat snakes, frogs, worms, and tiny insects. When rice paddies are flooded with water many insects and different tiny creatures live there, so when the paddies are drained and dry up again these are all killed. One grain of rice maybe involves the death of one hundred beings. Therefore, more prayer and compassion are needed even if one eats rice, barley or bread. Despite this, a vegetarian diet is much better than eating meat because there is no direct connection to killing beings. The vegetarian is thinking about eating pure, clean rice, not about eating insects. In contrast, those who eat meat know there is a direct connection between killing an animal and eating meat. Thus, the vegetarian view is more profound. Vegetarian food is provided naturally by mother earth. Rice grains have no soul or mind, and do not have any direct connection to killing because this is not actually meat from a corpse.

According to the Mahayana, one's motivation and awareness are very important. In many religions, animals, together with germs or bacteria, are not believed to have minds. If this were true, or one believes this deeply, then there is no bad karma in eating the flesh of others. According to Buddhism, however, animals do have consciousness. If one realizes this and still kills and eats them, bad karma (action, cause and effect) results automatically. This is because, according to the Vinaya, one has completely broken one's vows if the four conditions are complete when one kills an animal. For example, if a monk threw stones or weapons away behind a house and in doing so accidentally killed someone, no vows would have been broken, because he was not aware of this happening. Therefore, motivation is important for everyone who follows Lord Buddha, and one needs to watch the mind constantly. One should think of one's mind as a flower garden, that one naturally loves and cares for because one has planted and tended to it oneself.

The relevance of mind training is unchanging because people from all different countries, nationalities and cultures have the same needs. Therefore, mind training is Buddha's main teaching. Deity images, language, and traditional rituals, are different in each country, sect, or system. If a master of the three yanas from around Buddha's time saw the chanting, ritual, and mandala traditions being used by us now, he might find them very different. In his time, Buddha's teachings led many people to become good Dharma practitioners and bodhisattvas. They became very peaceful and gentle as they did the practices and attained the different levels of spiritual realization. That this still works today means that no mistakes have been made in the transmission of the lineages of the inner practice of mind training. Because it has not changed in any essential way, it still works. Gendun Chopel, the very learned twentieth century Tibetan scholar, said that the costumes of the deities are influenced by the culture of the country. For example, Avalokiteshvara is clothed like an Indian prince of ancient times. The costume is a reflection of the culture and the times. If Buddha had been born in Tibet, for instance, he may have been shown with a great deal of butter tea to drink, and a churn for making it. He may have described Sukhavati as having an abundance of the best butter and tea, and tea churns made of gems. Wherever Buddha taught, his purpose was to free sentient beings from suffering and lead them into enlightenment. The reason why images of Buddha have slightly different forms in different countries is that they reflect each culture's unique way of seeing things. I believe that the blessings remain the same. Therefore, the main transmission practice of training the mind is what is really important, and there is no contradiction of fundamental view. There is no need to make such criticisms as, "My way of conducting rituals and making costumes is correct and the others are wrong." The best attitude is to be very free and relaxed in one's practice. Guru Rinpoche Padma Sambhava said that in the Kali Yuga (degenerate age) it would become very important to establish the primordial natural wisdom of Samantabhadra Buddha's doctrine, so that liberation can be attained quickly. This means that the practice of bodhichitta is most important at this time.

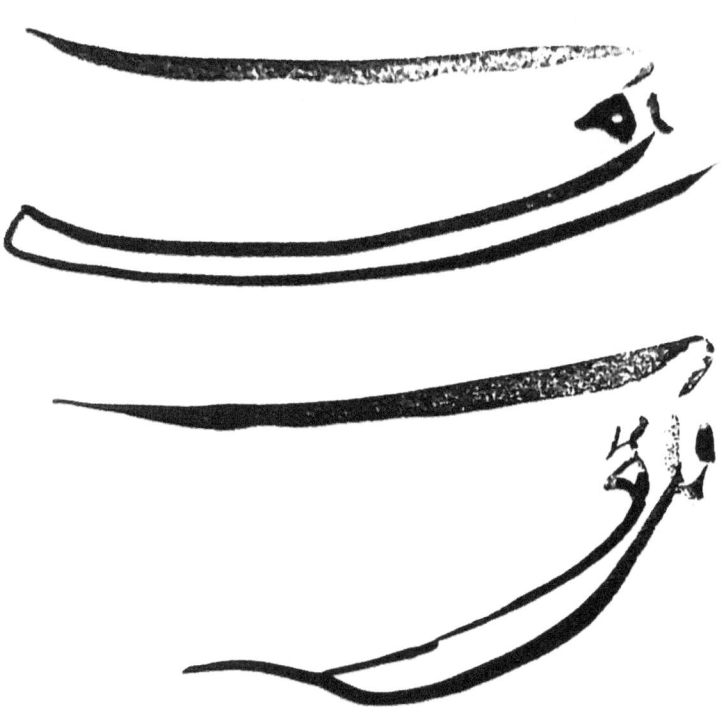

9
LOJONG

LOJONG IS GOOD IN THE BEGINNING, because anyone who has contact with this practice develops natural bodhisattva discipline and becomes gentle, in the same way that spring soil is very soft and whatever is planted there grows well. Lojong is good in the middle, as all the eighty-four thousand dharmas are included in it. Lojong is good at the end, as all sentient beings become one's best friends. Lojong is good for men, as they become Avalokiteshvara (Tib. Chenrezig), whose name means 'tearful eyes gazing with compassion upon sentient beings'. Lojong is good for women, as they become Tara, goddess of mercy, whose Tibetan name Drolma means 'liberator'. In one sense, Lojong is a great weight on the shoulders, as one takes all the struggles, problems, quarrels and violence of sentient beings onto oneself. At the same time Lojong is the lightest of all burdens as the practitioner becomes peaceful, gentle and happy, with compassionate loving-kindness for everyone.

There are three main deities connected with Lojong practice. Together, they surround Shakyamuni Buddha himself, who is golden in colour denoting the richness of enlightenment. These three deities – Avalokiteshvara, Achala (Tib. Migyowa), and Tara – are not simply a snow-coloured man, a sky-blue man and a turquoise-coloured lady. White denotes purity, blue denotes non-duality, and in ancient art green-blue was considered the prettiest of colours and was therefore used for ladies. As a combination of colours, green-blue symbolizes both serving all the sentient beings of the four directions and understanding the true nature of the dharmakaya. These four Kadam deities[1] symbolize the holding of bodhichitta, and are inseparable from bodhichitta. The word 'Lojong' means purification of the mind by means of love and compassion. It is a special word that was chosen by Atisha for people of genius, because whoever practices Lojong is really a king, a lord of the world, and this is very rare.

Through investigation one can see for oneself just how much suffering the negative emotions create. For example, one can see the extent to which unhappiness can be created within families, and how it would be possible for this suffering to escalate to such an extent that it could even lead to great wars between nations. One can see how a smart person can use pride and desire to conquer others, or to create great suffering for others in the form of sickness, starvation, death and quarrelling. One can also see how those who have great ignorance or stupidity create suffering for themselves. There is nothing one can do unless people change their mental attitude, because this suffering is created by karma (actions). Life just passes through states of suffering.

The root and fruit of all this suffering is the five negative emotions. When one realizes this cycle, one can see that it is very important to remove all negative emotions. The only method that will remove them is to use appropriate antidotes, because one must achieve complete realization oneself before being able to help other sentient beings. One cannot force suffering to cease, even by trying to use the power of wealth, weapons, or huge armies. Neither can one use eloquent lectures or exciting demonstrations of material power, because these methods do not touch the roots or seeds of suffering.

Through the practice of Lojong, anger is transformed into the positive emotion of love, love directed towards one's own self and others. If loving-kindness becomes much stronger than negativity, then negativity is automatically transformed into the positive. There is no need to view the negative aspects of the mind as being bad, dirty or one's enemy, because they are human emotions, one's own emotions. In order to transform them into loving kindness more meditation upon loving kindness is needed. Lojong practice is thus very important.

Atisha taught Lojong for the purpose of transforming mental depression and suffering into happiness and a relaxed mind. When one really loves, the negative emotions automatically decrease, just as ice automatically melts in hot water. It simply changes. Mahayana practitioners thus automatically focus love to others. When one does not experience this, it is because one still has some negative discrimination. If this is the case, one needs to try to change one's motivation through further practice of love and compassion. Whoever experiences this naturally-arising love finds that any feeling of anger or hatred that may arise is nothing, because it is never felt without awareness. Such feelings subside by themselves and love continues to grow stronger. This automatic love is impossible without, is inseparable from, and is a natural characteristic of, emptiness. Thus, love and compassion arise through the practice of Lojong meditation.

Firstly, one needs to realize that each sentient being possesses the causes of suffering, and to give rise to compassion. Secondly, one should try to subdue and cut off the negative emotions even while still involved in family life. Emotions themselves, however, are also a necessary part of human life. It is good to desire important things such as a good livelihood and a good home, and to care for one's family. Attachment, love and desire between husband and wife are necessary. Similarly, the desire to help one's neighbours, one's country or the whole world, and the desire for enlightenment, practice and meditation, are all important and good forms of desire. In the Mahayana it is important to be motivated by desire, such as in wishing to help the poor and remove poverty. It is important to feel the wish to remove the suffering of poor people, the wish to make them rich, and the wish to remove their emotional suffering. If the bodhisattva were to fight and subdue very evil people who are destroying nations, he would be motivated by good anger.

Similarly, envy of someone's good qualities can sometimes help one to become very successful in achieving good ends. For example, feeling envious of very warm families, the good education of others or skill in business practice, can become useful motivation. People who always help others can thus inspire one to improve one's own attitudes. However, this kind of motivation is not good if it leads one to fight or compete. Pride in one's own good actions, experience and realization, in one's good business practices, or in one's ability to make everyone happy and to please people with one's actions, are all good forms of pride. However, this should be the pride of feeling "Yes, I am acting correctly," otherwise pride can be dangerous.

Faith in one's beliefs is a form of good ignorance as it protects one from cynicism, for example, having faith in God the creator or in the law of karma (according to one's religion). In the case of Buddhism this means believing in the law of karma (action, cause and effect) without giving rise to doubt, even though one might not yet have a clear understanding of buddha nature. Actually, on this point of faith, one might say that the development of the modern scientific view of the world assists in understanding the Mahayana view. When scientific and Mahayana knowledge are brought together, they can clarify the meaning of the Dharma. Arya Asanga said that a bodhisattva who does not study the five sciences will never attain the level of omniscient one (Buddha). Of course, the 'five sciences' he was referring to are the ancient disciplines of language, logic, medicine, art and spiritual knowledge, which include eighteen different fields of knowledge.[2] Some areas of human knowledge are now much better developed and have progressed enormously since ancient times. Nevertheless, both modern and ancient knowledge have the same base, or root, in these 'five sciences.' Modern science can provide an even more subtle and detailed exploration of the first four of the five disciplines. However, the world also has some political and scientific philosophies that promote nihilistic views and so it is very important not to allow cynicism to block one's faith and confidence. In the Kali Yuga this is very dangerous. Therefore, it is important to hold one's beliefs and to have strong conviction that good action leads to good results and bad action to bad results. A husband and wife also need this kind of good ignorance, trusting one another and not investigating overmuch in daily life except to guard against harm.

Thirdly, it is necessary to wake up to absolute awareness. This means that one must meditate to achieve tranquility (shamatha) and then understand emptiness through insight (vipashyana). To begin with you need to know how to sit and how to focus. It is necessary to approach a teacher and ask how to do this. The best teacher is one who has realization. The alternative would be to go to the most highly qualified scholar who could explain the buddha doctrine. A person who has no experience of Buddhist practice and does not know the buddha doctrine can make mistakes and lead you the wrong way. In his book of advice entitled Letter to a Friend, Nagarjuna says that when a white house reflects the moonlight, it appears whiter still. Similarly, teaching and meditation can help to illuminate one's knowledge of Buddha Dharma.

In this way I have given a short explanation of the ancient Kadampa teachings. If you feel that it is correct, please, take it to heart, think about it, and continue to follow the teaching and practice of Mahayana. When investigating deeper one should especially engage in further study of the three yanas, including the Mahayana doctrines in the sutras and shastras, and the Vajrayana doctrines in the tantras. When reading the collection of the sutras (sutrayana) one discovers each to be an entirely amazing revelation of Buddha's teaching, of his knowledge, and of his miraculous powers. At each teaching, all the celestial beings and disciples of the ten directions gathered to listen. The sutras relate how the whole environment turned into a Buddha paradise and how Lord Buddha displayed his miraculous powers. For example, the time Buddha taught the Prajnaparamita on Vulture Peak (Tib. Jago pung ri) hill in Bihar, India, the small hill that you can see there now manifested as a jewelled mountain, and millions of celestial beings assembled from all the ten directions. These included nagas, naginis, gods, goddesses, and each class of universal being from all the directions of the nirmanakaya view of the universe. These demonstrations of Buddha's enlightened power of wisdom to manifest and bless, display the nirmanakaya (or conventional truth) view. I have read these stories and can see how special each sutra is. As these teachings are so wonderful, I want to emphasize that people should have more respect for them. The sutras are not ordinary teachings, they really show the nirmanakaya Buddha's power.

In conclusion, the root of Mahayana is compassion and loving-kindness. Compassion is the wish to remove the suffering of others. For example, on becoming aware of some sickness one must concern oneself with how to help. It is not enough to simply talk about compassion and helping to relieve suffering. Instead, one must actively assist from a very deep feeling of concern in the mind. For instance, it is very auspicious to have received the Bhaisajyaguru[3] (Medicine Buddha) initiation. However, it is not enough just to receive this, one must also use it to help others. This means to practice the Bhaisajyaguru sadhana with one million mantra recitations, until one receives some blessing experience from Bhaisajyaguru himself.

The best approach is to study to become a doctor, or to buy and give medicine to sick people for no charge if this is possible. In these modern times, it is difficult to do this completely free of charge, but the charge should be reasonable. When I was a teenager, I received medical training from my uncle and teacher in Nangchen, the famous doctor Taksar Tegchog. The teachings I received came from the lineage of Mipham Rinpoche[4] and my uncle was his student's student. Coming from a very wealthy family my uncle could afford to buy all the necessary medicine, and he never charged the people who came to him no matter how many came. I and some other students studied under him. First of all, he made us promise never to charge money for medicine but to be generous and unselfish instead; only after that did he begin to teach us. In Nangchen it was very difficult for a poor doctor to practice because many medicines were so expensive. This was because they included ingredients such as jewels, rare roots, woods, fruits and leaves that had to be obtained from India and China. It was very difficult, therefore, to make the promise not to charge.

I realize now that my uncle was a bodhisattva who wanted to help his patients from deep within his heart since, out of generosity, he spent a very great deal to help others. Also, doctors had to go out at any time of the day or night to help people, no matter if it was stormy or extremely cold, or whether they had to ride horses or walk. So many people asked for help that it was impossible to help them all, and some people would die. My uncle really had the heart of a bodhisattva because he shared everyone's sufferings. These days it is really difficult to avoid charging. However, if one does help administer medicine or help in a hospital, it is very important not to discriminate at all, but instead to treat everybody with equal concern.

However much one may engage in nice talk about healing and compassion, it is of no more use than the sweet singing of a canary if one does not actually benefit the mind and body of those who are suffering. Therefore, the Buddhist doctrine teaches that one should not satisfy oneself with sweet words, but should strive to be of real benefit to those in need through hard work, patience, and diligence. From one's heart, one should really involve oneself in the struggle to help relieve suffering. The four duties of lamas, monks, nuns, yogis and yoginis, are also good for lay practitioners to keep in mind:

1. not to insult others even though you have been insulted by them,
2. not to be angry with others even though they have been angry with you,
3. not to retaliate against others even though you have been offended by them,
4. not to strike others even though you have been beaten by them.

These four duties are very hard to fulfil, but if one has great self-discipline, it becomes easy to deal with the suffering of others, and easy to be of help. At one time the Buddha sent the Arhat Katyayana to teach in a rather uncivilised area of India. Buddha asked him what he would do if people paid no attention to him. He replied that he would think, "I am lucky that no one is quarrelling with me." He was then asked, "If they quarrel with you, what should you do?" and he replied that he would think, "Oh, I am so lucky that they do not beat me!" Buddha then asked, "Well, what would you do if they beat you?" and the reply was that he would think, "I am lucky they do not kill me!" Again, he was asked what he would do if they should kill him and his answer was that he would think, "They cannot kill my wisdom and peace and truth." If one has this attitude one succeeds, and cannot be harmed by anybody.

It is important to train hard in compassion and love if one wishes to become a Mahayana teacher. We who want to teach and help others need more training ourselves; otherwise it is like the blind leading the blind. For example, if one wants to bring peace to the world, one must first have peace in one's own mind. If we don't try to discipline our own hatred, discrimination, racism, sectarianism and selfishness, and become bodhisattvas ourselves, to engage in nice talk about Mahayana would be just like wearing a beautiful bodhisattva mask and dancing around downtown. Therefore, those who wish to help others should look inward to their own selves and try to increase their own practice and training. If one does not have the lineage, one cannot give Vajrayana initiations. If one is not a bhikshu or qualified abbot one cannot give ordination. Likewise, if one's own heart is not opened to compassion, love, and the compassionate attitude of bodhichitta, one cannot give bodhisattva vows.

In saying these things, my meaning is that bodhisattva activity is like a mirror with two faces – it reflects both oneself and the other, and benefits both. Both the teacher and the student must first practice Lojong, continuing for months and years, and try to gain real experience. This is like needing a good sharp axe to cut down a tree, otherwise you will never succeed no matter how hard you strike, because the axe will break and the tree will only become damaged and splintered. Once you yourself develop compassion and love, then healing, helping and bringing peace becomes very easy.

Many people get very excited about initiations, visualisation of deities, and meditation on shunyata. Talking about love and compassion is held in lower esteem as if these are a common and easy part of Lord Buddha's teachings. Really, to have this view means that one has no bodhichitta and that one is not yet progressing in the deepest heart teachings of the Buddha. It is very simple to talk of 'compassion'. Dharmakirti[5] says that compassion means wanting to stop the sufferings of others, and from the Mahayana point of view this is the defining characteristic of compassion. Though it is so easy to talk about, it is the hardest of all to put into action, and for this reason it is important to train strongly in developing compassion.

Even if one has no compassion, one can still benefit others if one can give a correct and scholarly exposition of the 'three baskets' (three vessels of the teachings), as it may help people understand the correct view of the dharma. People with good eyesight will avoid tripping and falling even if they are physically weak.

Sakya Pandita[6] says:

> However much the wise lack in skillful means, they will not follow the way of the fool.[7]

So, even though one's practice is really insufficient, one can still teach correctly according to how much one has learned of the teachings of the three yanas. Although this is very good, to truly become a bodhisattva it is very important to actually develop bodhichitta. It is much better for a Mahayana teacher to have bodhichitta and compassion than to teach about what it is.

As Guru Rinpoche Padma Sambhava said:

> Knowing hundreds, but failing to understand the most important one.

This is pointing out that it is possible to accumulate a great deal of knowledge and even become a great philosophical master, yet still overlook the most essential point, which is to actually clear the mind through bodhichitta. It is said that a parrot can recite "OM MANI PADME HUNG" but even though it utters the correct sounds only small benefit for others can result, great and true bodhisattva benefit cannot be produced.

One's motivation is very important. For example, if someone with a very selfish disposition gives rise to even a single kind wish to help others, it is much better than speaking colourful and pleasing words while loving kindness is forgotten. Shakyamuni Buddha related the story of a previous life when he was Dzawoi Pamo, a merchant in charge of a fleet of ships used to bring back gems from mines on an island in the middle of the ocean. One time his mother did not want him to sail with the fleet as she was afraid he would not return. However, he paid no attention to her and, as she desperately tried to hold on to him, he kicked her head and left. This action gathered a similar karmic result and finally led to rebirth in a hell-realm, where beings endured the suffering of having their heads continually tortured. There, he all of a sudden realized that there were so many others suffering the same misery as himself. He was moved to plead with one of the controllers of the hell realm to let all the others go free, and to turn all the weapons upon his own head. In response the controllers angrily chopped him down. He died and was immediately reborn in a higher realm. This good motivation, this compassion, was his first seed of buddhahood (enlightenment). In each subsequent life he progressed until there was no further achievement to be made and he became a Buddha. Thus, the initial seed of good motivation is very important.

If a very poor lady with neither money nor food to her name came upon others in a similar state and tried to relieve their suffering by stopping, talking to them and sharing what little she had, she would benefit them by virtue of her mind being pure. An example of this kind of behaviour is provided by Mother Theresa. Therefore, do not be frightened by the thought that you are not ready to help others, become a hero-bodhisattva, and as long as you have love and compassion, go ahead.

Shantideva says:

> And for him who has perfectly seized this mind
> With the thought never to turn away
> From totally liberating
> The infinite forms of life,
> From that time hence,

Even while asleep or unconcerned,
A force of merit equal to the sky
Will perpetually ensue.⁸

Therefore, if one is interested in love and compassion and has respect for the bodhisattvas, it means that one is very close to enlightenment and will soon be able to save sentient beings, few or many, according to one's level.

10
THE FOUR LIMITLESS THOUGHTS

May all beings have happiness and the causes of happiness.
May all beings be free from sorrow and the causes of sorrow.
May all beings never be separated from the great happiness that is sorrowless.
May all leave attachment to dear ones and aversion to others and
dwell in the equalness of all that lives.

THE MAHAYANA TEACHING is often referred to as 'the heart-teaching' of Lord Buddha because it was the seed of loving compassion that inspired his journey to enlightenment and, subsequently, at the moment of final enlightenment his loving compassion automatically reached its most powerful and exalted level, completely free from conceptual reference. Therefore, we also train in this attitude.

In the Mahayana the practice of bodhichitta is very important and meditation on the Four Limitless Thoughts – love, compassion, joy and equanimity – is fundamental in giving rise to it. The bodhisattva believes that space is infinite and that sentient beings fill all its vastness. As space itself is boundless, sentient beings are described as limitless. A true understanding of this is 'limitless wisdom' (Tib. tseme sherab). Sentient beings are all identical in that they are beset by conflicting emotions and experience suffering, no matter what their size, colour, or structure, whether they measure miles across or are so tiny that we cannot see them. Lord Shakyamuni was asked by a disciple to explain what the phrase 'limitless sentient beings' means. His reply was that when he looked at the ground beneath the wheel of a horse-drawn wagon, his loving wisdom-eye could perceive as many sentient beings as there are gods and men in the entire universe. This shows how much stronger the limitless love of the Buddha's mind is compared to one's own. The earth now has almost eight billion humans and there may be a hundred million gods in the heavenly realms. Buddha saw this many sentient beings just in the space beneath one wagon wheel.

Sentient beings arise from ignorance which cognizes an 'I', or 'self'. This becomes the cause of endless suffering and never leads to happiness. The bodhisattva has the means to relieve suffering. It is his or her responsibility to help other beings who experience great suffering and are in real need of assistance. To do this the bodhisattva needs to generate tremendous loving kindness. We want to help sentient beings, and even though we are presently still at the level of imagining helping, it is most important

Love

to generate this kind of wishing. All beings have natural and basic, true, buddha nature. Therefore, the power of our own buddha nature can actually extend to eventually liberate all sentient beings. This is the reason we practice. If there were no buddha nature, practice would achieve nothing. Buddha nature is the fundamental seed.

Also, according to Mahayana doctrine, one should adopt the view that each and every sentient being has somehow shown kindness to oneself just like the kindness shown by one's own present mother. So, during meditation one needs to believe strongly that all limitless sentient beings are one's mothers from previous lives, and furthermore that each sentient being has been one's mother not once, but so many times that all her blood from these previous lives could form an ocean, and all her bones, a mountain. This thought includes all beings, even one's enemies. This motivation which gives rise to tremendous compassion is very important. The compassion is limitless because it is the wish to remove all the sufferings of all one's mothers (all sentient beings), not just one of them. When praying and meditating, one's motivation is to remove the suffering and the causes of suffering of all one's mothers. As it might take as long as an aeon to help each sentient being in this way, one cannot be afraid. One must have a tremendously heroic mind. This is a very important aspect of the motivation to work so long and so hard for others, even to the point of giving one's own eyes or feeding one's own body to them if necessary. Moreover, such strength of mind is needed for helping each individual sentient being. Therefore, one needs limitless compassion. When beginning this practice, it is best to start by contemplating the kindness of one's present mother and how much one wants to repay her for this. Once this is very strong in one's mind, one can move on to thinking about neighbours, and finally, enemies.

Equanimity, where there is no disparity in one's attitude towards different sentient beings based on discrimination (such as between friend and enemy), is important if one wishes to benefit everyone equally. This is because all sentient beings are equally kind in that they all provide the opportunity to develop compassion, they are all equally involved in suffering and need help, and also the true nature of sentient beings is shunyata, which is basic equality. This is limitless impartiality, or equanimity. For example, if one wants even one sentient being to have good health, one also wishes this for all limitless sentient beings; if one wants to remove the suffering and cause of suffering of one sentient being by means of compassion, then one also wants the same for each one of the limitless sentient beings. Praying for everyone to attain happiness is limitless wishing. One wishes for the temporary happiness of each sentient being, the different conditions that will result in this happiness, and that this happiness will never change. For each sentient being one also wishes for the unchanging and sorrowless happiness that is the state of enlightenment itself, perfect awakening in dharmakaya. For example, if someone has good health one needs to pray that this will never change, or if someone realizes real joyful happiness in the heavenly realm in the company of angels, amidst beautiful flowers, trees, crystal waters, and music of many different instruments,

Compassion

one wishes for this never to change. Even though one is a bodhisattva, one can pray that a god of the realm of emanation will continue to emanate perfectly forever. One also prays that natural realization of buddha nature, achievement of the sorrowless state of nirvana, never changes.

The four limitless meditations are very important for those who want to practice the Mahayana. Patrul Rinpoche used the following similes:

> One's loving kindness for sentient beings should be like that of a mother bird who works hard to provide a warm, soft nest for her young and then cares for them in every way. The bodhisattva needs to care for sentient beings in this manner.
>
> One's compassion should be like that felt for the suffering of a mother who has no hands and so is powerless to help her only son who has fallen into a river. Because she cannot help him, she becomes more and more upset, and feels more and more love for her child. The bodhisattva needs to feel such limitless compassion for all sentient beings amidst all their different sufferings. The bodhisattva's motivation is a deep and heartfelt wish for beings to be free from suffering.
>
> As regards empathic joy, when a mother camel finds her lost calf, she is the happiest of beings. Similarly, the bodhisattva needs to feel such unlimited happiness when any sentient being experiences permanent or temporary happiness. Even in the case of temporary happiness, such as a sick person receiving medicine, a starving person receiving even one mouthful of food, those who are cold receiving warm sunshine, or those who are hot receiving cool breezes, one should rejoice and feel much happiness.
>
> Finally, one practices equanimity when one's loving kindness and benefit to others is free from discrimination and given equally to all beings of the six realms whether they be friends, enemies, or neutral. It should be equal in the same way that the mahasiddhas (enlightened sages of ancient times) held festivals for the benefit of all the people, and the feast was shared equally amongst everyone. One should demonstrate similar loving kindness, compassion, and equality, in all one's ideas and activity.

Joy

The Four Limitless Thoughts

Each of the four limitless thoughts has three levels of meaning. First, is the level of ordinary loving compassion which is directed no further than wanting to remove the suffering of sentient beings through one's compassion. This is ordinary help on a worldly level, not beyond apparent reality. This level of practicing the four limitless thoughts is of very great benefit and merit, but one still needs the second level. The second level is perfect understanding. In looking for the suffering of sentient beings one will find nothing substantial because everything is by nature conditionless. This realization is like viewing phenomena as dreams, illusions, mirages, the images of multiple vision, emanations, or reflections. It is the understanding that really there is no suffering and no one involved in suffering. This is the most profound Mahayana or bodhisattva view to hold while practicing the four limitless thoughts. The Buddha said that if one can meditate like this for even one second the merit accumulated is as vast as space itself. This is the true bodhisattva path of the four limitless thoughts. The third and most profound level is non-conceptual practice. This comes with the achievement of buddhahood itself. It is the limitless compassion of Buddha where everything appears enlightened and pure and there are no longer any waves of appearance of sentient beings. This state is the most powerful for helping beings, and is compared to clouds naturally giving rain, which gives life to fields, plants, and flowers. This rain of benefit is spontaneous and unceasing, continuing as long as sentient beings exist and suffer in the universe. The level of buddhahood is all-pervading.

At whatever level the bodhisattva practices them, the four limitless thoughts are of great significance. It is also very important to study the Mahayana doctrine taught by Lord Buddha and his holy followers, as it gives much detail on the practice of bodhichitta. If one does everything according to their doctrine then one can make no mistake. It is also very helpful to read the histories of the lineage gurus and to study their attitude and practice, as they were all bodhisattvas themselves. Their bodhisattva activity for the benefit of all sentient beings is very profound and limitless. Although one cannot copy this, one can try one's best to emulate them and make wishing prayers to be more like them. This is like a yak quickly eating as much grass as it can while keeping its eye on more distant pastures. One may not be able to act or have the same realization as great masters or the Buddha, but one can aspire to follow them and pray to be able to do so.

In his Mahayana teachings Lord Buddha said that he prayed to lead all sentient beings to enlightenment, with himself last. He also prayed that in the interim he would become light where there was darkness, a bridge where there was no way across a river, a home with beautiful land and meadows for the homeless, fire to warm those who suffer from cold, waters for those who thirst, and so on. I think it is because Buddhas and bodhisattvas have prayed in this way for previous countless aeons that we now enjoy this beautiful solar system, and our beautiful earth with its flowers, forests, gems, edible plants, healing medicines, and so on. I feel that all of this originates from

Equanimity

their bodhisattva wishing prayers, and maybe we can create similar benefit for sentient beings in the future.

When one sits and practices bodhichitta intensively many difficulties arise, such as emotions, defilements, and even sickness. The *Vajra Cutter Sutra* (Skt. *Vajracchedika Prajnaparamita Sutra*) says that as the great bodhisattva practicing the Prajnaparamita is purified many difficulties will arise, but this should not give cause for worry. For example, if one washes a dirty cloth the water changes colour as the dirt washes out, but this means that the cloth is becoming perfectly clean. Do not become depressed about one's inability to help at this stage but practice joyfully and happily, just like a master of ballet. If one practices Mahayana training without error one will gradually achieve higher levels of experience and it will become easier.

As Chandrakirti says:

> Then for the enlightened bodhisattva,
> the first cause of perfect enlightenment, giving,
> becomes his joy in giving even his own flesh if someone needs it,
> is reason for inferring the unimaginable extent
> of a bodhisattva's tremendous and selfless compassion.[1]

This idea of a bodhisattva giving his or her own flesh is further explained by Gampopa, who says that giving one's organs in this way is only beneficial if one can actually help someone, i.e., if the organ can be used. The ordinary practitioner of the Bodhisattvayana would not give in this way because not only would it be of no help but it would also destroy oneself (the practitioner). With achievement of the bhumis, the bodhisattva has the miracle power of enlightenment and then is able to help. For example, the Jataka history of Shakyamuni as an enlightened bodhisattva tells of an occasion on which he gave his eye to a blind person who could then see perfectly. When the enlightened bodhisattva prays in this way, the power of generosity is such that a new eye instantly appears as if nothing was ever lost.

You must study and meditate on Buddha's Mahayana teachings because this is the most profound practice. I believe that the strongest practitioner of loving compassion is one who possesses the very essence of Mahayana Buddhism. It is for this reason that the Mahayana is called the 'Great Vehicle'. This is not sectarianism because the Mahayana, or Bodhisattvayana, is Lord Buddha's heart-teaching. I hope all sentient beings may become qualified to practice the Mahayana, and through it achieve the absolute realization of shunyata and compassion that is without conceptualization.

11
A CALM MIND

BODHICHITTA IS VERY IMPORTANT for bringing about a peaceful mind. It brings calmness and clarity. If, when hatred arises towards someone, one is able to meditate on this person as being like a teacher because he or she is a cause for one to improve one's patience, this reduces hatred and results in great calmness. This happens because natural mind is itself always calm, just as a great ocean remains essentially calm even though its surface is continuously disturbed by different causes and conditions. In the mind, this kind of disturbance results in attachment and aversion to others, which endlessly multiply duality and discrimination between friend and enemy. Lojong, when practiced well, cuts through the problem and the mind becomes calm. This calm mind may be called bodhichitta. It is like a hook that brings with it many good qualities such as happiness and relaxation, and can also bring peace to one's family, friends, and country. As this calm arises from buddha nature, it radiates many qualities of enlightenment.

Someone once asked Lord Buddha to explain the point of his teaching. He replied that the point is to discipline oneself and make the mind calm. This is the goal of Dharma practice. No matter whether one practices Shravakayana, Mahayana or Vajrayana teachings, if the mind does not become calm it means that one's practice is incorrect in some way. This is true no matter how 'perfectly' or 'correctly' one appears to be doing the practice. It is like a set of scales by which to watch and measure one's practice. When one disciplines one's mind and develops a calm mind, then even upon seeing one's enemies one feels more positive, because the unpeaceful mind of hatred has been removed. If, upon meeting beggars, one has a wish to help them, this is a sign that the unpeaceful mind of greed has been removed. If one wishes to give medicine in response to seeing sickness, or simply wishes to visit and talk to patients in a hospital, this means that the calm mind quality of kindness is improving. If, upon hearing people fight and quarrel one feels sadness rising and wishes to bring them peace and happiness, this indicates a calm mind and is a sign of receding aversion. A calm and peaceful mind is similar to a smoothly running river on which one can calmly swim or boat. It is not like a fast-flowing mountain stream too rapid for peaceful swimming and boating, which is similar to a mind completely crowded with attachment and aversion.

The Kadampa Geshe Langri Thangpa was named 'Blackface' because he never smiled. The reason he never smiled was that he was always thinking of the sufferings of sentient beings. Even though he himself had many disciples and was a very famous Kadampa saint, he was never happy and relaxed. When he was young, his teacher Potowa asked him what meditation practice he would do. His reply was that through all his life until death he would practice Lojong. Potowa raised his thumbs (a gesture of great approval in Tibet) and said, "I never heard such good news as this! Good! Good! Good! Good!" Langri Thangpa said that during his life he would never waste even one breath, and that all of his breathing would be devoted to the 'sending and taking' practice of Lojong. This great wish shows that he had achieved the most calm state of mind. So please, if you should be beaten or insulted by someone, think, "This is my fault, mainly because my mind is not calm. It is in fact a reflection of my uncalm mind." This is true because uncalm mind is a main element in provoking an attack. However, this kind of experience can happen even if one does have a calm mind due to the ripening of one's past karma (action), or such an incident may be the result of a combination of both causes. While both causes are one's own fault, the latter is more difficult to escape.

Furthermore, even when you are kind to someone and they are good to you in return, you should think that this is only the other person's kindness, "I have really done nothing for this person when I compare it to my wish for him to have both the permanent happiness of enlightenment, and temporary worldly happiness. Even though I want to do so I am not yet able to lead him to full enlightenment, and so I can only pray for the ability to do so." At the same time, you should recognize that this good result comes because your mind is just a little calm with bodhichitta. In this way one reduces pride, which is the biggest obstacle to developing a calm mind. Pride is like a stone lying in the ocean. Even if it remained there for millions of years it would never become soft. Pride is the same as an inverted cup that cannot accept anything.

Lord Buddha's mind was very calm, clear and disciplined, so much so that even wild tigers, lions and elephants became tame in his presence. They would bow down to him and would never harm him. He never needed an army, bodyguard, or weapons, because his loving compassion protected him. If the mind is not calm but is in fact full of attachment and aversion, then no matter how perfectly costumed and religious one looks, it is quite worthless. On the other hand, for one whose mind is calm it does not matter if he or she wears rags or armour, or holds weapons, because the mind is calm inside. This is just like the silkworm that looks unpleasant yet produces beautiful thread from inside, or like the Bodhisattva Manjushri who wields the sharpest of swords in a threatening attitude yet never strikes; instead, he simply holds it, beginninglessly and endlessly. The sword itself represents the ultimate nature of reality. Buddha's teaching is not concerned with external appearances; the aim is to liberate the mind. Buddha never held the belief that happiness and sadness come from somewhere else. What is outside is unimportant. If a person's mind is completely full of the negative emotions, yet he or she wears the robes of the highest sangha and bows down in the temple shrine room, it is the same as being a tiger. Buddha really runs away when such people come inside the temple.

If one has a very disciplined mind that harbours no hatred and is completely full of Lojong qualities, even if one appeared outwardly crazy, such as going naked, or wearing snake skins and demon masks, one would be Buddha's heart disciple. I think that all the buddhas and bodhisattvas of the ten directions would come to visit such a person. In Lojong practice one first meditates on oneself and others as equals. The second meditation is to develop more love for others than for oneself. Lastly, one meditates on exchanging one's own happiness for the suffering of others. One practices to improve each meditation until it is strong and stable before progressing to the next step.

All Mahayana and Vajrayana teachings are practiced with the purpose of calming the mind. In this respect the most effective technique for Vajrayana practitioners is tranquil, calm shamatha meditation and the non-dualistic awareness meditation of Mahamudra that leads to enlightenment. If it is not easy to do Mahamudra practice because of mental or physical disturbances, then one should do Lojong. For Mahayana practitioners Lojong is the most effective source of a calm mind. However, this practice is undertaken only as part of intensive Mahayana training. It is not to be done if the ego is strong, because self-interest or hoping for too much causes worry and an uncalm mind.

For dharma practitioners in whom the Four Dharma Thoughts[1] are not developed (described as 'dry seed'), there are practices that can be used to calm mental disturbances. In the case of anger, close one's eyes and visualize one's surroundings transformed into a heavenly environment such as Sukhavati or Tushita heaven, where everything is crystal and goddesses shower cool milk over one's body. Then move to a cool place or shrine and sit, letting the air circulate, and breathe very gently twenty-one times. When the mind becomes calm, consider the situation constructively, such as thinking positively about one's family. If the mind remains calm, one can then read a little about loving compassion from a book.

When strong jealousy disturbs your life, put yourself in the other person's position and put him (or her) in your position. Then imagine him being jealous of you in the same manner, and continue for a little while like this. When feeling his jealousy begins to bother you, tiring your mind and making you feel a little upset, open your eyes and think, "Oh, I am the one who is doing this – to him. Sorry! There is nobody being jealous of me." Then gently breathe in and out seven or twenty-one times. On the outward breath see your jealous feelings going out and away from you, and on breathing in feel very calm and peaceful.

If one feels too much disappointment, open the windows to let in fresh air and then lay down. Relax the body and breath as much as possible, feet resting straight out with heels down, and arms at one's sides with the mala held in one hand. Concentrate on the touch of each bead between your thumb and finger and, without any mantra, concentrate strongly on each bead as it passes. After completing one round, breathe out very gently through the mouth, keeping your mind on the breath. This will calm you down.

There could be many reasons for feeling proud, such as wealth, physique, intelligence, personal qualities, and so on. One should go to one's shrine room and sit down. Begin by thinking, 'Why am I proud?' If it is because of education and knowledge, one should first think of Manjushri. Think of how one cannot compare with Manjushri, before whom kings, queens, and enlightened beings bow down in praise of his knowledge. Next, think of how people emulate, praise and read the works of the best scholar in your chosen field. Consider, "Compared to this who am I? I do not get awarded such high honours or have as many people paying attention to me. My attitude is simply an inflated bladder of pride." Now visualize yourself as a bladder filling up with your pride just as if it were being inflated, until, in one sixth of a second, it suddenly explodes from the pressure. Repeat this seven times, again and again. Gently breathe in and out seven times. On the outward breath pride leaves as a yellowish colour; breathe in softly and gently. If you have time, get up very smoothly and gently and prostrate before the shrine in a relaxed manner. This is especially effective when practiced before the Tripitaka or a Buddha statue. It is important for a Buddha statue to contain zung zhuk (blessings) and be blessed by a consecration (rice-throwing) ceremony. But, even without these, one should still do this practice, and pride will gradually diminish.

Please all do your practice even though it might be difficult. This is the dark age, and in these times, it is very hard to subdue self and develop a peaceful mind.

12
SHAMATHA
(Tranquility Meditation)

SHAMATHA MEDITATION (Tib. Shinay; Eng. Calm abiding) is of great importance in all three yanas of Buddhism. In general, all shamatha practices are the same, although each tradition or sect may employ different techniques.

The great Mahayana master Shantideva says in the *Bodhisattvacharyavatara*:

> Having understood that defilements are completely overcome
> by vipashyana endowed with shamatha,
> first, I should strive for shamatha.[1]

The reason one engages in shamatha meditation first is because it is through this practice that one loses attachment to the world and thoughts come to rest. For example, if one wishes to see a golden fish in a lotus pond where many bubbles, waves and turbid water obscure one's vision, it is necessary for the water itself to become tranquil. It is only then that one can look into it to see the golden fish. Similarly, if one wishes to give rise to enlightenment, the disturbances caused by ordinary worldly thoughts and emotions that make enlightenment difficult to achieve, need to be conquered first. The source of thoughts are the five senses: seeing, hearing, smelling, tasting, and touching. These may give rise to mental grasping and attraction to the 'five royal pleasures', or to negative feelings and rejection, or to indifference. Attraction to pleasurable sensations can be a strong stimulus for thought production. For example, strong attachment can arise towards friends to the point that one can no longer control one's thoughts. Alternatively, if the sensations are unpleasant, negative emotions give rise to the production of negative thoughts. The five royal pleasures are beautiful form, music, scent, taste, and touch. They are abiding characteristics of the kamadhatu (Tib. dod kham), or desire realm. The Mahayana and Shravakayana teach that one needs to maintain the Vinaya precepts as a foundation for shamatha practice. The reason for this is that the Vinaya is very effective for teaching strong renunciation of samsara and for cutting off attachment. The *Bodhisattvacharyavatara* describes the next best course of action as going to a cave or forest where there is only the moon shining by night, the sun by day, and the singing of birds; a place where one has few possessions, and eats and sleeps less. In such a place, even if one were with a friend, one would talk less. This kind of situation very effectively cuts off thoughts and attachments, and shamatha arises quickly.

For lay sangha members who are involved with worldly or family matters, the best foundation for shamatha practice is to follow a daily timetable, together with special retreats for periods ranging in duration from years, to months, to days, or even to hours if family considerations present difficulties. During shamatha sitting it is very important to relax and try not to be disturbed by thoughts about business or other problems. If this is difficult then it is better to sit for only a short time. Lord Buddha said that even concentrating for the length of time that it takes an ant to run from one's brow down to the tip of the nose, results in great merit and purification, and bad karma accumulated over many lifetimes is removed. This is because, although one might feel this is "just shamatha practice," in this short period one actually contacts one's natural Buddha mind. While one may sit perfectly, if problems and thoughts arise to disturb the mind, the calmness and clarity of shamatha cannot be achieved. However, this situation is not necessarily an absolute waste. One time a monkey mimicked a certain bhikshu whom it saw sitting in meditation in a cave. Through simply copying the bhikshu, the monkey eventually became an arhat because of the inherent power of the sitting posture itself. When sitting it is better not to hold the mind too tightly, but rather to seek the balance that is best for oneself where the mind is as calm as possible.

Shamatha mind is the very important primary foundation. At the beginning of one's practice it is not good to jump to vipashyana or straight to Mahamudra as this would not be a safe route for achieving good results. This would only be effective for someone who had tremendously strong devotion (Tib. mogu) – such a practitioner is known as 'instantaneous one' (Tib. chigcharwa). It is generally best to climb gradually, in a more discriminating manner – this kind of practitioner is known as 'the practitioner of the graduated path' (Tib. rimgyipa). Most practitioners, however, belong to the category of 'uncertain one' (Tib. thogalwa), as they follow a combination of both paths. Both ordained and lay people practice these paths. The time taken, whether long or short, is unimportant; what matters is to practice as patiently and precisely as one is able.

The place one uses for shamatha sitting needs to be clean and tidy. It can be in a quiet place or small room at home. If one is a Buddhist practitioner or has respect for the Buddha, one should place a nicely shaped representation of Lord Buddha before one. This can be a picture, statue, or painting. Some attractive flowers and burning incense or sandalwood should also be placed there. The buddha image should be elevated slightly higher than the practitioner. If one does not like to have these it is not important, a quiet room with plenty of light is sufficient. In either case, one needs a cushion to sit on. One can use a good Japanese 'zafu', or a Tibetan cushion which is usually a square design called a 'small samadhi seat' (Tib. samten bol chung). This is a one-and-a-half-foot square cushion filled with deer hair, wool from a big-horned sheep, or certain grasses. The cushion should be about five inches thick and very strong and hard. If the weather is very hot, one should meditate in a place that is a little cool. If it is very cool, one needs a warmer place.

One should prepare oneself before meditating, as one has to remove anything that bothers the mind before sitting. Say to oneself, "Now I will forget all mental business, problems, troubles, disappointments, nervousness and unpleasantness, and I will never allow them to arise during meditation." It is better not to meditate when feeling too distracted. First try to relax a little, or recite something short and simple like the six-syllable mantra of Chenrezig, so that one has calmed down a little before meditating. If you go ahead anyway you will be unable to control the situation and meditation will be disturbed, just as the Yangtse river flowing over rocks will no longer flow smoothly, but will tumble and churn. Like trying to take a clear video through a contaminated lens, the picture will never be good. Also, from the Mahayana point of view, one should think, "I am going to attain enlightenment on this very seat for the benefit of all sentient beings," and then entreat all the root and lineage gurus and the most holy Lord Shakyamuni (the most disciplined and enlightened being) for their help. This is like washing dishes before you eat from them. In meditating one is going to a festival and banquet of enlightenment, and therefore one must first be clean.

When sitting down, it is very important to sit in the seven-point position of Vairochana Buddha.[2]

These seven points are, sitting with:

1. the legs crossed in the vajra, or full lotus, position.
2. the spinal cord straight.
3. the shoulders straight, but naturally loose, with the arms resting downwards in a relaxed circle, such that a cuckoo (bird) could fly through the curve between the arm and the body.
4. the hands in the gesture of equipoise, upturned, with the right hand resting on top of the left, and the thumb tips lightly touching.
5. the neck bent slightly forward so that the head tilts down about one inch.
6. the tip of the tongue resting on the upper palate.
7. the eyes naturally open looking straight ahead, then lowered until the gaze rests just above the tip of the nose.

This position balances the elements of the body, allowing the energy to flow freely, thus controlling emotions as well as mental and physical disturbances. All seven of these physical disciplines should be maintained during meditation practice as even a little mistake in the position, such as leaning a few inches to the left or right, or forward or backward, can create problems. The beginner may want to learn good posture by sitting in front of a big mirror with a plumbline hanging centrally from the ceiling. By comparing one's sitting posture with the line one can practice the correct posture. A horizontal line on the mirror at the correct height for the top of the head can also help one to become aware of any shortening of the posture.

If it is difficult for the legs or because of health to assume the full vajra position, one should try the relaxed half-lotus position and change sides from time to time. Alternatively, one could try a chair, or it is helpful to include intervals of walking meditation before pain begins. If the practitioner wants to engage in long periods of meditation, a smooth piece of sandal or juniper wood can be placed under the chin to support the head. It is very important to be comfortable rather than forcing and squeezing oneself.

When the meditation session is finished, first move the shoulders forward several times, then the neck forward and back, and circle the head to the left and to the right. Hold the arms straight out in front and open and close the hands several times. Get up very gently, and stand for a few seconds before moving around, do not immediately start moving around quickly. This meditation is good for meditators from all the three yanas as it is the foundation, of meditation. (There may be some slight differences between schools, such as eye position, for example.)

During shamatha meditation one needs to remove the five causes of disturbance (Tib. nyepa nga):

1. The disturbance of laziness (Tib. leylo), where one does not try to engage properly in shamatha.
2. That of forgetfulness of instructions (Tib. damngag jedpa) where one forgets the different techniques for shamatha sitting.
3. That of dullness and agitation (Tib. gyingwa gopa). Dullness, or 'sinking', is losing awareness due to the disturbance of a slight darkness or fogginess of mind, or to mental sluggishness. Agitation, or 'scattering', describes a state where thoughts do not settle due to mental unruliness.

The antidote for dullness or 'sinking mind' (Tib. gyingwa mugpa) is stronger awareness and clear contemplation. One needs to radiate tranquility and "lift oneself up." If one's environment is very hot, one should wear less clothing, eat lighter food or seek a cooler area in which to sit. Allowing the breeze or the fragrance of flowers or grasses and herbs through the area can be beneficial. It may also be helpful to move into a better lit area. A remedy for sleeping is to splash one's face gently with cold water or to engage in walking meditation for a while. The antidote for agitation, or 'following thoughts' (Tib. gopa), is to think about the impermanence and suffering of samsara that permeates the world and the universe. Then when sadness arises one should contemplate one's breathing. Worry and resentment (Tib. gyopa) can be remedied by trying to forget problems that arise in the mind and focusing contemplation on just one subject until the mind becomes tranquil. In this case, it would initially be best to focus on a very beautiful and fine-featured statue or thangkha of Lord Buddha, or to visualize him sitting before one on a lion throne, very youthful and radiant and in deep one-pointed concentration. If disturbing emotions arise, one should immediately stop one's meditation; do not continue while they rise as this will make sitting more disturbed the next time. It is always better to finish one's meditation when it feels good, because this is the experience that will be brought to the next sitting. It is very important to follow this kind of advice as a beginner. Later, when one is more experienced, calm mind comes easily and disturbances are all controlled.

4. That of non-application of antidotes (Tib. nyenpo ngon par du mi gyipa). This inactivity results from sinking and tiredness.
5. That of over-application of antidotes (Tib. nyenpo ngon par du gyipa) when the mind is already calm. This over-stimulates the mind and prevents it from settling.

These five causes of disturbance are the greatest hindrances to the shamatha experience.

There are eight antidotes, or 'mental combinations' (Tib. dujay) to remedy the five hindrances. The first four of these prevent laziness:

1. Earnestness (Tib. dunpa) in wanting to concentrate.
2. Diligence (Tib. tsolwa) in striving to maintain one's concentration with sharp awareness.
3. Faith in (Tib. daypa), and respect for what one is doing.
4. Perfect ease, or watchfulness, (Tib. shin jang) which recognizes whatever arises in meditation. This prevents thoughts from proliferating and maintains the purity of concentration which is the nature of all shamatha.

In general, the antidote to laziness is diligence. The first duty is to know that shamatha practice is essential as it is the foundation for all the meditations of the three yanas. The second duty is to make rules and a timetable for oneself. The third duty is to practice shamatha meditation with care and delicacy. These three together form the basis. If one of these is missed, Shamatha realization will not develop properly and one might then follow the wrong path. Therefore, one needs to push oneself – this is the meaning of diligence.

The antidote that overcomes forgetfulness (Tib. jedpa) is:

5. Memory (Tib. drenpa), or mindfulness. In the same way that a gardener attends to his flowers and is always careful lest he neglect or accidentally cut some, one needs strong mindfulness.

The antidote for dullness and agitation is:

6. Vigilance (Tib. shezhin), or brightness and alertness of mind.

The antidote to non-application of antidotes is:

7. Mental exertion (Tib. dujeypa), confidently (Tib. sempa) or joyfully engaging in shamatha meditation. This has the three qualities of joy, bliss, and perception, which dispel sinking and scattering by a constant mindfulness that is always watching for them and applying different antidotes as soon as they arise. This is like a hawk in the sky that constantly watches the ground, sensitive to the smallest movement, and then immediately swoops down to pick up any mice it sees. This watching mind is aware of the strength of the antidotes, and aware if one forgets the antidotes, therefore it is ready each time. As it increases in strength, this mind brings more antidotes into use.

The antidote to the over-application of antidotes is:

8. Equanimity (Tib. tang nyom). When shamatha meditation becomes very strong, one should not continue to hold it too tightly. At this point one must relax a little and rest in equanimity – the eighth and final antidote.

These eight antidotes continue to be of great importance to shamatha practitioners as long as the five disturbances continue to arise. The practice can be compared to taming wild horses. Once a horse is tame it no longer needs restraint or the whip, and the rider can then just relax and ride along gently. It would be a source of disturbance to beat a tame horse. Atisha said:

> If you engage in shamatha meditation without correct contemplation then you will never attain perfect shamatha realization, though you practice for one thousand years.

Therefore, one must always follow the appropriate sutras, and practice shamatha correctly. Shamatha meditation is of the utmost importance and one's aim must be to give rise fully to this experience. One also needs the help provided by the six powers:

1. The power of hearing (Tib. thopay tob), or study of the techniques of meditation.
2. The power of contemplation (Tib. sampay tob) or continuous investigation, which identifies what is correct and what is incorrect during meditation.
3. The power of mindfulness (Tib. drenpay tob).
4. The power of vigilance (Tib. shezhin gyi tob), or awareness.
5. The power of enthusiastic perseverance (Tib. tsondru kyi tob), or diligence, which means not letting experiences such as difficulties, boredom, dislike, interest, or disinterest, disturb one's practice.
6. The power of familiarity (Tib. gompay tob), or mind itself which is not separate from shamatha.

These six powers bring the benefit of the nine stages of improvement in settling the mind:

1. Mental settling (Tib. nang jog), the stage of focusing with ease upon whatever object of concentration one chooses.
2. Continual settling (Tib. gyundu jogpa), the stage of finding it easy to maintain concentration while guarding against distraction.
3. Patch-like settling (Tib. lanti jogpa), the stage of easily detecting distracting thoughts or absent mindedness, and returning to one's concentration.
4. Close settling (Tib. nyewar jogpa), the stage of perfect placement, whereby one easily maintains and increases sharply focused and one-pointed concentration, without tension or tightness.
5. Subduing settling (Tib. dulwar jaypa), the stage of mastery, where one further subdues sinking and scattering through recalling the benefits of shamatha which is the ground for all subsequent high experiences of enlightenment.
6. Pacification (Tib. zhiwar jaypa), the stage at which the disinclination to meditate arising from laziness or forgetfulness is rejected through recognition of its consequences.
7. Complete pacification (Tib. nampar zhiwar jaypa), the stage where it is easy to eliminate conflicting emotions and other disturbances as they arise, through applying appropriate antidotes.

8. Single pointed dwelling (Tib. tsechigtu jaypa), the stage of always finding it easy to engage in deep and profound one-pointed concentration.
9. Equal settling (Tib. nyampar jogpa), the stage of achieving the power of equanimity. The mind becomes very settled and there is no longer any continuous need for antidotes, nor are there worries about meditation. The causes of thought are easily controlled, and returning to contemplation is effortless.

Throughout the stages of shamatha practice one applies the four kinds of attention:

1. Painstaking attention (Tib. drimti jugpa).
2. Repeated attention (Tib. chaypa dang chayti jugpa).
3. Uninterrupted attention (Tib. chaypa mepar jugpa).
4. Effortless attention (Tib. tsolwa mepar jugpa).

The first power, that of hearing and study, brings one to the first stage of settling the mind (mental settling). Once one has received the initial shamatha instructions and had a chance to ponder them, then upon starting the practice one already has more control of the mind. Initially, thoughts seem to arise constantly like a stream cascading over a waterfall. This is not a problem; it is simply that one was not previously aware of how many thoughts constantly arise in the mind during the course of daily life. The second power, that of investigation, brings the second stage of settling the mind (continual settling), where the mind is sometimes calm, and sometimes has thoughts arising. At this stage, the third hindrance, that of dullness and agitation, is stronger, and one needs to apply the first of the four attentions, painstaking attention. The third power, that of mindfulness, brings the third stage of settling the mind (patch-like settling). At this stage thoughts arise if there is a cause for them, but otherwise the mind is settled. Now one is aware when the mind becomes busy and quickly goes on to apply one-pointed concentration. Now that one's concentration is stronger, one does not allow the mind to drift into thinking and one enters the fourth stage of settling mind (close settling). The fourth power, that of alertness, leads to the fifth stage of settling mind (controlled settling). Now one's mind is more tame and controlled, and it becomes more pleasant and joyful to meditate. This leads into the sixth stage of settling the mind (pacification), where one automatically sees the causes of agitation as they occur and quickly abolishes the thought process. The fifth power, that of enthusiastic perseverance, brings one to the seventh stage of settling the mind (complete pacification). Between the third and seventh stages of settling one needs to apply the second attention, repeated attention, as one's practice of shamatha changes from time to time. Sometimes it is controlled, and sometimes disturbed. The principal characteristic of the seventh stage is that negative emotions become easy to pacify and this brings one to the eighth stage (single pointed settling), where all the remaining thoughts become easy to pacify. This is a high, one-pointed shamatha state of samadhi which is completely undisturbed by dullness and agitation. This settled mind state is very powerful. Here one uses the third of the attentions, uninterrupted attention. Shamatha sitting is no longer troubled by thoughts. This can be compared to being in control of a wild elephant and riding on its back. The sixth power, that of familiarity, brings one to the ninth stage of settling mind (equal settling) where the master completely controls the elephant.

When these nine qualities are all very well established, the finest and most perfect shamatha experience arises. This is the same as taming an elephant, because he is then always easy to control, and will automatically do what his rider wishes. The rider is very relaxed and joyful and even if he or she plays the flute it will not disturb the mount. This is the highest achievement of one-pointed mind, very close to the true state of shamatha. However, if mental and physical bliss (Tib. shin jang) do not arise at this stage, then the perfect experience of shamatha has not yet been achieved. During the ninth stage, a coarse experience of bliss may be briefly experienced, but more shamatha meditation is needed for the profound experience. The end result of shamatha is the complete attainment of a perfect and refined mind and body. If this arises, then one has reached the peak of worldly shamatha achievement.

In the *Abhidharma* it says:

> This shamatha experience cuts through mental and physical sufferings and problems and removes all defilements.

This is the same as a very tame elephant that will follow wherever one goes, stay where one wants it to, or play with one in the meadow. Shamatha brings with it a very great accumulation of worldly virtue and it becomes easy to use one's mind and body for any spiritual practice, just as gold can be used to make every kind of jewellery. It becomes easy to subdue the negative emotions and to control both positive and negative actions. One also becomes able to heal one's own sickness and easily dispel one's tiredness.

It is said that there are three principal experiences of shamatha; these are blissfulness, clarity of mind, and absence of thoughts. When these three arise, one must avoid attachment to them and to the feeling that one is experiencing enlightenment itself, because such arising of pride and attachment leads one into mistaken ways. Shamatha is a very important meditation. Do not give it up. This would be throwing away the opportunity of achieving enlightenment. Do not leave this practice for something that appears more interesting, as this would be no different than throwing away or breaking the engine of a car while carefully looking after the exterior.

13
VIPASHYANA
(Insight Meditation)

BOTH SHAMATHA AND VIPASHYANA (Tib. Lha thong) are very important for the practice of Mahamudra. Shamatha is practiced first as it is a grounding meditation, and a method or antidote by which one controls the energy of the mind and makes it tranquil. By itself, shamatha is limited to bringing peace and tranquillity; to progress further one needs vipashyana meditation.

DEVELOPING THE BASIS FOR VIPASHYANA MEDITATION

Once one's accomplishment in shamatha meditation has become quite strong, the constant strong mindfulness in applying antidotes that was needed to establish it is no longer necessary. When one meditates it is easy to enter the state of shamatha, which resembles the smooth flow of a great river hardly disturbed at all by waves. It is at this point that one begins to practice vipashyana meditation. Vipashyana means 'realizing the true nature of phenomena through the wisdom of discriminating awareness'. The basic posture and methods for concentration come from shamatha meditation. One stays very relaxed, the shoulders drop down and the spinal cord rests in a natural and straight position, without tension. In this position one then relaxes in shamatha meditation for a short while and allows everything to settle, just as suspended debris settles, or bubbles disperse, in still water. One is then ready to begin investigating one's thoughts to see where they originate and where they go. This is done by allowing a single thought to arise, and then watching it.

BEGINNING VIPASHYANA MEDITATION

After the initial period of tranquillity meditation, one begins by concentrating upon a deity that one finds easy to visualize, such as Chenrezig, or one's own special deity. Looking at the visualized form of Chenrezig one can see that he is white in colour, with four arms and beautiful ornaments, and that he is seated upon a moon disc in a lotus flower. While meditating, think that Chenrezig's white colour is that of compassion, that his four arms symbolize the four limitless meditations, that the moon disc upon which he is seated signifies that his compassion leads sentient beings to enlightenment, and that the lotus flower symbolizes his complete freedom from samsaric existence. Looking at this very beautiful mental image one should then investigate where it comes from. Is it part of one's own body, or is it external? Imagining that it is external, investigate by asking whether it really exists outside of oneself. If so, then why can one not actually, physically, touch it? When one looks in this way one sees the image as clear and external, and simultaneously as not existing externally. Its nature is voidness. This is the same as the moon's reflection in a pond: while the moon's image upon the water's surface is clear, no top, middle, or bottom exists. This is the awareness that form is emptiness and emptiness itself is form. One should hold this experience for as long as possible, or until one's concentration weakens.

Looking again at the visualized image of Chenrezig that could not be found to exist externally, one should now search for it internally. Look carefully to see if it is located in some part of the body. Next, search for it in the mind. If one considers the Chenrezig and the mind to be the same, look to see what mind is. Does it have colour or arms? If it has colour, is it white? Looking at the shape of the mind – is it shaped like Chenrezig, does it have arms, and so on? Investigating thus, one can see that mind cannot be only one colour, cannot have arms, and so on, and therefore one cannot establish that the mind is Chenrezig. Therefore, this visualization must be a manifestation of the mind. Its nature is the same as the nature of thoughts, which have no basic existence. They are like clouds arising in space and vanishing into space, after which they cannot be found again. When one has looked carefully one should then rest in this experience.

One has found this Chenrezig to have no basic existence. In the same way everything else is a manifestation of the mind. Whatever arises in the mind has no ground for existence, it is just an illustration of the mind, and is naturally empty. Like a mold that gives shape to clay, mind creates concepts which shape phenomena. Whatever you see, whatever you detect, is this mind structure. Each sentient being's conceptualization of reality is very different. Human beings may see water as a drink, but for most animals it is their home. Celestial beings see it as nectar, but for hell beings it is like molten lava, and hungry ghosts see it as a horrible, poisonous liquid. Thus, while each sentient being is perceiving the same object, it is not conceptualized the same way. First, mind illustrates, then, phenomena occur. For example, looking at a piece of wood, mind decides what shape it could make. First, mind makes the shape, such as a table, or a figure that could be carved. One can then apply legs, top, and so on, to make a table. A separate, external object – table – is thus made. However, this external object was created by the relativity of the pieces of wood, mind, and cause and effect. There was no table or figure in existence in the piece of wood, but now it is a beautiful table or a statue. First mind illustrated and then things changed. Now the word, the name, has also changed to 'table', or whatever creature has been sculpted. Everything has the 'shape' of the mind. Continuing to investigate in this way one finds all inner and external phenomenon have no inherent existence, they are like the reflection of the moon on water. Just as in a dream or a reflection in a mirror – appearance is empty. Following investigation of coarse mind (conceptualising and visualizing mind), contemplate the subtle mind (mind in a gentle and quiet state of stillness, the ocean of mind settled). Coarse mind can be compared to a painting on the canvas of subtle, tranquil mind.

Now look at this meditator and illustrator, the mind itself. Where is its source? Does it arise from the body, from external sources, or from the five aggregates? Where does it end? Where is it staying now? Investigate these questions and look carefully. The past has gone and cannot be retrieved and so is naturally empty. The future has not yet arrived and so it is also empty. The present instant itself has no existence as it is related to the past or the future and does not exist as something separate. Practice continually in this way until intrinsic mind appears, and one experiences the natural mind of wisdom, free from dualistic self-existence.

Next, one can change one's visualization, to Manjushri for example, and repeat the investigation, also asking oneself where the visualization of Chenrezig has gone now that a new one has arrived. One can then see that there is no place to which it has gone, it was just a manifestation of the mind. Then where has the image of Manjushri come from? It has not come from a different source; it is also a manifestation of the mind. When one investigates what space it occupies, and then what time it occupies, and which comes first, one finds that this image has no existence in time and space. This shows that it is without any trace of independent arising, without going, and without staying, yet at the same time appearing. In this way mental appearances are like waves on the ocean. A wave is not different from the ocean. It arises from the ocean and it returns to it. The next wave that arises is no different in its defining characteristics from the one that preceded it, yet at the same time they are separate. Each single wave is not separate from the ocean, yet at the same time is not the entire ocean. This is a simile for the rising of thoughts in the mind. The concept of duality is destroyed when one sees that waves are not the same, yet are not different.

Once again one should look at the mind and determine whether it is many appearances, or just one. If it is one then how can so many thoughts and appearances arise? Therefore, it cannot be just one. If one tries to see it as many, one can see that if it cannot be one, then it cannot be many. Therefore, everything is just manifestation. All arising is produced by cause and effect and relativity. A piano, for example, is only created by causes and effects bringing together all the parts in relation to one another. When one can find neither one mind nor many minds, one should meditate on this point.

INVESTIGATING THE EGO

Next, one should think about how all the suffering of beings in samsara arises from ego – the belief in an 'I'. For example, in thoughts such as "I am cold," "I am happy," "I am hungry," "I want fame," "I hope," or "I am going to be disappointed," there is always the underlying basis of a strongly held concept of 'I'. One should investigate this 'I' itself. Is 'I' the same as the body? If so, one should look carefully at the body – what is it? The body is divided into many different parts, such as two arms, two legs, a head, etc. If each, for example the head, is body, then why do we need the other parts? If each part is body, then we would have many bodies. Why does one need all these parts together if each is body? If we have many bodies in this way then each piece should be capable of representing body. Look carefully. One may consider each part as body, but each part can be divided even further into skin, muscle, etc. Then where has the body gone? One can continue dividing the parts still further until there are only cells and atoms, and with continued investigation these too can be divided. Is the cell the human being? Is it the body? Is it the cell that is this important basis for 'I'? There are millions of cells, so which one? It is impossible for a cell to be the basis for 'I'. Just as a house is not its bricks. There is no basis for an 'I' in the material body.

Now, one can investigate to see if 'I' is the same as the mind. If it is the same, why does one say 'my mind', or 'my knowledge'? If mind belongs to 'I' then where is 'I'? So, mind is not 'I.' The mind can also be divided into thoughts, feelings, and so on, such as "I'm happy" or "I'm sad." Now, the thoughts "I'm happy" and "I'm sad" are completely opposite to each other, so which is 'I'? If one is 'I' it follows that the other cannot be, because they cannot be the same. Therefore, 'I' cannot be thoughts or feelings. Following this reasoning, thoughts of the mind are the same as cells of the body or bricks of the house. One may think of the body or the mind as the same as 'I', or different from 'I'. If either seems the same as 'I', investigate as described above. If different, then where is this 'I'?

Consider the chariot. It looks like one thing but it can be taken apart into pieces such as the spokes, axle, and so on. Each piece does not represent the chariot. The name and relative truth of the chariot refer to the whole thing. Similarly, when all the parts of the body are gone there is no basis for 'I'. Thus one cannot find any basic or fundamental body. What then is the body? In this way one establishes that there is no real existence of the body and, therefore, there is no basis for the concept of 'I', the ego. To what then can one attach the ego, when there is no place for it? Where is it? On investigating whether it is resides in the head, one divides and destroys the head. Where then is the 'I'? Continue investigating all the parts of the body, hunting for 'I' in this way, until both body and 'I' disappear, and so are seen only as delusion, because there is no such thing in existence as an 'I'. When one realizes that there is no 'I', it follows that there can be no 'my', as nothing can belong to an 'I' that does not exist. 'I' and 'my' are just delusion. Investigate this completely and concentrate on this point of tranquillity. This calm and clear point is very important. It is like the first phase of the new moon, the start of the meditation path that leads one to enlightenment.

This analytical meditation leads to discriminating awareness. It is not the same as ordinary investigation such as research in the fields of science, physics, or mathematics, as it involves searching for true reality by cutting through the block of delusions. While investigating, one is also in the shamatha state of mind, and it is important not to lose this during the practice of vipashyana. Once one has settled into shamatha one should investigate with it. This is like birds that can fly so far through space, through clouds, lights, and elements. They are still flying in space although they pass through all these things. These two meditations go together. Shamatha and vipashyana are inseparable.

Next, one should further investigate the concept of one's own existence by looking at feelings such as "I am hot," "I am cold," or, "I am hungry." If one cannot find a truly existing body or ego then who is it who feels? As one cannot find a truly existent body then feelings must also be natural emptiness. For instance, if one were to touch one's left toe to a fire it would be burned. Look to see what is burning, is it the body, or 'I'? Look again to see who feels the pain, is it the body (toe) or 'I'? One cannot find an 'I', but nevertheless one thinks, "I am burning;" so look to see if the toe and 'I' are the same or separate. If they are the same, then if one also burns the right toe or a finger, there must be another 'I' attached to that toe or finger. In this way it follows that one could find many 'I's. Therefore, feeling is also a delusion. Really nothing is burnt. If there is no 'I' then who is burnt? If the feeling is in the toe, then why does the mind feel? If feeling is in the mind, then why does the toe feel pain? Investigate again.

INVESTIGATING PHENOMENA

There are two alternative ways to meditate:

1. Meditation and concentration is the ordinary approach.
2. Investigation and meditation is the scholarly approach.

One who has limited knowledge of doctrine can engage in direct sitting with little investigation, while the more scholarly can engage in wise study of the Buddha Dharma, first investigating, and then meditating. Both ways are very good. The former is a more direct practice of sitting and contemplation where understanding of the true nature of reality arises by itself. This is a simpler route on which it is not necessary to engage in much thinking, study and investigation. Through this route of the rising of the one-pointed mind, tranquility, great clarity, devotion, guru yoga, patience, and renunciation of existence, achievement is realized. This is like cutting a tree at the root whereupon the branches and leaves naturally fall.

The second route establishes each point of logic and so uncovers this system of relative (conventional) and ultimate truth. Phenomena, the five aggregates, and the ego are investigated through discriminating awareness according to the scriptures of Lord Buddha and the commentaries of many scholars such as Nagarjuna and Asanga. In this way the practitioner cuts through ego and finds natural mind. This is the same as cutting a tree down slowly, piece by piece, beginning with the leaves, then the branches, and so on.

Both of these methods are good as they suit people of different dispositions. It is not that one way is better or more important than the other. In this dark age there is not much time for prolonged study before proceeding with meditation. Therefore, it is best to go to a meditation master and take instruction from him or her. Then meditate in a cabin, or some other suitable place, where one can follow the meditation instructions one received, and so directly discover the four kayas of Buddha in one's own mind.

In order to follow this path, one needs several things. Firstly, one needs devotion to the guru. This devotion is known as 'the head of meditation'. The blessing of the guru is the best way to remove hindrance and to meditate without error. Secondly, one needs compassion for sentient beings, such that one regards others as one with oneself, and loves others as much as oneself. Meditation upon compassion is the most important antidote to errors on the path to enlightenment. Thirdly one needs renunciation, which is known as 'the foot of meditation'. Fourthly, one needs to sit in shamatha and vipashyana which is known as 'the body of meditation'.

Basically, the best approach is to concentrate on what one's guru has given one to do, without guessing or reading about the next stage. One should move forward with the guru's guidance, otherwise there can be a blocking of real experience and understanding. After giving Gampopa the Six Yogas of Naropa and Mahamudra, Jetsun Milarepa told him that he had a further profound teaching that he would give to him later. Gampopa was very excited as he waited for this, until, finally, he requested this most precious teaching. Milarepa then showed him his bottom, the skin of which was very calloused from sitting so long on cold rock, and said that this alone was his most secret teaching. This means that one needs to meditate all the time because genuine Mahamudra experience is beyond words. It cannot be received or found intellectually. Mahamudra can only be achieved by letting it arise from experience.

Milarepa told Gampopa that one day his devotion would no longer be the same, as he would come to truly think of Milarepa as the Buddha Vajradhara, and on that the very day he would achieve perfect realization of Mahamudra. Gampopa wondered what this could mean since he felt that his devotion was so strong already that it could not possibly increase further. However, later on, when he achieved Mahamudra experience when meditating in his retreat in the Gampo mountains, a tremendous devotion to Milarepa arose. In that moment his earlier experience of Shamatha, Vipashyana and devotion became comparable to an eggshell, out of which emerged the true experience of Mahamudra. Therefore, one should simply sit and practice more Mahamudra or Maha Sandhi, as these are the intrinsic Vajrayana points of view in meditation.

Ordinary meditation may sometimes give one the feeling of great experience, such as the arising of non-conceptualisation, radiance, or great bliss, or one may experience great difficulties, such as the arising of strong emotions that disturb one's concentration.

Vipashyana

Whatever happens one should view these objectively, simply as experiences, whether they seem good or bad. At such a time, it is more dangerous to bind oneself to one's experiences through attachment as this creates stronger ego, and is misleading. It makes no difference whether one is bound by chains of gold or chains of iron. Gold, however, is more seductive. Rather, one should remain natural and free without blocking anything, just as the garuda flies through space. Milarepa said that even good experiences are gone when one achieves Mahamudra. So, it is important to sit and practice continuously and not worry about anything at all. Whatever happens, happens. However, it is not enough to practice sitting without some knowledge. One also needs the help of the accumulation of merit and so one should always practice the six perfections. On the other hand, study alone cannot lead one to the goal of profound Mahamudra. Sitting is also essential, because when one holds and considers one thought another naturally arises, and this is a continual process – thus thinking binds one like a chain and one never becomes free from the process of conceptualization.

Moreover, Padma Sambhava said:

> Though your realization is like space, continue to take delicate care of one's mind.

If one wants to obtain something profound one needs a finer grind with a sharper blade. Similarly, if one wants a very clean cloth, one requires stronger detergent and more washing. It is the same with insight meditation, one needs to look more at what things are and this makes the nature of things clear. Therefore, if one does not practice investigation, one's practice will not be clear like the clear light of sunrise. There will be no realization of the true nature of mind, dawn will not come, and the sun of realization will never rise. This is the reason why Lord Buddha gave very extensive teaching that fills hundreds of books, why Nagarjuna established the Madhyamaka school, and why Arya Asanga taught the Yogachara school. All these are ways of investigating the true nature of mind and gaining the realization of enlightenment.

14
THE POWER OF EMPTINESS

A FREQUENTLY HELD MISCONCEPTION about the wrathful Vajrayana deities is that they represent a form of demon worship. Mahakala, for example, has a wrathful face and holds a different weapon in each hand, while Mahakali rides a mule in an ocean of blood, and her palace is constructed of human bones and decorated with innards. No matter how wrathful a human being can be, it is nothing compared to the wrathfulness of such deities. However, their wrathful appearance represents the subduing of evil gods, and thus these deities really embody the antidote that subdues ordinary hatred and anger. Terrible deities or places such as these do not actually exist; really there are no oceans of blood or mountains of bones. The deities are activity emanations of the five dhyani Buddhas.[1] No deities with such profound meaning can be found anywhere else and therefore it would be a great misconception to view them as objects of demon worship. They are purely a spiritual technique used for purifying negative mind. Lord Buddha's love and compassion manifested as the wrathful deities to provide sentient beings with a method for subduing the anger and hatred of our own minds. He was also providing an internal means for removing external hindrances that cannot always be pacified through peaceful activity. All evils, devils, and hells are created by anger. Once one reaches the first bhumi, anger is pacified.

The wrathfulness of such deities arises from the great compassion of bodhichitta, of enlightenment, itself. Compassion energy is like fire that burns all things with very sharp energy. Compassion is at its strongest once complete enlightenment is reached, and can then be manifested as wrathfulness if the need arises. Fire may come from wood, but fire itself is very pure energy. Compassion is the same, and the angry quality of the wrathful deity is pure compassion. Just as fire gives warmth and transforms everything it burns into energy, the wrathful deity subdues all things and turns them to enlightenment. After wood catches fire, the flame will not turn back to wood again; the wood has gone. Similarly, nourishing manure can help to produce a beautiful and fragrant flower. Upon reaching enlightenment, Milarepa no longer needed wrathful practice of this kind because he had completely subdued his own anger, which was transformed into infinite love and compassion.

It took a great length of time for Buddha to attain his perfect human form (nirmanakaya). This form no longer has ordinary (samsaric) elements, DNA, or cells, because each cell has transformed into luminosity and vajra elements. This is the reason why Buddha is able to manifest each cell as a buddha field. When the sun shines in the sky it lights the earth, at the same time darkness is gone – everything is clear. Similarly, at the level of Buddhahood, ordinary genetic form has gone, transformed by mind. This process took six years of practice in solitude for Buddha. For this to be possible, each part of a sentient being's cells must evolve into the buddha body through the accumulation of merit and wisdom. It thus took many lifetimes for Buddha to eventually reincarnate into a body where each cell had so evolved. This is the final rebirth of the bodhisattva.

Each of the six realms of beings has one Buddha acting for their benefit and Shakyamuni became the Buddha for the human realm. Lord Buddha was now ready for full enlightenment, ready to complete one more life, as Shakyamuni. He took human form because he needed to use human language, behaviour, culture, and food, in order to work principally for human beings. Genes basically come from the mind, in the sense that mind is the source of all our actions (karma), and it is actions that carry one into each particular rebirth. While the genes and cells of each life come from one's parents, it is past actions that carry one to those parents. It takes many aeons to purify karma and complete the development of primordial wisdom so that the dharmakaya is attained. Once this is accomplished one attains nirmanakaya form. As this form does not have ordinary genetic programming with elements, cells, and blood, its attainment precludes any return to a samsaric form. Samsaric genetics comes to an end. Buddha was beyond ordinary human biology, just as sunlight dispels darkness. An aura of light extended for a full arm's length around his body, his feet never actually touched the ground when he walked, cloth did not touch his skin, and even if food was rotten, it became the most delicious as he ate. This is beyond mundane conceptual explanation. This form is the emanation of the power of enlightenment. In the Mahayana, it is at this point that the Buddha returns in endless emanations to help all sentient beings – continuing until all are led to enlightenment and none remain. This activity is just like lotus seeds producing more lotuses for as long as the garden of sentient beings exists.

Buddhists believe that firstly, wisdom is attained through understanding true natural emptiness, then compassion is generated, and that these two elements (wisdom and compassion) constitute the energy of mind. This energy leads to a tremendous change in living structure, just as a seed of barley develops and grows when it has the two conditions of moisture and soil. In this life, the samsaric condition is that of the aggregates which lead to death, while natural energy continues to carry these two elements. As spiritual practice develops stronger compassion and understanding of emptiness, this energy increases. One can then use the samsaric physical form to accumulate merit, for example, helping the needy, making prostrations and mandala offerings, visualizing deities, reciting mantras, etc., even to the extent of becoming able to give one's own flesh for the benefit of another. This activity creates further merit, thus further increasing one's mental strength and energy. This continues, until upon reaching enlightenment there is no further to go. It is in this way that tremendous new energy of loving compassion develops.

Lights shone from Mahamaya's womb just before the Buddha was born, and he emerged from his mother's right side, representing spiritual life (as opposed to the left side, which represents samsara). Buddha walked immediately after his birth and pointed a finger to the sky and said, "I am the perfect one." Not being born in an ordinary way indicated that he was not taking worldly birth. Being able to walk and talk at birth showed that he was already a manifestation working for sentient beings. He would have no more worldly existence, and his biological system was not an ordinary one.

Vajrayana teaching is so direct that it is capable of leading ordinary, sinful people to enlightenment in one lifetime. In such a case, the natural human body one is born with does not have the time to transform. Marpa Lotsawa's rude character continued from his youth throughout his whole life, but upon reaching enlightenment his rudeness was no longer the same – it became a manifestation of enlightenment. Eventually, Marpa Lotsawa attained a vajra body, which is the total enlightenment body, without genes, cells, and so on. In this union of luminous mind and illusory form (sambhogakaya) all the ordinary genes, DNA, oxygen, energies, and ordinary conscious and subconscious mind, are totally transformed by the Vajrayana method, just as special sand can be transformed into crystal or pure glass.

The weapons held by the wrathful deities represent emptiness. Today we could replace any symbolic weapon they hold, such as the arrow, with the atomic bomb. Emptiness is absolute truth. There is nothing that has power beyond this.

Emptiness possesses seven qualities:

1. **Uncuttable**. Emptiness, however, can completely cut through all relative (conventional) conceptions, realizations, beliefs, and confidences.
2. **Indestructible**. Each level of emptiness realization that one achieves breaks through the previous level. This continues until one reaches the first bhumi when, like seeing the first sliver of the new moon, one first sees the true nature, the emptiness, of interdependent origination. This is embracing prajna, the Mother of Wisdom, Mother of the Victorious Ones of the Three Times. It is the beginning of enlightenment. Whereas different pleasant visions or philosophies cannot destroy one's understanding of emptiness, emptiness can destroy all of them.
3. **Solid**. Other devotions, faith, trust, belief, or comfort (either worldly or spiritual), may appear very solid but there are points of

view which can destroy these so-called solid beliefs. No one can ever destroy the solid understanding of emptiness.

4. **Unchanging**. Everything changes – personality, behaviour, karmic fortune, and so on. Uncertainty is inherent in everything. For example, a rooster knows exactly when dawn will break, but if it is reborn as a donkey, it no longer knows. Similarly, Buddha's regent Mahakashyapa had achieved the highest vision and power of Vedic religious practice, but meeting Buddha completely changed the nature of his realization. Realization of emptiness cannot be changed.
5. **Even**. When one achieves complete enlightenment through realization of emptiness it is very even, the same as flying above the clouds. Inner peace arises, and everything can be seen in very delicate detail.
6. **Impenetrable**. Worldly siddhis, realizations, powers, or miracles, cannot penetrate emptiness. However, emptiness penetrates them without barrier, like sunlight passing through a crystal.
7. **Invincible**. Ignorance, anger, desire, and all negative thoughts, cannot defeat the realization of emptiness. Even if one has no realization, the practice of emptiness meditation from time to time can defeat them all. The achievement of complete buddhahood means these are completely defeated.

In the oral transmission lineages of Mahamudra the stages of meditation (Tib. gom rim) culminate in the lama pointing out the mind – a direct meditation that opens the mind to its primordial, natural purity, variously called Buddha, Tathagatagarbha, Guhyasamaja, Kalachakra, Hevajra, Vajrayogini, clear light, natural emptiness, or liberation pervading all samsara and nirvana. This direct awareness of intrinsic knowledge is found in the oral tradition of Mahakashyapa through to Bodhidharma and his lineage of Chan/Zen. It is also in the Vajrayana lineages of Buddha Dorje Chang (Skt. Vajradhara), through Saraha, Nagarjuna, Shabaripa and Maitripa down to the Kagyu patriarchs Marpa and Milarepa or through Nairatmya to Virupa and down to the Sakya masters, or from Buddha Kuntu Zangpo (Skt. Samantabhadra) through Garab Dorje and down to the Nyingma masters. All of these show the way to practice the necessary foundation work for the journey to understand the true nature of phenomena. If one wants to eat tsampa (ground barley) one must first plant the seeds to produce the barley; likewise, if one wants realization, these preliminary practices are essential. This is very important. The realization of emptiness means that one is awake all the time. Emptiness is also called the Perfection of Wisdom, which is the Great Mother of Enlightenment.

15

THE SPIRITUAL FRIEND
(Tib. Gewa'i shenye)

THE TEACHER WITH WHOM ONE TAKES THE BODHISATTVA VOW is extremely important and should be regarded with deep respect as a very precious jewel, because he or she is bestowing the very seed of enlightenment. In doing this, the teacher becomes one's spiritual friend. A dharma friend like this who is able to give the bodhisattva precepts is very rare and therefore difficult to meet. Even though one were never to see this teacher again, one should always think of him as a permanent guiding light in the darkness. This is very important because the Mahayana is the most profound teaching of Lord Buddha and is the path to full enlightenment. One should never act against one's spiritual friend by engaging in gossip or any other actions that arise from lack of faith or negativity. This is the worst mistake the Mahayana student can make. It would not matter to the spiritual friend if he or she were beaten or made the subject of slander or gossip by the student. But it would be very serious for the student as this would destroy the seed of enlightenment, and thus the very value of becoming a Buddhist would also be lost and destroyed. Nowadays, many people who take bodhisattva vows do not even recognize the spiritual friend later on, and if they meet him by chance on the street fail to even acknowledge him.

Those who have been unaware of the importance of their attitude towards the spiritual friend should realize their error. The *Sutra of the One Thousand Buddhas* tells how each Buddha first received the seed of enlightenment from his Mahayana Dharma friend, and how each became a Buddha because of this seed. This sutra never mentions the teachers who gave refuge or initiation; importance is only given to the teacher from whom they first received the bodhisattva vows. This means that you should not forget the teacher from whom you received this precious seed. Do not take these vows in a casual or forgetful manner. If you seriously want to take the bodhisattva road, believing that enlightenment is something worth achieving, then the teacher from whom you receive this seed is the most important. Even if you leave this teacher, you must always continue to recognize that you gave rise to the bodhisattva mind with him or her.

Here in the West, there is a great openness to the most profound Mahayana teachings of Lord Buddha, which is due to the ripening of good karma. The attitude one holds towards the teacher is of central importance when taking any of these teachings, so please do not forget this. You need to remember that you first became a Mahayana

practitioner when you took the bodhisattva vow, and see that should you ever come to lack faith in your spiritual friend, it would be reason to feel very deep sorrow before all the Buddhas and Bodhisattvas of the ten directions. It would also be reason to feel very deep sorrow before all sentient beings, because when you took the vows, you promised to become their saviour.

The Vajrayana spiritual friend is the external manifestation of Buddha, the one who gives the direct introduction that opens you to self-liberation, and as such, he or she is very, very important. The Vajrayana spiritual friend is the only one who can give the direct and profound initiation teaching, the direct introduction to Mahamudra or Ati, to those who are suitably qualified vessels for receiving the teachings of this dharma vehicle. Keeping samaya is of very great and fundamental importance to those who receive this teaching. One's individual guru, who introduces one to the teaching, also explains the samaya relationship between the Vajrayana teacher and student.

Every morning
calling to the Guru
loneliness
gives energy

16
DEVOTION
(Tib. Mogu)

Before one practices Vajrayana meditation, it is very important to receive initiation. At the time of initiation, the guru himself is both Vajradhara and the deities, and as such bestows upon the student the seeds of the four kayas. This is the transmission of the blessings of body, speech, mind and nature, that transcend worldly values and endow the student with the authority to be equal to Buddha. This opens the door to enlightenment. The guru also gives the student a special deity name. After initiation the teacher is then the root guru (Tib. tsawai lama) and the student becomes a samaya holder and Vajrayana practitioner. Samaya is the foundation, and devotion is the blessing. 'Devotion' means that, for the student at the time of initiation, the teacher is the vajra master and opens the door of buddha nature. In the worldly sense this is the great kindness of the guru. The vajra master germinates and nourishes the seeds of the four kayas and cultivates profound devotion, which is the soil of awareness. As this is the same as Shakyamuni Buddha's activity it is the special kindness that the vajra master shows, leading the student to enlightenment and the ending of suffering. The vajra master feeds the tiny chick until it becomes a strong garuda and takes full flight. The necessary condition for this is that the student have strong samaya. Those reborn in the present time are too late to receive teachings directly from Buddha, or even from great siddhas like Milarepa who completely achieved Buddhahood. But the present guru, be he or she a mahasiddha, a noble bodhisattva, a bhikshu or bhikshuni, a yogin or yogini, highly realized, or an ordinary man or woman, is providing the same service for the student as teachers of those great times in the past.

In this dark age, humankind is losing the high qualities of the bodhisattva, which are loving-kindness, patience, and diligence in practice. This is happening because the force of negative emotion and materialistic values is increasing in strength, causing many problems and much distress for people. In such times, spiritual strength is even more important. Therefore, one should carefully keep samaya and devotion, and realize that the guru and one's practice are inseparable. It is very important to maintain faith in this way. Do not to allow one's view to be influenced by negative ideas that make the root guru or any of the teachings of the three yanas appear ordinary.

Some great students who meditate in solitude recite the guru-yoga prayer, *Lama kadrin chen chenno* (*Kind guru turn to me*) in a loud voice at the break of day when the ravens take flight in the light of early dawn. In great students, devotion and emotion are not separate. If the disciple's attitude towards his own lama is such that the guru appears ordinary in comparison to the deity or the Triple Gem, then the blessing received is also of an ordinary quality. This is so even though the student may call to the guru a hundred million times. If the student's attitude is that the guru is Buddha, then the blessing is that of Buddha. If the attitude is that the guru is Chenrezig, then the blessing is that of Chenrezig. The degree of blessing one receives is measured by one's attitude. If it is high then high blessings are received, if middle then middle blessings are received, if low then low blessings are received. For those who have the attitude and feeling that the root guru is inseparable from the deity and is really Vajradhara, holder of limitless compassion and limitless power of blessing and kindness, calling in this way is like turning on a television to allow passage of the images to the screen. Even if the guru himself is just an ordinary lama, these blessings pass like an electric current and all the power of the deity or Triple Gem comes to the student – just as images can be seen on the television screen although they come from elsewhere. The blessings of the deities come through from the guru. He radiates great blessings through all his six senses, his breathing, touch, and so on. The power of these blessings depends upon the devotion of the student.

There are many stories about devotion. One history of ancient times describes a very great student who saw his guru as identical with Vajradhara and prayed with deep devotion. He reached complete enlightenment. When his guru died the student looked into the five buddha realms to see where he had gone, but was unable find him. Still looking, he was very disappointed to find that his guru had been reborn in samsara. Even though his guru had an ordinary mind, the student's own devotion had led to success. A good attitude of body, speech, and mind on the part of the student pleases the guru, because the guru is a great source of blessing and representative of all the buddhas of the past, present, and future. Therefore, the mahasiddhas of ancient times prayed for 'the nine attitudes that please the tsawai lama'. These include listening to the tsawai lama and viewing whatever he or she does positively as a skillful means of teaching the student to subdue self. Once a vajra student accepts his or her root guru he or she should thereafter always hold this view of him as the tsawai lama – thinking that all his or her actions are good and all his or her words are truth.

It was for this reason that in ancient times a student first spent many, many years watching to see if his or her teacher was perfect or ordinary, a good lama or not, before requesting initiation from him or her. There is no samaya connection between student and teacher before initiation when the relationship is just the same as between friends, or between a school teacher and student. But after receiving the teachings of the three yanas, especially the four abhishekas or introduction to the ultimate nature of reality in Mahamudra or Ati, there is a samaya connection, and the view of 'root guru' becomes necessary. In the Vajrayana system, the title of 'tsawai lama' means that both the student and the teacher chose one another before committing to any connection, that the student has received the vows of the Shravakayana, Mahayana and Vajrayana from this teacher, and that special Vajrayana initiation has also been received from him. In the Kagyupa view, the guru who introduces the student to the Mahamudra is the root guru. Nowadays, some people think of the guru from whom they receive refuge as their root guru.

A vajra student who conceives of the teacher as ordinary, or who has many negative ideas about the teacher and therefore no confidence in him, has the wrong attitude. Even if this student were to meet Lord Buddha, he or she would retain his or her negative outlook and be unable to see the high qualities of the Buddha. There is a story about bhikshu Legpay Karma who served and was a student of Shakyamuni Buddha for many years. Legpay Karma became very jealous, until finally, one day, he told the Buddha that he could see nothing special about him other than his six-foot wide aura, and that otherwise they were both the same. Saying this, he left. This means that he could not help breaking samaya, because his karma was just that way, but in doing so his negative attitude caused him to collect much negative karma. Even the most enlightened being, Buddha himself, cannot change this or help a person who completely blocks himself in this way, because the seed of faith is blocked by the negative view. This also means that there is no karma between the student and the teacher, so Legpay Karma should not have gone to Buddha in the first place if he could find no holy teachings there. Even if a student's official standing is much higher than that of his guru, an attitude of pride will cause him to lose his noble and good qualities. As an illustration of this, there was once a student who became a very famous teacher. One time his root guru attended his class dressed as a beggar. The student was very embarrassed and pretended not to see him. After the class was finished, he rushed to see his guru where he was staying with other beggars, but upon making prostrations to him his eyes fell out onto the ground. This happened because he was lying to his guru and did not really respect him. However, in that moment his negative karma was purified. Feeling very sorry he asked his teacher to forgive him, whereupon his eyes miraculously returned to normal.

If some negativity towards one's teacher should arise, it would be better to tell him or her about it frankly with full openness and confidence. This is very important between the root guru and the student because the relationship between them is the most enduring and confident to be found on earth. Positive motivation and confidence towards the guru are necessary and need to be carefully preserved. If any little negativity is allowed to build up on either side it will lead to damaged samaya, just as a fungus can grow in food. If one feels negative and unsatisfied with the guru, one should try to heal the situation openly through confession and forgiveness. If the student and guru really do not want to continue the relationship, it is better to leave peacefully, and throughout the rest of one's life never to gossip or hold any bad attitude of body, speech, or mind towards this guru. In this way no samaya is broken. This is important because the Mahayana teaches that the guru's bodhisattva connection to the student is infinite. For this reason, the best thing is to have confidence in each other. This, and having openness of heart towards each other, is the first step. Secondly, one should try to follow correctly when given Vajrayana teaching and instructions to develop devotion and samaya. One should value the guru's spiritual guidance and spiritual kindness rather than looking at his worldly qualities. Thirdly, even if it seems that the guru never practices, his or her Vajrayana samaya-holding student must do so all the time, and not be lazy. For example, one very devoted student of Ananda, who thought that Ananda must be very highly realized to be serving the Buddha, became an arhat in one week under Ananda's instruction. He could then see telepathically that Ananda was not highly realized. When the student asked about this, Ananda replied that he was too busy serving to practice. After Buddha Shakyamuni's parinirvana, Ananda became an arhat in just one week. Therefore, the student's main priority is to maintain right view and right conduct. Right conduct includes devotion, practice, and always being positive towards the teacher and the Dharma.

Mipham Rinpoche said that during his studies he could not tell the meaning of many of the ancient Nyingmapa tantric texts; he found them very difficult to understand. However, he never lost faith in the doctrine. He felt only that his understanding was poor and that there must be a profound meaning nevertheless. In this way he continued his studies and never gave in to doubt or disbelief. This was a good omen, as he later came to a complete understanding and realization of the deep meaning of the Nyingmapa doctrine and found these difficult texts to be the essence of the Vajrayana.

17
VAJRAYANA

'Full enlightenment' as used in a Buddhist sense means full buddhahood, beyond worldly being. By contrast the term 'enlightenment' applies to those who have attained the first bhumi and beyond – beyond any worldly stage of mind. It cannot apply to ordinary practitioners because 'ordinary' signifies that they are not yet purified of defilements and have not yet accumulated enough merit. In contrast, the term 'Sangyay' (the Tibetan word for Buddha) indicates the full purification and accumulation of merit.

Vajrayana teachings are usually appropriate for the most intelligent students in whom all five negative emotions are very strong. For these students, the purpose of the Vajrayana teachings is to transform the emotions into enlightenment energy and thus quickly achieve enlightenment itself for the purpose of saving other beings. For these people, the teachings of the other yanas are too slow and gentle. Therefore, reading the character and mind of such students, Lord Buddha provided different techniques appropriate for their liberation and realization of buddha nature. The practice of Vajrayana is very, very dangerous – one can fail. It is clear that if one wished to swim across the River Ganges, one would die unless one was a skillful swimmer. Meanwhile, an expert and confident swimmer could cross very quickly. The five negative emotions, the very things that Shravakayana strives to discipline and purify, are actually utilised in this practice, just as fertilizer is used in farming. The Vajrayana employs superior methods of discipline and purification and is a more direct path, leading to the same result as the Mahayana – that of achieving full enlightenment. However, there is great danger, because instead of achieving enlightenment it is possible to travel in quite the opposite direction. This can happen if one does not properly understand the graduated study and does not follow the practice as a qualified Vajrayana vessel. By way of example, there was the man who practiced the Hevajra sadhana and recited one billion mantras while on retreat in a cave. Although his visualization and patience were very strong, he did not have a proper understanding of the path, since his only motivation was to gain power. After death, he was reborn as a demon with nine heads.

All three yanas employ different methods but the aim of all Buddhist practice is the same. If a patient wants a cure for cancer, it does not matter what kind of treatment he or she undergoes as long as it heals quickly. The most precise and swift method for complete healing is the best, so long as no mistake is made. But it is also possible to

make a mistake and even cause death. It is the same with the three yanas. The aim of all Buddhists is to become enlightened in order to cherish sentient beings and lead them to happiness. This view is the essence of Buddhism.

People who are not qualified do not understand Vajrayana teaching and do not think it is a way to enlightenment. They may think that it is some kind of magic practice, mental power, or demon worship. People who think this way do not understand and are not qualified to do the practice. This is either because Vajrayana is naturally beyond their comprehension, or because they are training first in Shravakayana and Mahayana teachings. Therefore, Vajrayana practices are not really public teachings. Vajrayana is very popular nowadays and, because of this, people need to realize that it is necessary to receive initiation and hold samaya if one wants to practice. Holding samaya is the maintenance of sacred commitments undertaken at the time of the initiation. One could say that initiation and samaya are like the axle of a vehicle. If these are missing one will be unable to progress with any of the different Vajrayana practices, or they may even lead to failure. Initiation and samaya are of great importance in the Vajrayana as they are the root of practice. This is as true today as it was in ancient times, and remains true as long as one continues to practice. While many other things can change or be improved upon, such as rituals and costumes changing to fit different cultural backgrounds, certain things cannot be changed without losing the very foundation, the ground, of the practice.

It is said that with Vajrayana one can remedy even the worst negativities. The five inexpiable negative actions, the gravest sins that one can commit in one's lifetime, are:

1. to intentionally hurt a Buddha or a representative of the Buddha (one's own tsawai lama) so as to draw blood.
2. to murder one's father.
3. to murder one's mother.
4. to murder an arhat or a mahasiddha.
5. to divide the sangha through slander, or by instigating quarrelling or fighting.

Through Vajrayana practice, it is possible for anyone who has committed even these five grave sins to achieve enlightenment in his or her very lifetime. Such is the tremendous power of the directness that distinguishes this vajra technique. Through this great power of purification samsaric hindrances are overthrown, dualistic binding is released, and the endless chain of cyclic existence is broken. The practitioner thus quickly realizes the union of luminous mind (dharmakaya) and illusory form (sambhogakaya). This is enlightenment itself.

Even for ordinary people Vajrayana is very beneficial, because when receiving initiation one receives the highest blessing of body, speech and mind. Nowadays, every person who meets vajra masters receives some initiation or mind transmission and probably now holds some degree of samaya. Guru yoga practice that arises from the heart and is strong in faith and confidence is therefore most important. In this regard there are the Four Sessions Guru Yoga prayer and the Six Sessions prayer for purifying and healing broken samayas. The qualities of the guru are explained in many different ways in the different schools, but in the short form 'guru' means someone who has the proper lineage, who themself practices, who follows the tradition properly, who has tremendous compassion for sentient beings, and who does not lead the student on the wrong path. Great lamas of ancient times have said that even if all these qualities are not complete (and it is difficult to find teachers with all these qualities in the Kali Yuga) the teacher must have the principal attitudes, which are loving-compassion for sentient beings and practicing shunyata training all the time.

The precepts of Shravakayana masters are not the same as those given in Vajrayana initiations. To take refuge in the Shravakayana is to take refuge in a holy one for the benefit of oneself, and endeavour to become like him or her by purifying oneself. In this case, one views the Buddha as very holy and high and oneself as very low and impure. Upon receiving Vajrayana initiation, one receives the authority to become united with, and inseparable from, the deity. This is potentially very dangerous because the self is no longer ordinary, and therefore one needs more samaya (Vajrayana precepts). In this case the self is one with the deity; one becomes Buddha. This situation can be either very holy or very dangerous depending upon one's attitude. To keep the right attitude one must practice, and must keep samaya. The worst attitude is to think that as a Vajrayana practitioner one is now free to do anything and does not require the mind of renunciation of ordinary delusion. A snow lion can leap from mountain top to mountain top, but if a fox tried to follow, it would fall and be killed. A person holding such a mistaken attitude would be like the fox.

If one follows Vajrayana instruction properly, and is therefore a great samaya holder and practitioner, there is no block whatsoever on the path to enlightenment, even in family life. This remains true even for someone who is very powerful in samsara, such as King Indrabhuti.[1] Another example would be the great and powerful Kublai Khan who received the highest anuttarayoga initiation of Hevajra[2] four times from Sakya Lama Phakpa,[3] and completed the practice of all the yogas.

The causes of breaking samaya are lack of knowledge, lack of respect, lack of mindfulness, and strong uncontrolled negative emotions. As these arise for everyone until the first bhumi is achieved, one therefore needs purification. According to the Mahayana doctrine, the achievement of the first bhumi is accompanied by certain signs that are explained by Chandrakirti in the Madhyamakavatara.[4] Scholars argue this point. The most scholarly Sakya Pandita held that those who claim to have achieved the first bhumi must manifest the signs. Some Kagyupa lamas have said that this is not necessary because mind can achieve this level while the body remains ordinary, like a garuda in its egg. After death and leaving the ordinary body, all the signs then manifest in the intermediate state. Sakya Pandita and many other scholars find it somewhat odd to believe that mind can achieve the first bhumi in life while the qualities are achieved in the intermediate state. They argue that this is like the sun rising today and the light coming tomorrow. Debate aside, upon achieving first bhumi one can no longer fall back into delusion. Until one achieves this most profound point of realization of emptiness one must take care of one's samaya.

There are fourteen root and eight branch samaya commitments. According to the Anuttarayoga teachings of the most scholarly Manjushri emanation, Sakya Pandita, the root samaya vows are broken by:

1. thinking or saying that the guru is bad, and feeling disgust towards him. (Simply feeling angry with the guru does not completely break one's commitment.)
2. breaking any of the vows of the three yanas because one is against Buddhist teaching or does not feel it is important – together with failing to confess.
3. having anger or hatred towards any Vajrayana practitioner as they are all one's Dharma brothers or sisters. If you share the same guru this is even heavier. If you have also received initiation together in the same mandala it is the heaviest. 'Anger' means harbouring the mental attitude that he or she is 'my enemy.'
4. giving up love for any single sentient being and instead wishing them pain, suffering, or misery – together with failing to confess.
5. giving up the Mahayana's main heart teaching of bodhichitta, that of wanting to lead all sentient beings to enlightenment, and also giving up love and compassion because of a weak mind that asks, "How can I possibly protect sentient beings from suffering?" – together with failing to confess.
6. criticizing, giving up belief in, the Vajrayana, Mahayana or Shravakayana, as not being the way of enlightenment, or disregarding it for the same reason.
7. showing Vajrayana equipment and secret activities, and teaching Vajrayana rituals and mudras, to someone who does not have the necessary initiation.
8. not understanding that one's body is intrinsically the five buddhas, and so viewing it with disgust and treating it badly.
9. not understanding and doubting knowledge of the emptiness view where 'all phenomena are naturally empty and free from extremes', or holding and creating wrong views about it, for example,

eternalism, nihilism, and so on.
10. making friends with or showing loving behaviour towards those who do harm to the guru, disbelieve the buddha doctrine, or who harm or hurt many sentient beings.
11. grasping and holding the nihilistic view that everything is completely empty, even though the view of emptiness is beyond words and concepts.
12. causing others to lose faith through improper practice of Mahayana or Vajrayana. However, if another loses faith through no fault of one's own, samaya is not broken.
13. rejecting the special samaya substances during ganachakra festivals.
14. criticizing women, for example saying and believing that a woman is of 'low' birth, impure, ugly, and so on. This is important because women symbolize the emptiness of transcendent wisdom.

The eight branch vows are broken by:

1. thinking of taking a consort who is not qualified due to not having samaya commitments.
2. engaging in bad jokes, or mocking, teasing or quarreling with others, at a ganachakra ceremony.
3. referring to the special samaya substances by ordinary names during ganachakra ceremony, or using the special Vajrayana names at other times.
4. not doing one's practice properly according to the Vajrayana tradition but giving others initiation or showing them the sadhanas.
5. pridefully showing different Vajrayana mudras when it is not necessary, even to those who do have initiation.
6. upsetting a sincere student who wants to practice properly by teaching contrarily to their wishes.
7. failing to do deity practice and guru yoga for a full week during a stay at a Shravakayana practitioner's place.
8. giving teachings about high initiation to people who have only received the first level of initiation and no higher.

The sadhana of Vajrasattva (Tib. Dorje Sempa) is the best method for purification. If one says one hundred thousand Vajrasattva mantras, all previous negative karma is purified. If one recites between twenty-one and one hundred a day, the negative karmas of the previous day are purified. If this is done daily without fail, the Vajrayana practitioner can keep the mind pure. Three things are necessary in order to receive the

Vajrasattva sadhana: the initiation of Vajrasattva; the textual transmission; and the explanation of the practice. To do this practice one also needs proper motivation, which means that one must have the four correct powers. One's samaya should be purified daily with the realization that what is to be purified is one's damage to, or breaking of, samaya, and that the cleansing agent, the means of purification, is the four powers. These four aspects are very important as they are necessary for purification.

The first of the four powers is faith in the blessing power of the Triple Gem (Buddha, Dharma and Sangha), making supplication to them and the guru, and requesting their help to purify oneself. This request is made before holy objects, such as a stupa, statues or sutras. If no such object is available, one may visualize the Triple Gem. Other holy objects that have the power of blessing are hair, cloth, bone, or ashes of the root guru, or the guru's handprint or footprint made with saffron water on a white silk cloth. This is because once the guru has given one the Vajrasattva initiation, he or she is one's Vajrasattva; if he or she has given one Hevajra, he or she is Hevajra; and so on. The guru is inseparable from the Triple Gem. If one feels that one's samaya with the guru or with a vajra sister or brother has been at all damaged, one needs to explain clearly, apologize and perform ganachakra ceremonies.

The second power one needs is faith in the blessing power of regret. If samaya has been broken knowingly, it is particularly important to remember this and to make a mental confession. It is important not to forget it. If one does not remember any specific damage, it is still important to make a general confession of any harm to, or breaking of, samaya, because one is continually doing this through ignorance. If an item of one's clothing has a dirty spot, one concentrates on working to clean that area with one's hands and detergent. However, as the cloth gradually becomes old and dirty then the whole garment needs to be washed. For the ordinary human being harm to one's samaya accumulates in this way over the days, months and years. Even though one may consider oneself very pure and holy there are one hundred thousand samayas that can be broken. When confessing one needs to generate the power of regret. One Nyingmapa text on special purification called *Cry of Confession* begins with the words, "Oh, what sadness I have. What am I to do?" Engendering this emotion is very important, otherwise confession is mere words and not purification.

The third power is the blessing power of antidotes for negative karma. How effectively antidotes can be used depends on the person and their level of practice. But in any case, it is important to do one's best for oneself and others. The antidotes are the circumambulation of temples, correct prostrations, producing new holy objects of the Triple Gem (statues, books and stupas), giving medicine to the sick and food and clothes to the needy, helping everybody in all good ways, reciting mantras and sadhanas correctly, meditating for periods of years, months or days, giving rise to special bodhichitta for all sentient beings, building temples, monasteries, guest houses and travellers' hospices, reciting sutras, rescuing sentient beings, and helping people to become friends.

The fourth power one needs is the power of resolve to desist from negative action. Some lamas say that one should simply resolve never to break samaya again in the future. Lama Tsong Khapa cautions that this can be a lie because we damage or break samaya unknowingly, due to ignorance, and so it is better to resolve to try in any way one can to stop breaking samaya.

These four powers comprise purification from the point of view of the 'provisional, relative, or conventional meaning' (Tib. drangdon). This is required to interpret the intended meaning. They are very important because we live life on the relative or dualistic level. Thus, a relative level of purification is required as a means of approaching the ultimate. The other form of purification is the 'certain, ultimate, or definitive, meaning' itself (Tib. ngedon). Ngedon is the contemplation of the true nature of all phenomena, which is the point of liberation. If one looks at things as they are, seeing their non-dual nature, this is the best purification, because it cuts through the very fabric of duality. This means that one must intensively practice Mahamudra or Dzogchen meditation. If one does not meditate and merely understands that everything is shunyata and pure, there is no purification. When Milarepa was introduced to Dzogchen he thought it was too easy and there was no need to do anything, so he just slept and achieved nothing. So, his Dzogchen master sent him to Marpa Lotsawa.

'Duality' signifies the multitude of ordinary beliefs, ideas and concepts held in the mind. Religious people can build even more clouds of concepts and beliefs than other people, and thus become even more distant from reality as this fog obscures the true nature. From beginningless time up until now, sentient beings have bound themselves to samsara by their own delusions. These delusions seem very real but have no basis. If one has true realization, one then understands that the confession, the confessor (the union of the vajra master and Vajrasattva), and the antidotes, are all a kind of game played on the battlefield of samsara, a game that is never won or lost. Existence and non-existence depend upon each other. But if one looks directly, both become opposites, and so cannot be one thing. If one looks at how they appear to be related, one sees that if one is missing, the other cannot be. Therefore, there is no one, no other, and no both. And so, ultimately, they are a delusion. By waving a cloth in the air one can make many patterns and designs; however, these are really just built up by moving individual threads.

Concepts are uncertain and change all the time. One person may believe something but another may not see it the same way. For example, one person may think a young lady is the prettiest in the world, while another does not find her pretty because he has a different cultural conception of beauty. Yet another may be her old boyfriend who considers her to be the worst of all and whose notion of her as pretty has disappeared, while another may think she is the best and be very attached to her.

Similarly, purity and impurity are relative conceptions that are dependent upon one another. Therefore, the most effective Vajrasattva practice is to realize there is neither purity nor impurity. This realization can cut the root of all hope and fear, pain and pleasure, and so on. Until one achieves absolute purity and while still dealing with the relative world, one continues to need the purification practice of Vajrasattva. If a chick tries to fly before its wings are ready it will fall and die, so it is important to stay in the nest until the wings are strong. When one realizes absolute (ultimate) truth it is the same as a crystal. Purity and impurity are then seen as just relative conceptions. A crystal does not need polishing or not-polishing because it is pure crystal by nature. It has always been pure and there is no need to clarify it further. If one realizes there is no duality then one realizes the primordial purity of phenomena. Delusion has no existence. Vajrasattva practice can cut delusion because this practice represents the point of absolute truth and transcends confusion. Therefore, if you experience happiness or sadness, it is just the game of the emotions and the different manifestations of delusion. This form of purification is the 'simplest' and most effective, but it is also the most difficult. One first has to climb the ladder of 'provisional meaning' in order to reach the house of 'certain meaning'.

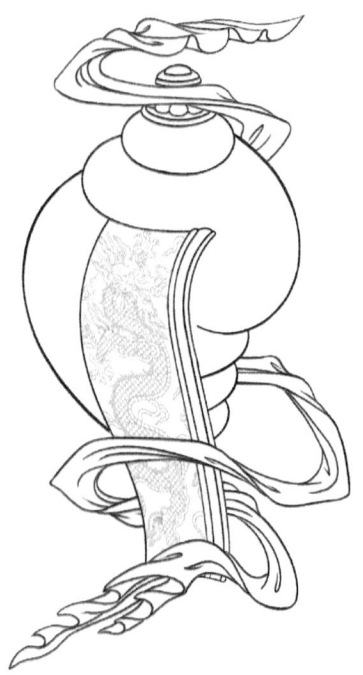

18
THE THREE YANAS

THE SHRAVAKAYANA, MAHAYANA AND VAJRAYANA are all Lord Buddha's teachings and as such all share the same principal purpose. Their methods differ because they are designed to meet the needs of different students, each of whom has his or her own karma (action) to mature and ripen, as well as individual levels and types of intelligence and wisdom to work with. Different ailments, such as a headache, foot injury, or toothache cannot all be treated with the same medicine because each requires its own particular treatment and care. Medicine that helps cure one ailment may aggravate or be quite ineffective for another. Consequently, Buddha taught countless techniques in order to benefit beings of various disposition – as many as were necessary.

According to the Nyingma tradition there are nine principal yanas[1] which can be grouped into the Causal Vehicle of Dialectics (Tib. Gyu'i tegpa) and the Fruition Vehicle of Tantra (Tib. Drebu'i tegpa). The Causal Vehicle is more concerned with the Four Noble Truths, and the basic condition of suffering and its causes. These teachings involve more investigation and meditation in order to apply appropriate antidotes for the seeds (or causes) of suffering. Antidotes are the different techniques used in meditation to effectively pacify all negative thinking and the products of ignorance, namely desire, anger, pride, jealousy and greed. The emphasis of these teachings is purely on self-liberation, and the result of the practices is achievement of the egoless stage of nirvana. However, this does not mean that there is less loving compassion involved, it is just that some people are less drawn to think so much of the suffering of others and less motivated to seek the liberation of others before that of themselves.

This collection of teachings is suited to the kind of lay practitioner who prefers to give up wealth and physical pleasures. Such people can more easily follow the Shravakayana path which involves realizing that egoism is the creator of both suffering and the delusory world of the five skandhas, and can more easily generate the practice of analysing both samsaric and spiritual phenomena, thereby attaining self-liberation. These teachings are also suited to those practitioners who have a tame mind, such that it is easy for them to experience contentment and satisfaction living a homeless monastic life. The Shravakayana teaches greater mindfulness of physical karma (action), both negative and positive, and taking vows for subduing self (ego) in order to lead the practitioner into nirvana. It is a wonderful path. Through these teachings Buddha saved many sentient beings from the suffering of samsara and led them into enlightenment.

The purpose of the Mahayana teachings (also known as the Bodhisattvayana) is the same as the Shravakayana in that it is designed to cut off egoism and lead the practitioner into nirvana. However, some people have a greater interest in sharing their goodness to benefit and help others. They worry little about themselves and seem to have been born with stronger habits of love and compassion. Buddha taught the Bodhisattvayana for such people, providing them with a method of practice that makes more use of meditation on compassion and love for the endless numbers of sentient beings, that involves tirelessly extending care to others, and that promises to liberate all sentient beings leaving not even one single being behind. These practitioners accomplish the six transcendent perfections that derive from the two bodhichittas.

The first of these is conventional bodhichitta: the practice of compassion, love, and cherishing others with the wish to lead them to enlightenment. The second is ultimate bodhichitta: the absolute truth of the essential emptiness of all phenomena that are realized to just be manifestations arising from and dissolving back into empty space. This practice is a very strong means of accumulating merit and pacifying the negative defilements. Once negative karma and thoughts are cut off at the root there is then little reason to be concerned with exercising control over one's physical actions. For instance, so long as it is undertaken solely for the purpose of cherishing others, it is even possible for a bodhisattva working for the benefit of sentient beings to engage in negative actions without worry of falling into lower realms.

In this way, Mahayana methods lead one into nirvana. The Shravakayana nirvana is one of 'non-returning'. It is the end of suffering just like the extinction of the flame of a butter lamp. In the Mahayana the generation of bodhichitta (compassion for all sentient beings) is gradually strengthened until, upon reaching enlightenment, it is generated automatically and spontaneously. This nirvana is not one of extinction. It is like the rising of the sun in the sky, whose light naturally radiates, warming the earth and helping things to grow. The self-cherishing mind automatically declines through this practice. The degree to which this is achieved depends upon the level of realization of the bodhisattva practitioner.

In the Shravakayana, the body is seen as an impure and unpleasant substance. Decoration of the body, the wearing of jewellery and the possession of wealth are considered hindrances to the development of disgust for samsaric life, the basic condition of which is suffering. Therefore, the aim is to reduce and reject such activities, and thereby abandon desire. The Mahayana also sees that the conceptualization of things as good or bad, precious or non-precious and so on, is caused by basic ego-clinging leading to aversion and attachment, anger and desire. The approach here is to remove the very cause itself through meditation on the essential emptiness of all phenomena, while love and compassion subdue all the negative emotions such as anger. The Mahayana view of emptiness cuts through our deluded states of mind with the same result as Shravakayana practice because ego is pacified. However, the Mahayana has more skillful means for benefitting sentient beings.

In the Fruition Vehicle of the Vajrayana, the ego-mind itself is transformed into primordial wisdom. Right from the outset everything is viewed as the realm of enlightenment and there is no concept of duality, such as purity and impurity. Thus, this practice also cuts through the negative emotions and karma and leads to the realization that there is no such thing as 'atman' – an eternally existent 'I', or self. The Shravakayana sees the body as impermanent and impure. The Mahayana sees ego-mind as a dream body of the nature of an illusion, where there is naturally no existence even though the mind cognizes duality – like trying to paint on space. The Vajrayana sees the five skandhas as enlightened forms, the mind as primordial wisdom, and all male and female beings as the circle of enlightened beings. Therefore, in the Vajrayana view there is no room in the mind for ignorance, anger, jealousy, egoism, or negative karma (activity). When a highly qualified Vajrayana vessel such as Indrabhuti, Guru Rinpoche Padma Sambhava, or Machig Labkyi Dronma[2] receives initiation, the ego is immediately purified and he or she is led instantly into the experience of enlightened mind. However, for Vajrayana students in general, initiation is the seed of enlightenment.

Consider angry activity: The Shravakayana teachings prohibit angry activity as it is seen as a cause of suffering. In Mahayana teachings angry activity is also seen from the conventional point of view as something bad that should be stopped. It is viewed as the worst activity because it destroys the Mahayana vow by which one became a bodhisattva to benefit sentient beings. At the same time the ultimate understanding is that everything is delusion, thus in reality there is no existence of anger in either time or space. In the Vajrayana everything is seen as part of one buddha circle, or mandala, where all males and females are enlightened beings and the negative emotions are transcended, becoming true, natural, primordial wisdom naturally free from the two extremes of existence and nonexistence, (i.e., all the sixteen points of shunyata). Sakya Pandita said the Vajrayana and Madhyamaka views (Tib. tawa) of this are equal. In this field of enlightenment there is no possible cause or condition for angry activity to occur and so it is naturally prevented. This view is therefore the antidote for negative action. When one realizes the true nature of reality the root of violence is obliterated. Vajrayana has the same basic reasoning as the Mahayana; however, the different rituals and methods of practice of the Vajrayana path can be used to subdue the evil mind of those who engage in the ten wrong actions[3] and lead them into the true, natural state of enlightened mind (Skt. jnana). In this way negative beings have been liberated by wrathful bodhisattva activity. If people have not pacified anger it can lead to a whole range of problems from small fights to great wars where many people are killed and a tremendous amount of suffering is created.

In the Mahayana view, should it ever become necessary to kill in order to protect others and save many lives, such action has to arise out of great compassion and also because there is no other possible solution. Here, great compassion means both the compassionate wish to protect the victims, as well as compassionately wanting to stop the potential murderer from engaging in his negative actions. This is the same as the story related in the history of one of Lord Buddha's previous lives as a bodhisattva, when he killed an evil man in order to save the lives of five hundred sailors. Under ordinary circumstances both the Vajrayana and Mahayana prohibit this kind of physical action. Such activity can only be undertaken by those who have the power to either liberate the mind of the sentient being who is killed, or to restore him to life again afterwards. Only the mahasiddhas – enlightened bodhisattvas who have complete realization of shunyata – would be able to do this, and only if it was necessary. The mahasiddha Tilopa caught and ate live fish in front of his student Naropa in order to upset him, and thereby expose the doubts he was holding towards his teacher. Tilopa afterwards freed the fish, which flew back whole and unharmed into the water. Someone asked me why doesn't a fully enlightened being such as this use this method to liberate all sentient beings? Buddha Shakyamuni or Avalokiteshvara have the power to liberate all beings without exception through their buddha activity. This limitless activity of loving compassion provides both temporary relief of suffering, and the key to the gate of absolute liberation – i.e., the Dharma teachings that provide for the purification of action (karma) and the accumulation of merit and wisdom. However, even though the sun has the power to illuminate everything, there are still shadows.

Each and every sentient being carries tremendous negative karma (action, cause and effect) and no one can change the inevitable fact that this will lead to suffering, just as a seed planted in good soil with good water will grow. Only the individual himself, through repentance, can purify his own negative karma.

Negative actions arise from ignorance and are continuously produced in the mind, speech and physical continuum of sentient beings. Good actions produce happiness and good conditions as inevitably as the seed of a medicinal plant will mature into a medicinal plant. Bad actions produce suffering as inevitably as the seed of a poisonous plant will produce a poisonous plant. The essential buddha nature, or tathagatagarbha, of samsaric beings is obscured by their own actions just as gold is hidden in stone. A Buddha's activity is as limitless as sentient beings' creation of dualistic action. The best way to stop the production of dualistic action is to practice Buddha's teaching of absolute bodhichitta or enlightened mind. This is illustrated by the legend of Avalokiteshvara (the 'Bodhisattva, Great Bodhisattva, Chenrezig') who has one thousand arms and eyes, and eleven heads. It is said that this form came about as a result of a promise he once made to Amitabha Buddha that he would not become fully enlightened until all six realms of samsara were completely emptied, with not even a single sentient being left behind. He sealed this with an oath, "May my body break into a thousand pieces if I break this promise." He then continued to work for many aeons until he thought he had liberated the countless multitudes of sentient beings. But when he looked from the peak of Potala mountain he saw that not only were there just as many beings as before, but their number had increased and there was even more suffering. Feeling the situation to be hopeless he momentarily lost patience, breaking his vow. In that instant his body broke into a thousand pieces, and his head into eleven. Amitabha blessed all the pieces and they transformed into one thousand arms and eyes, and eleven Buddha heads. Avalokiteshvara's thousand arms are emanations of the one thousand Chakravartin (Universal Dharma) kings, and his one thousand eyes are emanations of the one thousand Buddhas of this kalpa (eon). Amitabha told him, "Sentient beings' karma (action) is never-ending so do not lose patience, but continue to work to liberate them from suffering." Avalokiteshvara then resumed his work for sentient beings with both wisdom and compassion.

Accordingly, even if Tilopa killed all the fish in the waters of the universe, countless more would appear. So it is for all creatures, as countless more constantly come into cyclic existence and will continue to do so, produced by their own karma. From the Mahayana point of view the beneficial activity of enlightened beings is limitless, just as the emergence of sentient beings into cyclic existence never ends. For example, the water flowing down a mountainside can be contained by a dam, but if the source of water is unending the dam will not be able to stop the flow. Eventually the water will flow over and around it in all directions. I believe that Tilopa must have liberated countless sentient beings, especially fish since this is what he ate, but that he did not show this miraculous liberation to everyone – only to his special student. Mahayana Buddhism believes that for Buddha Shakyamuni, as for all who are enlightened, all phenomena are naturally enlightened. It is said that Tilopa achieved full Buddhahood; therefore, in his realized view, everything was part of the mandala of the deity and he had no dualistic view. As he was fully enlightened, he experienced no duality or delusory environment. If all was enlightenment, he must have experienced no earth, no ocean, no river, no fish, no stars, no mountains, no continents, no sun, no moon and no sky, because these phenomena only appear as the result of ripening previous karma. For Tilopa there was no difference between him and the fish, because the buddha nature of the fish was not separate from him. Therefore, when he liberated them there was no really existent killer, no fish, and no action of killing, although from the samsaric viewpoint these would be perceived as existing. Their bodies instantly turned into ganachakra and their minds to full enlightenment, thereby reaching the end of all suffering. This was therefore an act of great compassion for these creatures, one that depended on Tilopa's own siddhi. Also, these fish were ready to meet Tilopa in this way because of prior connection, they may have been his disciples previously and were in their last rebirth as fish or other animals.

'Buddha' means completely free from ignorance and even the defilement of tendencies. This is just like the sun's rays. While the sun itself has no consciousness, ideas or dualistic mind, its light brings benefit wherever it radiates, removing darkness and allowing flowers, trees and colours to be seen. Not even one single blade of grass is missed by the sun's energy as this has helped it grow and given it colour. The benefit that results from enlightenment continues uninterrupted for as long as sentient beings themselves exist.

The famous eccentric Drukpa Kagyu saint, Drukpa Kunley (1455–1529),[4] killed many mountain goats and deer in order to pay his family's taxes, in meat, to the local ruler. He specified that all the bones and skin must be carefully set aside. Afterwards, he put these together and restored the animals to life, free to go back into the mountains once again. In both this example and that of Tilopa, nothing was killed. Killing is completely prohibited unless one is able to restore life or liberate the mind of the being that is killed, such as sending it to the realm of Amitabha Buddha. Lord Buddha's principal teaching prohibits the ten negative actions. I mention this because in Vajrayana practices associated with wrathful deities such as Vajrakilaya or Mahakala, there are many rituals for destroying evil. However, these are in no way similar to the black spells used by sorcerers of ancient times when they tried to kill or harm their enemies. In Vajrayana Buddhism wrathful activity arises out of great compassion, infinite love for the sentient being, and the understanding of primordial wisdom. It brings benefit for the liberation of sentient beings, thus extinguishing the suffering realms of existence. The kind of miracle shown by Tilopa in this story was only possible with the natural power of realization he had achieved. In Vajrayana's absolute view everything is one buddhafield: there is no killer, no victim, and no action of killing, and so, automatically, there is no cause for killing. In conclusion, all three yanas hold the belief that killing is bad and should be prohibited. While their approaches and methods differ, their aim is the same – the avoidance of killing.

Each of the three yanas also holds its own particular view of other negative actions of body, speech and mind. For example, as long as certain conditions are met, both Mahayana and Vajrayana allow bodhisattvas to engage in sex. However, this must be necessary in order to benefit another being and not used to indulge any selfish desire or lust. The bodhisattva Dawa Zhonnu, a great and enlightened bhikshu, once met a very old lady in the advanced stages of leprosy. Her body was so ugly and rotten, and smelt so bad, that no one could bear to go near her. He perceived that her mind was very hungry for sex with him and that if he rejected her, it would drive her to kill herself. Out of deep compassion he decided to help her when she beseeched him, and after apologizing for breaking his vows he slept with her even though he knew that he was creating negative realms for himself in the future, as well as contracting the disease. As a result of this she was saved from committing suicide, and he, having accumulated great merit and positive karma through his compassionate activity, quickly attained full enlightenment. This shows that in Mahayana and Vajrayana the most important consideration is one's motivation, so that should such actions be undertaken the reason behind them is love and compassion, and the physical action itself is not the principal motivation.

If one asks why in Vajrayana it is possible to practice with a consort, I think the correct answer is that this practice is a means of purifying the mind of the five negative poisons, and so attaining the 'union of illusory body and luminous mind'. I have heard of some people confusing Tibetan Vajrayana with Hindu tantra, but in so doing they utterly misunderstand the Vajrayana. The manifestation of the deities in Hindu and Buddhist tantric rituals may appear to have some similarities but these are superficial. Vajrayana is actually the most profound of Buddha's teachings because it cuts off egoism and delusion, leading beings to enlightenment in a short period or even in just one lifetime.

In the Shravakayana tradition it is important to portray enlightened beings with shaven heads and monastic robes like Buddha in his nirmanakaya form, to show their manner of discipline. This implies that any alternative such as the Vajrayana manner of yogis and yoginis shows they are not high Buddhist sangha. However, it seems to me that the former costume is more an expression of the first yana or stage of discipline, where the practitioner cuts off attachment to hair, body and decoration. Whereas when full dharmakaya and sambhogakaya enlightenment is reached, these teachings no longer apply and it is no longer necessary to always wear this costume, as was the case for the great Indian masters of the eighth century: Virupa who promulgated the teachings of the Hevajra Tantra[5], Guru Padma Sambhava, and Saraha – the holder of the Mahamudra lineage. In fact, there is even some uncertainty as to the correct Shravakayana costume because in each Buddhist country the costumes of Buddha and the deities vary according to local culture and custom. This is apparent in the variety of Buddhist sculpture, painting, and ways of thinking. The deities are enlightened manifestations of Buddha, and Vajrayana and Mahayana art portray them wearing jewellery, embracing consorts, and in various positions of dance. They are portrayed in this way because both disciplines believe enlightenment signifies freedom from duality, and that with full enlightenment all phenomena, the skandhas, elements, movement, sound, time, space, and so on, are also enlightened. It is not possible for bad karma or immoral poses and costumes to manifest within the field of enlightenment. This includes all the deities, which offer a variety of means of attaining liberation to suit people of differing character.

Generally speaking, there must be the realization that the three kayas, dharmakaya, sambhogakaya and nirmanakaya, represent the mind, speech and body of enlightenment, respectively. The first is ultimate, non-dual, enlightened mind. The second is the infinite and spontaneous display of luminous enlightened mind. The third provides physical contact with liberation itself for the benefit of the sentient beings of the different realms. Shakyamuni is the nirmanakaya form of the Buddha, and his costume represents both disciplining the negative aspects of samsara and freedom from samsara. This costume, that includes a shaven head, wearing saffron, red, yellow, or blue dharma robes and holding an alms bowl, symbolizes transcending ordinary samsaric life. It displays the holding of right view, right speech and right action by the sangha, like a pure crystal or flower. Those who come to hold this discipline by taking ordination and receiving the costume do so as a result of tremendous previous good karma. Even if just one, or four, or one hundred monks or nuns live in a country, then that country is very fortunate, because these people are very respectable, are the object of offering alms, and are a source of great blessing and merit.

In the Shakya clan of Nepal and in Thailand, all boys must become ordained sangha for a short period of time during which they wear robes, shave their hair, beg with an alms bowl, think of self-discipline and precepts, and recite sutras. I think this is wonderful, as for each person it seems like planting and cultivating the seed of a medicinal plant in good soil. I hope many people will follow this custom because in this spiritual dark age, a time of materialistic interests, quarreling and fighting, it is difficult to become a holder of this great and holy nirmanakaya costume for one's entire life. Receiving this transmission or lineage for even a short period is very important in times such as these when people's lives generally have many obscurations and difficulties. Everyone should make a wishing prayer to have the opportunity to become a holder of this nirmanakaya costume as a bhikshu, bhikshuni, or novice, either in this life or in a future lifetime, as this is the best moral virtue.

The vinaya history tells of a time when the kingdom in which Buddha resided was threatened with war and invasion by a neighbouring king, who was intending to kill everyone. Buddha told his disciples not to worry as he would prevent any invasion. Requesting that the invading king and general be brought before him, Buddha manifested as a very powerful king in full costume surrounded by a large army. The king was so frightened by this display that he stopped the battle. Lord Buddha thus established peace and ended the fighting. If it were true that the monastic costume is always essential then it would follow that Buddha himself broke precepts by appearing as a king, even though it was really a method of protecting and saving the people of the two warring kingdoms. Manifesting like this in no way detracted from Buddha's enlightened activity and duty to save sentient beings. The Vajrayana view of this event is that Buddha always remains in the universal enlightenment level of equanimity, therefore he remained pure and lost nothing by wearing a king's costume. Like a pure crystal mountain that reflects a myriad of rainbows in the sunlight, Buddha produces many manifestations while never changing or staining his crystal-like purity. Vajrayana deities are like these rainbows.

Some people are upset when they see Vajrayana deities depicted with their consorts, as they consider this quite inappropriate for enlightened beings. They react this way because they are either too involved with sex themselves, or very negative towards it, believing it to be a very bad and dirty activity. Some Mahayana and Shravakayana practitioners consider the Vajrayana to be no different from the histories of the Hindu gods that contain many references to sex and fighting over consorts, and portray them wearing jewels or cemetery ornaments. Unlike these mythological histories, the accounts of the Vajrayana deities contain no mention of them fighting over consorts as in ordinary life. These practitioners feel that an enlightened being must be celibate. On analysis, it can be seen that this is a very dualistic and one-sided view.

Careful study of the three yanas reveals that they are no different in principle or purpose even though they do have different points of view. Moving from arhat, to bodhisattva, to vidyadhara,[6] activity becomes progressively deeper and wiser and the methods used to reach enlightenment become more and more profound, until the deepest method can lead to enlightenment within the span of just one life. Hunger can be satisfied by drinking soup, eating cooked food, or eating raw food. The purpose and benefit of eating is the same in each case. However, someone who cannot eat raw food does not have to discriminate against those who do, and if someone dislikes liquid food they do not necessarily have to be antagonistic towards someone who likes it. If one cannot use all three methods together, one should choose the one that feels most interesting – in this way Buddha offered choices to his followers. It is not necessary for someone who prefers to live on nothing but milk to demand that others must do the same.

Again, I wish to try to clear up some mistaken views about the Vajrayana. Those who hold the vinaya precepts might feel that the purpose of Vajrayana practice is sex. If so, this is because they do not have a clear understanding that the three yanas are all Buddha's teachings, providing a variety of methods to benefit all sentient beings. Such a view is possibly due to individual attachment or aversion to sex. The Vajrayana neither encourages nor is negative towards sex, which is a natural and universal samsaric function, as is eating food, putting on clothes in the morning, or sleeping in a bed at night. What the Vajrayana does emphasize is stopping the causes of suffering and wanting to heal suffering. In the Shravakayana the view of the impurity of body and negative mind is used as a meditation method to lead one to the stage of an arhat – the stage of enlightenment that is beyond the concepts of purity and impurity. Similarly, blissful sexual energy can also be used as a cause of enlightenment by certain people who have strong sexual energy and are very intelligent, as was the case for many of the Eighty-Four Mahasiddhas, the principal Indian masters of the tantras in the mediaeval period. Any negative phenomenon can be transformed into goodness if used properly. Therefore, there is no contradiction between the Buddhist yanas and practitioners should practice with devotion rather than criticize those who follow the other paths. Lord Buddha fulfilled his bodhisattva vows – he promised to provide different methods for all sentient beings to achieve liberation, and never to refuse any type of person.

This particular misunderstanding of the Vajrayana is due to the fact that worldly sex is a very visible and pleasurable energy. However, like eating delicious food or wearing fine and fashionable clothes, sex involves desire and attachment and strengthens the ego, creating hatred and lust that in turn produce suffering. The Vajrayana never views the male-female manifestation of the deities to be contaminated with these negative emotions nor with worldly sexual energy. Even at the first bhumi level the bodhisattva is free from worldly lust or attachment. These deities are aspects of the thirteenth bhumi level – the highest stage of enlightenment – so how could desire, lust, attachment and other negative emotions remanifest at that level? Ordinary pleasure is transcended and replaced with a cause of enlightenment that is wonderful. Therefore, when one sees the male-female union aspect of the deity, the activity they show does not mean that sexual activity is necessary in Vajrayana practice.

Also, from the Vajrayana point of view, ordinary worldly sex is not considered sinful or dirty – all holy beings come from parents by this process. Women in general are not thought of as bad, dirty, or very low in comparison to men – in fact they are generally more physically handsome than men. The female consort figure is very important because the Vajrayana has inherent respect for the 'female principle' and female energy. One is therefore breaking samaya and creating negativity if one despises any woman. One is also wrong to think that ladies are considered important for the sensual pleasure of male lay practitioners of Vajrayana.

By and large, human beings have created mainly male-dominated societies. Men have powerful bodies with more strength, while ladies are naturally weaker. Also, the male sex drive is mainly directed towards obtaining sexual pleasure with younger women. In this sense, when a young lady marries the couple are very happy with each other but later on when she becomes old, they lose interest in each other, and then jealousy and competition can arise between them. Consequently, men have developed and apply many negative attitudes towards ladies. In many instances this has led to women being seen as second-class humans. In India it used to be the custom to burn the wife when the husband died, but if the wife died the husband was never burned. This was because a widow was considered 'unclean' and to have a negative influence; this idea was not applied to a widower, however. Ladies have suffered a great deal as second-class citizens. Even though Lord Jesus had great loving compassion and never mentioned such an idea, hundreds of thousands of ladies were tortured and burned alive towards the end of the mediaeval period in Europe.

Even in Buddhism the Shravakayana and Mahayana both regard ladies as second-class people since, for example, they do not respect nuns as highly as monks. The biography of Guru Rinpoche Padma Sambhava, the Pema Kathang, says that once women receive high ordination the duration of Buddhism will be shortened. This attitude is based on the idea that ladies have weaker fortune and are an object of lust. However, Guru Rinpoche's consort Yeshe Tsogyal later said that her energy had increased the duration of Buddhism by thirty years. Some nomadic people in the Khampa region of eastern Tibet do not allow ladies into their homes unless they are relatives or friends, while men are free to go everywhere. In some Hindu and Jain traditions, it is believed that, unlike men, women can never become enlightened. In some other religions with extreme views, women are not allowed to participate in society or receive an education, and are expected to cover their bodies all the time and never talk to men. If a lady becomes a prostitute or sleeps with a man who is not her husband, she has to be killed. Also, some cultures practice genital mutilation of women, cutting out the sensitive tissues and sewing the labia together until marriage, thus depriving their women of sexual pleasure and causing much suffering by way of infection and medical complications.

In contrast, the Vajrayana view is that ladies are very important because the female is a manifestation of wisdom. The female principle is the play of emptiness, the cause and effect of liberation. As representative of the true, natural, sensual beauty of the elements of the universe, the female consort deity symbolizes compassion, infinite beauty, consummate bliss, and the profound enlightenment form itself. If one does not understand this, then the male-female aspect becomes a source of lust and desire. This universal bliss energy of enlightenment creates infinite space on both the ordinary and absolute levels. On the ultimate level, it is described as 'neither coming nor going, neither one nor many.' Vajrayana is the most profound method for removing delusions and confusion, and realizing the true nature of the mind and skandhas, leading to the five kayas – liberation itself. Liberation is beyond concepts or words, but its qualities of infinity, compassion, love, and blissful form, are symbolized by the female consort. All females are considered to be manifestations of this energy whether they are ordinary or enlightened, and therefore they cannot be viewed negatively.

The Vajrayana teaching says that all human females belong to one of the four groups of enlightenment consort. The first of these is named 'with lotus', the second is 'with deer', the third is 'with elephant trunk', and the fourth is 'with conch shell'. The characteristics of each group are mentioned in all four sects of Vajrayana in Tibet. For example, Milarepa's consort was Tashi Tseringma, the goddess of Mount Everest. Wishing to serve Milarepa, she and her four sisters said, "If we possess these four qualities may we help you attain final liberation from the vajra body and achieve the union of luminous mind and illusory body?"

Milarepa replied:

> In the lineage of Lord Naropa
> the main practice is prana and chandali
> The best offering of all is karmamudra.
> The lotus one is very charming and blissful,
> the conch shell one is very joyful instant mahasukha,
> the deer one is very subtle and without duality,
> the elephant one is perfect realization of shunyata;
> free from any fault you are Tashi Tseringma.

Therefore, all ladies are good representatives of primordial wisdom. This is why the main Anuttara tantras of the Vajrayana school state that the fourteenth root samaya vow is not to harm, criticize, or harbour disgust towards any woman, as this could lead one into the vajra hells. A young Vajrayana consort is recommended as the most qualified because youth possesses the special five qualities and five pleasurable sensations. This is not discriminating against older women; it is natural. When a flower is too young it is not yet perfect, when it gets older it no longer has complete beauty, the best time of the flower is between these two. Thus, youthful form is the best for a consort of a high yogi like Milarepa. Furthermore, mahasukha does not mean ordinary orgasm, which is merely samsaric sexual pleasure. That is not the key that opens the door to enlightenment. If it were, then it follows that pigeons, roosters, and hippies must all be enlightened. This is further evidenced by the fact that a male can achieve orgasm in many different ways even without karmamudra – like a flower with no honey. Some Tibetan pujas contain a confession prayer that includes reference to sex as a natural but sinful activity, but one needs to think about this further to ascertain whether or not it is true. If natural sex is a sin, then why is it a universal means of reproduction? Even a Chakravartin king or queen, saints, or holy men (prophets) came from sex between their mother and father. In the case of reproduction, it seems that sex is like a cause or seed whose fruit is the birth of children. Therefore, this has nothing to do with virtue or non-virtue, nor with sin or not sin. Eating, sex and sleep are daily worldly functions of sentient beings. For this reason, Buddha says that engaging in sexual misconduct, such as adultery or immorality, is when sex becomes a sin. When certain high yogis attain karmamudra it is a virtuous activity, as was the case for Milarepa and most of the Eighty-Four Mahasiddhas. Great lamas such as Sakya Trizin and the late Dilgo Khyentse Rinpoche are also highly qualified. Never believe that sex is sinful activity. Sinful means bad karma (activity), so if it is sinful then how could such highly realized bodhisattvas continue to incarnate? If bad karma is not purified then self is not free. Karma binds beings to samsara just as the criminal must serve his or her sentence in jail – throughout this lifetime one must therefore do purification practice. Making these points does not mean that I have respect for sex, I am simply giving my analysis.

The male consort deity such as Kalachakra is a manifestation of beginningless and unceasing great vajra energy. This can cut through dualistic worldly pleasure and unite with luminous mind. In the Vajrayana view male energy is like the sun's rays and female energy is like the soil and seed of enlightenment. Ordinary or wrongly-used sex is a creator of samsara. It is a great source of pain, pleasure and lust and is therefore very deeply involved in the suffering of samsara. Vajrayana masters have said, however, that for some exceptional people such as Tilopa, proper use of sexual energy becomes a vehicle for achieving full enlightenment in a very short period of time.

Because the Vajrayana understands that the female aspect has this great quality of bringing enlightenment energy, it uses this as a cause of enlightenment. The other

Buddhist schools do not believe this and conceptualize the female form merely as unpleasant and a source of samsara. When animals run in the meadows, they unknowingly destroy flowers; only the bee understands that the flower contains a tremendous amount of honey. A person who finds a large piece of gold but does not know what it is, might throw it away because it is too heavy and difficult to carry. But someone who knows it is gold can use it to make beautiful shrine ornaments, jewelry and temple decorations. The character of people such as King Indrabhuti, Saraha, Tilopa or Naropa, etc., was such that when they were young and living ordinary lives, they had tremendous attachment to females and could not renounce them. As such people cannot become ordained and follow Shravakayana or Mahayana practice, they could almost miss the opportunity for dharma practice and nirvana. The Buddha saw this different mentality clearly and therefore provided the tantras and Vajrayana. Certain other types of people are very good at following the Shravakayana path to enlightenment which is simple and straightforward, however it is also a long process that may take many lifetimes. These two approaches have different attitudes and moral conduct.

Between enlightenment on one side and samsara on the other, is a great battle. Some Shravakas are very successful and become arhats, but some lose patience. If this happens, they feel personal shame, and people feel disgust towards them because they have broken ordination, so then they lose hope of becoming an arhat. This sense of shame arises because the mind is convinced that samsara is negative and that endeavouring to become an arhat in this life is the only method possible. If one is perfectly successful on this path, keeping pure morality and a pure monastic life, it is then a great field of merit and therefore very good and respectable. This is why we take refuge in the sangha. However, other people find it difficult to follow this path properly. Buddha perceived that the energy of sexual union can be used as a means of leading some beings to enlightenment (nirvana) quickly, in one lifetime or less, no matter how sinful they were. This method could purify such beings even if they had been sinful over many lifetimes, or had killed their mothers or fathers, or destroyed the three religious objects (of refuge) – the three worst sins. Buddha therefore taught the tantras to these students and opened the gate of Vajrayana by giving initiation. The second and third initiation includes the karmamudra (consort). It does not even matter if one carries very negative karma, as did Milarepa for instance. When Milarepa's student, Rechungpa, asked him, "You are the greatest enlightened person – whose incarnation are you?" Milarepa replied:

> Your question shows the greatest lack of faith in the Vajrayana. I am not an incarnation, I am a sinful person, but the Vajrayana is the greatest of methods, leading to enlightenment in this lifetime even for such a sinful person as myself. So, I attended a qualified teacher like Marpa and practiced the Vajrayana teaching, and now I am fully enlightened.

Even though these two categories of practitioners are qualified to follow different disciplines, the essence of Lord Buddha's teaching works for them equally, leading both to liberation from samsaric suffering and the achievement of enlightenment (nirvana). The different conceptual framework of the two classes can be analysed. In one, the five skandhas of the human physical form must be seen as very ugly and unpleasant, like a rotting skeleton. By this method one becomes free from desire and attachment. Just as an ugly larva changes and emerges from its cocoon as a butterfly, so one leaves attachment and is longer bothered by the sensual world. In the other (the Vajrayana) a beautiful lady is seen as a female deity whose form is even more beautiful than that of a human being as it does not have flesh, bones, or blood, and is beyond ordinary worldly beauty. By taking refuge in the dakinis and practicing dakini energy the practitioner is then freed from worldly desire or lust. This is the same as a tiger cub born very beautiful and energetic, becoming a powerful tiger. Therefore, these are both very respectable techniques provided by the Buddha.

Someone who is especially qualified can practice both the Shravakayana and Vajrayana techniques together. Such a person is naturally disciplined, has less attachment and is very intelligent – having very deep understanding and wisdom. For example: Atisha, Gampopa, Longchenpa, Je Tsong Khapa, Sakya Pandita, Ling Rinpoche, Chobgyay Trichen Rinpoche, Karmapa, etc., have been great holders of the three yanas – each being a celibate bhikshu, a bodhisattva, and a high Vajrayana yogi with very profound inner realization of Vajrayana teaching. There have also been many lady holders of the three yanas. For this type of holy person Mahamudra and chandali (Tib. tummo) serve in place of physical karmamudra practice, so these great lamas have nothing to do with worldly karmamudra.

Whoever wishes to know more about the Vajrayana first needs to find an accomplished vajra master and then be accepted by him as a qualified Vajrayana practitioner. Secondly, he or she must then receive the Shravaka and Mahayana training and certain vows before studying the Vajrayana doctrine, and even then, cannot practice Vajrayana without initiation or talk about it publicly. Therefore, before one can criticize the Vajrayana it is necessary to make a complete study of Lord Buddha's teachings. The greatest scholar Jamgon Lodro Thaye, said that according to the Tibetan scholarly custom, five major topics must be studied prior to Vajrayana, these are: Vinaya, Abhidharma, Prajnaparamita, Madhyamaka and Pramana. To complete the study, one then continues with Kriyayoga, Upayoga, Yogatantra, Anuttarayoga and Atiyoga. At this level of intellectual knowledge, one is then able to make a conceptual judgement. However, it is necessary to meditate further if one wishes to reach the experiential level. If one has not completed these, criticism of Vajrayana can have no real basis and would be the worst form of poisoned speech; this would create the worst karma for oneself, as it would be no different from physically harming the Buddha by cutting his body. This does not mean that I myself know all of these and chose the Vajrayana as the best one, but my great and profound teachers, holders of the three yanas, have all told me this. I am simply passing on their message to those of discriminating mind.

In Tibet, masters such as Atisha, founder of the Kadampa; Gampopa, founder of the Kagyupa; Sakya Pandita, Lama Pakpa, Kunga Zangpo, the founder of the Sakya Ngorpa sect; Rongton Sheja Kunrik, founder of the Sakya Tsarpa sect; Tsong Khapa, founder of the Gelukpa; and Khyungpo Naljor, founder of the Shangpa Kagyu, are all examples of monks who were perfect vinaya holders (bhikshu) while at the same time being great bodhisattva practitioners and great masters of the Vajrayana siddhis. Each is like a golden vessel filled with honey-nectar into which is dropped a wish-fulfilling gem, because all three paths stay together. This is how one reaches complete understanding of Buddha's outer, inner and secret teachings: the external world of the five fields of sensation, the inner world of mental manifestation, and the secret world of the divine natural mind. If one does not completely understand the three yanas it is very important to study and practice them.

The Shravakayana concept of practice could never accommodate the Vajrayana one because of the Shravaka view of the human body as unpleasant, comprising dirty substances, and being impermanent and shameful. Only in the Vajrayana view is this not the case at all. Instead, the body is actually considered to be the basis and raw material for the nirmanakaya form. It is considered prettier than flowers since they cannot talk or think, being only a combination of elements. The elements of the body are seen as primordially pure and beautiful, and therefore portrayal of deities in union does not depict impure objects of mind in any way. Mental discrimination creates negative thinking alongside of it, if this happens one cannot see the deities without getting very upset. This is how wrong ideas are created. On the other hand, if one understands the meaning of the Vajrayana paintings one is then very positive and respectful. People who do not understand are really superimposing their own mental picture onto the deities and thereby creating a very strong feeling of discomfort. Once such ideas arise, even the energy of Vajrayana deity practice in one's shrine room may make it feel desecrated. Meanwhile this feeling really comes from oneself and is self-applied. Every teaching of Lord Buddha is a different route to the discovery of the true, natural state of mind.

There are also very wrathful Vajrayana deities, some of which bear the faces of different animals. This aspect of Vajrayana practice has also been misunderstood by uneducated observers who have mistakenly conceived of it as demon or animal worship. Really, these wrathful deities are being used to symbolize a particularly significant truth – that compassion and primordial wisdom cut off ordinary anger and ignorance. These angry forms do not destroy or eat oneself or others. The animal face represents the ignorance that we generally consider to be negative and the root of samsara. However, the true nature of ignorance is non-discriminating awareness, the profound primordial wisdom of the dharmadhatu. Therefore, when a deity displays an animal face this signifies the purification of samsaric ignorance. Ignorance has no real existence, and the concepts of right and wrong that result from samsaric ignorance are also naturally non-existent, pure, and all-pervading like space. This is also symbolized by the fact that both the body of the deity and the animal face manifest together in one form. In the true nature of mind, ignorance ultimately has no duality, and is most profound as it is itself transformed into enlightenment. Therefore, unlike some ancient shamanistic mythologies where gods and goddesses with animal heads are believed to really exist, the deity does not demonstrate a form of animal ignorance, nor does it possess the powers of certain animals. For example, an actor may portray a variety of characters for the audience by changing costumes and make-up, but he really remains himself all the time. Just so with the different deities whose enlightenment is unchanging while each presents a particular negative aspect of the practitioner transformed into the enlightened level. Each aspect of enlightened energy purifies a corresponding negative energy, and this combined meaning is represented in each deity that is shown with an animal head. This could be compared to a troupe of international dancers where the unique costume of each culture clearly indicates the dancer's nationality. A Mahayana or Shravakayana practitioner, however, may not feel faith towards this idea, or find it interesting.

Wrathful deities thus signify the purification of the five poisons of the mind, such as anger and passion. The deity is not showing his or her own anger, for example. Such deities are necessary for certain practitioners, just as different sicknesses require their own appropriate treatments. These special wrathful forms are the source of two blessings for the practitioner. Firstly, they supply the practitioner with very strong energy to subdue the kind of hindrances that are manifestations of the five poisons. Wrathful deities can never create anger or hatred because they are not demonstrating anger. Sometimes parents have to be wrathful with naughty or bad children but this does not mean that they feel deep hatred towards them, they are actually acting compassionately for their children's benefit. The wrathfulness of the deities symbolizes all the qualities of enlightenment such as compassion and love. The second blessing of these deities is that they lead the practitioner into enlightenment very quickly, based on belief that wrathful energy is much stronger than ordinary energy. Those who do not understand Vajrayana seem to have a great deal of confusion about this, however Vajrayana practitioners, both past and present, have been led quickly to enlightenment through the practice of these deities; thus, the practices are very useful. They also bring a much more comfortable and happy mind to the practitioner than does meditation on the body as a skeleton, or as rotting and impermanent.

Therefore, I think that Vajrayana practice bestows great significance upon both the Shravakayana and the Bodhisattvayana as it brings them both to completion in enlightenment. While Vajrayana both resembles the essence of the other two yanas and includes them both, they do not include the Vajrayana. I hope that this does not give the impression that I consider my way to be the only one and others to be wrong. The mind is powerful; it creates samsara and nirvana. The manifestations of samsara are limitless and very powerful but the manifestations of enlightenment are a trillion times greater. An enlightened being can manifest as a limitless number of different deities if it brings benefit for the liberation of sentient beings. Enlightenment is neither male nor female. It cannot be measured by ordinary conceptions because they are as narrow as the eye of a needle, while enlightenment is as wide as open space; the one cannot be compared with the other. Therefore, one should not try to fit enlightenment qualities, benefit for sentient beings, and the aim of liberation of the ego into enlightenment, into one's own set of preconceived ideas. Buddha taught different types of Dharma teaching, so one should not try to accommodate everything to the view of just one of these. As the wide variety of beings constantly produces worldly conceptions, different cultures, backgrounds, religions, philosophies, living traditions, and views, one cannot apply only one set of criteria. It is better to regard Lord Buddha as very kind and great to teach so much, and then while feeling that the particular approach one has chosen is good for oneself, generate respect for all Buddha's teachings and all the different Buddhist schools.

Nowadays, there are numerous Tibetan Vajrayana Buddhist monasteries being constructed in holy places in India (such as Bodhgaya), and in the Far East. The shrine rooms of these usually house only a statue of Lord Buddha, and do not include the other Vajrayana deities in order to avoid disappointing international Shravakayana believers. I think this approach is very wrong. The Vajrayana believes in the three kayas: the dharmakaya (enlightenment itself) which is formless, the sambhogakaya which is the manifestation of enlightenment in the form of the deities, and the nirmanakaya which is the physical form of enlightened beings. For this reason, we are very fortunate to be able to use these forms in temple decoration. What need is there to hide them? It is very discriminatory to prevent practitioners from making prostrations before representations of the Vajrayana deities. When this negativity enters a temple, it has already become impure. Shakyamuni spent many, many lifetimes accumulating the two merits until he finally took birth as Siddhartha and reached full enlightenment. Considering this, it seems that we are despising his great efforts if we do not respect primordial natural enlightenment itself and the great Vajrayana concept of the different levels and manifestations of enlightenment that he taught. When we Vajrayana practitioners prostrate before male-female representations of the deities our attitude never involves worldly thoughts or feelings about sex, as might be the case with an ordinary samsaric photograph. Instead, we believe the deities to be sambhogakaya manifestations of Buddha Shakyamuni, enlightenment that is primordial, beginingless and unending. Shakyamuni is the nirmanakaya manifestation of Buddha, leading the life of the twelve great deeds, renouncing the life of a householder. He manifested in this way for the purpose of bringing all of us sentient beings of Jambudvipa to liberation through face-to-face contact. Once enlightenment has been achieved there is no longer any attachment to a home, as enlightenment is beyond all concept of home, and no longer any need to carry the homeless view. Therefore, I think that those who hold the Vajrayana teachings should build statues of the Vajrayana deities and display them in the shrine rooms.

Hindu tantrikas claimed that many Vajrayana deities are merely different manifestations of Shiva or Vishnu, and, consequently, this greatest heart teaching of Lord Buddha was absorbed by the surrounding Hindu culture as Buddhism was destroyed in India after the 12th century CE. While Buddhism disappeared without a trace, Hindu teachings were very visible. Because general Buddhist teaching, and especially those of the Vajrayana, became absorbed into Hinduism at that time, Hindus think the Vajrayana deities are manifestations of Hindu gods and that Buddhist teachings come from Hindu teachings. As an example of a similar misunderstanding, we now say that spaghetti is an Italian food; even though this food originally came from China, nobody says it is Chinese. Although I mean no disrespect to the Hindu gods, and respect Shiva as the leading worldly god of the Himalaya who resides on Mount Kailasha in Tibet, they are not at all the same as Vajrayana deities such as Kalachakra, Chakrasamvara, Hevajra, Yamantaka, Ganapati, Arya Tara, or Vajrayogini, none of whom are found in the Hindu pantheon. Not understanding this, Hindus have applied the names of their gods to Vajrayana deities, and other people have come to accept this as true. There are some Vajrayana deities and Hindu gods that have the same or similar name, such as Ganesha; however, many people also share a name in common, such as John, but are not the same person. In the mind of the Vajrayana practitioner, Ganesha is a Vajrayana deity, while a Hindu practitioner believes that Ganesha is a Hindu deity. No one can say that Ganesha is primordially Hindu or Buddhist, and so neither can judge the other. There is no universal or primordial law that says Ganesha is only pure Hindu and not Buddhist, thereby suggesting that Buddhism borrowed this deity. Hinduism takes the view that because some of its elements such as the Vedas are older than Buddhism their Ganesha must obviously predate the Buddhist one, and thus confirms its Hindu origin. Buddhism asks, "Were the Four Noble Truths first, or did Hinduism come first?" Well, the Four Noble Truths are pure Buddhist teaching. Historically, Buddha may have taught these after the emergence of Hinduism, but their truth transcends time. Although the deities are somewhat similar to Hindu gods in appearance and also have their own associated mantras and yogic practices, if one looks carefully, one can see that they are completely different; they have a different purpose and lead to a different achievement. The very basis of these two views is different, because Buddhism does not have the Hindu concept of atman nor any belief in external superbeings. Instead, Buddhism is based on the Four Noble Truths, the Eightfold Noble Path, and the ten paramitas. We know they are Vajrayana deities because their descriptions are found in the Buddhist scriptures and people who follow pure Vajrayana use these practices. Vajrayana practitioners never conceive of their practice deities as Hindu because in their view the fundamental seed is different. As well, the Buddhist deity Chakrasamvara is depicted stepping on Shiva and his consort. This illustrates that the Hindu and Buddhist deities were separate from the beginning, and that the founders and views are different.

There is clear evidence that this absorption of Vajrayana deities into Hinduism is occurring even in the present day, as some Theravada Buddhist countries say that the deities are not truly Buddhist but are actually mixed with Hindu ones. Vajrayana has many similarities with Hinduism, but just because Hindu sadhus shave their hair and wear saffron robes one cannot say that Theravadan monks have copied their costume. This view is the same as the common Tibetan expression: "My father's cup is the cleanest in the world," which means that one holds one's own beliefs to be the only truth. It is like proclaiming to know much more than Shakyamuni himself, or that his knowledge is limited in comparison to one's own. If you say there is no such thing as pure Vajrayana, namely that it is mixed with Hinduism, then you will not be able to understand the Vajrayana. In this case, it would actually be more appropriate to think that Vajrayana is not an authentic teaching but only a mixture of Mahayana and Shravakayana, because then you may actually be starting to understand Vajrayana Buddhism. Why? Because the Vajrayana includes the Shravakayana and the Mahayana. However, neither of them can include the whole of the Vajrayana, just as a gallon container can hold three litres of water but a one litre container cannot contain a whole gallon. For this reason, Vajrayana practitioners must display and clearly explain the richness of their deities, rituals, ceremonies, and meditations, as this will preserve them and keep the differences between the Hindu and Buddhist tantric traditions clear.

Buddha did not teach the Buddhist tantric practices publicly. People have many different individual views and karma (action) and thus need different methods for mental discipline. This type of teaching is suitable for students who are very talented, have strong mental and physical energy, and have strong attachment to worldly pleasures. Shakyamuni gave this very spiritual path to lead such people into enlightenment by the method of transforming their own energy into buddhahood. In early times, images of Vajrayana deities, vajra and bell, and mudras, were very secret; they could not even be seen without initiation and were never displayed publicly. This is because these symbols are so easily misunderstood. As I mentioned earlier, the purpose of these teachings is to provide an antidote to samsara, to samsaric suffering and the causes of suffering. If this purpose is forgotten then one has taken the wrong path. Were these teachings public, those as yet unready and unqualified to study them would be led astray. Therefore, Shakyamuni taught these only to students with the capacity to understand them. The vajra master chooses students who are thus qualified for the Vajrayana. For such students these teachings lead to a great increase in respect for Lord Shakyamuni. This respect is much stronger than that of students of the other classes of Buddhism. This is because the Vajrayana disciple comes to a full realization of all the functions and qualities of the three kayas of Lord Shakyamuni. If a crystal ball is placed on a white cloth, it turns white, if placed on a cloth of five colours it turns to those five colours, but all the while it really remains the same. In the same way, the tantric deities are different manifestations of Buddha himself and are absolutely inseparable from him. Therefore, for the Vajrayana practitioner, if there are one hundred deities, this means that he or she can develop devotion and confidence in Buddha that is one hundred times stronger than for one nirmanakaya form.

Shakyamuni manifested in different ways in order to liberate his followers, thereby providing them with a variety of skillful methods by which to overcome suffering and the causes of suffering. For some followers Shakyamuni took the form of a monk wearing saffron-coloured dharma robes, with a golden appearance and the one hundred and twelve marks of the beauty and glory of the nirmanakaya. The Vajrayana considers that the Buddha manifested in as many different forms of wrathful and peaceful, male and female, deities as were necessary, thereby completing the full spectrum of practices needed to lead beings to enlightenment. Buddha embodies the enlightenment qualities of body, speech, enlightened mind, quality and activity (Skt: kaya, vak, citta, gunaratna and karma, respectively). Each of these five qualities manifests as different mandalas of deities that purify the five unvirtuous emotions. These unvirtuous emotions are the threads of suffering that weave and hold the fabric of samsara. The Vajrayana is therefore the best method for purifying these in a short time. The methods of the other Buddhist schools are much more gradual, as it takes many lifetimes – it is said 'eons' (Skt. kalpa) – to reach enlightenment. Those who are qualified to practice the Vajrayana need not worry that it takes kalpas, because this method leads to Buddha Vajradharahood in a short period of time, possibly even a single lifetime. Therefore, those who naturally have strong faith and understanding of Vajrayana are extremely fortunate. So, it is better for those who do not understand not to criticize the Vajrayana. Ancient mahapanditas say that one cannot see what is beyond one's reality, therefore there may be doubt about some dharma teachings, and in that case, it is better to leave them alone.

Further to this, some western publications about Buddhism state that the Vajrayana idea of transcendent knowledge developed from Hinduism; and another western scholar holds that Buddhism must be authenticated by science. I do not think either of these are correct views to take. If it is said that at different times in history some aspects of religions came from outside sources, then it follows that all religious rituals could have originated from elsewhere. I think it is disrespectful to say this. Historically and spiritually the Vajrayana is one of the great schools of Buddhism. It was founded by holy people before the advent of modern science so how can anyone be the judge of this? That would be the same as judging Jesus, Mohammed, Buddha, or the Hindu sages. Some things that are claimed could be right but other things would be wrong. For example, if it was claimed that very high bishop ordination does not come from Lord

Jesus, then from where was it copied? Such rituals are produced within the religion itself and are not due to connections between religions. Every mythology has a history, and each religion has a mythology. There are many different mythologies – they cannot all be the truth. Some might accord with scientific theory about the physical world but this kind of reasoning could not fathom, for example, a Buddhist meaning that may be deeper and altogether different. Furthermore, other religions believe that everything was created by God, and while modern science does not agree with the notion of an Adam and Eve, it cannot prove they did not exist. Therefore, there is nothing wrong with belief. It is better for a follower to believe everything in his or her religion because in each case believing has some great meaning and healing power for the mind. When one achieves full buddhahood then everything is beyond belief or non-belief, truth or non-truth. There is no argument and no need for debate between science and religion. Milarepa said someone asked him, "Are you a great and virtuous man?" and his reply was, "First I did sinful and unvirtuous deeds, second I did only virtuous deeds, and now I am beyond both."

Upon careful analysis one can see that the Vajrayana is a more direct means of transforming the mind into its true, natural state of enlightenment, because in Buddhism it is believed that everything is created by karmic mind. For example, the form of a beautiful girl would have been created gradually by mind and karma (action, cause and effect) over millions of years, as changes in the combinations of the elements were brought about by the involvement and interaction of feelings, perceptions, consciousness, and the imprints of positive and negative karma. One can analyse this further by going back thousands of generations to a time when females may have looked quite different. They may have looked very ugly and unpleasant by current standards, with form more like an ape. The differences between males and females are the result of previous karma. Since there is natural attraction between males and females, when this attraction occurs the female may subconsciously feel that she wants to be even more attractive. As this feeling increases, so do feelings of pride and of beauty. Each time this mental process happens it produces further change. In this way the separation in male and female form slowly widened, with the female gradually developing more beauty and becoming more involved in making herself beautiful. This has finally resulted in the present, very beautiful, form of the female. A beautiful girl may also have had a beautiful and generous mind in previous lifetimes, she may have made beautiful offerings, had great patience, and been of benefit to everyone around her. This kind of karma leads to beauty in subsequent lives no matter whether one is male or female. In these two ways one can see that everything is a process of cause and effect generated by mind.

This process can be seen in other animals as well. The male peacock did not have such beautiful plumage a million years ago. Because of a strong desire to have a means of attracting and securing a female partner, this same mind process slowly created his beautiful feathers. In all animals, either the male or the female must have beauty.

Similarly, a yak's horns or a tiger's teeth have not come about just by coincidence nor have they been made by some person or some evil force, functions of the mind are involved in their creation. Over many millions of years this kind of creature developed the feeling and perception of needing some security and means of self-defence. This feeling of defence in the mind slowly led to the material evolution of horns. In this way the mind brings everything into existence. In some beings a subconscious feeling of difficulty in eating slowly led to a feeling in the mind of wanting to chew strongly. This led to the very slow and gradual production of teeth, part of the skeletal structure, and the hardest and strongest part of the body. This process involves the coming together of many causes such as desire, anger, greed, hunger and thirst. Without mind it could never happen.

Therefore, all universal phenomena are manifestations or creations of mind itself. Each sentient being's point of view is different from that of others; they do not all see things the same way. For example, some see water as a place to live, some as a drink, for some it burns like molten metal, for some it is a poison and some are neutral towards it. Sentient beings are made up of the five skandhas. An external phenomenon such as a rock, for example, is part of the five elements, part of form. The mind first discriminates between liquid or solid, regarding them as completely different. Thus, the two opposite concepts of soft or solid arise, and rock is then understood to be solid. Subsequently, further divisions are created by different karmic tendencies and carried by mind: such as 'iron', 'rocky', 'gold', 'silver', and so on. All of these are also concepts arising from mind. An endless number of such concepts can arise because this phenomenon is contained in karmic mind. But there is no such thing as primordially existent or established 'rock' in the universe. Rock is compounded of many elements. This is what Buddhists describe as dependent origination.

It is said that many millions of lifetimes before reaching enlightenment Lord Buddha was an ordinary sentient being. At that time his form was not the same as his subsequent Buddha form that was created over so many lifetimes of practicing love and compassion. This practice transformed his mind, producing the extraordinarily beautiful nirmanakaya form, or rainbow body, of Buddha. This beauty had gradually developed with each life as a result of the virtuous activity of the mind.

People say that if you worry too much you will get old fast, but they do not completely understand how the mind plays a part in causing this to happen. When the mind is upset or depressed, the feelings of anger and sadness distort one's natural conceptions. This in turn causes the physical elements of the body to change unnaturally and one begins to look old. Natural mind has innate qualities of freedom, peace, wisdom and natural feelings, which function properly to bring about the sequential stages of youth and ageing. Anger and sadness block this natural flow of physical time and space, disrupting the natural progression.

Shells, that provide safe homes of many varied shapes and colours for molluscs, are another example of defences that have been created by mind. This creation happens when certain mental functions and the background karma (action) of the mind combine with time and space in just the right sequence. Buddha mentioned that nothing can happen without the appropriate cause and effect, and mind can do nothing on its own without the right connection with cause and effect. However, when karma (action, cause and effect) brings all the different physical elements and adequate time and space together in just the right combination, then the functioning of the mind can bring about this gradual process of evolution, leading to a physical creation that completes this cycle of events. The next cycle may take many million years and change the physical body once again. The results of this subsequent process of creation would be different from the first, because the actions of body, speech, and mind would not be the same and would lead in a different direction. Also, a single negative or positive action (karma) by itself cannot instantly lead to a result; the right conditions are also necessary, which is the reason why this process takes such a long time.

Maybe, many thousand years from now, human beings will be bigger and stronger both physically and mentally. If this occurs, it will be brought about by the five skandhas and mental functions becoming stronger and more complex, and wisdom and knowledge increasing. Thus, humans would need a longer lifespan in which to use their increased powers of thinking. They would also need a more spacious environment and improved energy flow within their bodies. It may be that over the next many thousand years human conditions will continue to improve. This would be brought about by the functioning of karma-mind. Even though it is possible for physical changes to appear, carbon, oxygen and hydrogen, etc., are needed. How can the capacity of something be improved, for example, how can a bird's feathers and wings develop with so fine a structure, and so on? This must involve karma-mind (carrying the seed) and the elements working together to slowly produce a bird. For example, a being may have the karma to be reborn as an animal; mind carries the karma but the set of conditions that can give rise to (cause) this are also necessary. The modern idea is that first you need the carbon, hydrogen and oxygen, and so on, but how can you prove that these alone will make an animal? This is a like a modern 'big bang' theory – even though these elements are needed how can you prove they carry the seed of something like a feather's structure? Why should elements take the form of DNA? Maybe DNA is produced by karma-mind? Think about this. Jainism says that all universal space is filled with soul, or bardo mind. So, Jains always cover their faces, and do not even shake hands strongly to avoid hurting anything. Maybe elements like hydrogen and oxygen carry this kind of karma-mind and qualifying conditions relative to each other, like seed and fruit, to produce different forms of life. But this takes a long time, maybe a billion years, because the necessary conditions are also important. This is dependent origination (Tib. tendrel). How can science prove that carbon, hydrogen, oxygen, etc. created all the different sentient beings? Why would this happen in the first place? Which came first, birds wishing to fly, or wings? Mind is strongly involved – the wing is produced by mind because the condition of certain sentient beings made them want to fly. Mind then found the right elemental conditions and slowly produced wings, and flight.

Maybe at that future time when people might be bigger and stronger, they might also be more intelligent than at present, and Vajrayana teachings may thus be much stronger and more profound, and include one hundred times more teachings. It is predicted that when Maitreya, the next Buddha, comes he will be very tall, and people at that time will enjoy very long lives and general prosperity. This kind of good result is caused by positive actions. On the other hand, if humans use their lives to act negatively the human body will shrink in size, conditions will become bad, and the human life span will become very short. This is all possible because basic mind itself has no beginning, no end, and no form. It cannot be reduced to physical elements. This is like space the size of one sesame seed equalling universal space. The power of the mental energy involved is tremendous. Vajrayana teachings cannot be taught to minds that are underdeveloped or feeble, or which hold to a small view. Humans are one hundred times more intelligent than animals, and although with proper training we can teach discipline and right action to an animal (for example, not to kill or steal), it is not possible to teach it the more profound Buddhist teachings because the necessary conditions have not yet developed.

Scientists say that everything is the product of the process of evolution, a statement that supports the view that humans have not been created by an external superbeing, such as Brahma or Shiva. If humans had been created by such a being it would not be possible to change his laws in a million years, unless he himself were to be destroyed. It is said in Hindu mythology that Shiva will eventually destroy all life; but having created pleasant things what need would there be to destroy them? Everything continuously declines, growing old and being destroyed. Phenomena have only a brief existence. It seems to me that if Shiva likes to destroy, it would be better for him to do so without causing suffering by making everything disappear instantly, in the space of one millionth of a second. These gods regard themselves as the most powerful of beings, indestructible, victorious and free to do as they please.

It is not that I am opposed to any spiritual mythology, but that it is always important for us to be free to discover the truth. Theistic philosophy maintains that the power of the gods is beyond the scope of the human mind; however, from early man to the present this same human mind has created everything, including all the different beliefs, names and views that are held today. Everything is impermanent, including ideas themselves. It is for this reason that so many different and even opposing ideas have come to exist.

In Hindu theistic philosophy the three principal gods are credited with three functions: firstly, creation by Vishnu, secondly, preservation of what has been created by Brahma, and thirdly, destruction of what has been preserved by Shiva. These three functions are like making torma cakes in the monasteries from barley, that are then placed on the shrine and protected from insects, rot and damage, and finally smashed and destroyed when the ritual is finished. This theistic view is incompatible with the concept of impermanence and karma (action), or of evolution itself, which involves a constant process of change from one instant to the next created by ever-changing causes and conditions. In his very first sermon Lord Buddha explained that all combinations are impermanent, and he repeated this teaching at the very end of his life when he passed into Parinirvana.

Creation is purely a coincidence of causes and conditions, as a result of which something appears. Thereafter, when the conditions change, the appearance must also change. This is what is known in Buddhist philosophy as dependent origination. Mind itself is beginningless, and in light of this even a modern scientific measurement of thirty billion years becomes as nothing. We count and measure time, but the mind itself is timeless. We consider thirty billion years to be very long but if we completely imagine the view of beginningless time, one hundred years is like a mere fraction of a second. If we consider the dimensions of the universe and its galaxies in the same manner, the galaxies become as small as single spider webs with their different shapes and patterns. As a small example we can look at the present city of Toronto, where one thousand, or a few hundred years, ago there was probably not a single house, light, restaurant or word written on a wall, and thus see how much we have created in only a short span of time. If we look carefully, it becomes apparent that the city has not appeared by itself but has come about through the involvement of timeless energy, human mental activity, perceptions, feelings, imaginative concepts translated into words and actions, and the elements.

This reasoning shows that the way we discipline the mind has specific results and what we practice is accomplished. This is how certain people transform their energy into enlightenment energy by means of Vajrayana practice. Although theists believe that gods have the power to create, preserve and destroy, I think this is physically impossible. The Buddhist view is that the creator is desire, while ignorance is the preserver and anger is the destroyer. This is a very beneficial point of view because each individual functions in these three ways. As these three functions are subject to action cause and effect, and impermanence, one can change them through the practice of the three yanas. It is much easier to transform desire, ignorance, and anger than to change the three gods. How does one do this? While each yana actually has methods of practice that are antidotes for all three of these, each yana is stronger in one area.

Mahayana methods of practice emphasise the antidote for ignorance, Shravakayana methods emphasise the antidote for anger, and Vajrayana methods emphasise the antidote for desire. Therefore, I think that whoever follows, respects and listens to Lord Buddha must accept all the three schools of Shravakayana, Mahayana and Vajrayana. All three share 'one taste' in that they all bestow great knowledge and serve to open the wisdom of the practitioner. I mentioned earlier my belief that the true, great Vajrayana masters have a greater understanding and respect for Buddha than do practitioners of the other vehicles, and never hold the view that Shakyamuni is in any way lower than the Vajrayana deities. All three schools have the same view: that Buddha freed himself from suffering, completely purified the root cause of suffering, achieved full enlightenment, and will never return again to samsara. All three schools agree that the causes of suffering are negative karma (action cause and effect) and ignorance.

19
KARMA AND DEPENDENT ARISING

LOOKING AT MIND ONE FINDS CEASELESS ACTIVITY, but all of this is just dreams. Consider the relationship between cause and effect. If one supposes that cause comes first, which implies an original cause without antecedent, then it follows that cause cannot be dependent upon effect. If an effect is already established, then cause becomes meaningless. In fact, cause and effect are mutually dependent, and it is this dynamic that produces all the different appearances of phenomena. If cause and effect were independently established (and therefore unrelated) they would 'destroy' each other. Change would be impossible. Colours and shapes would always remain the same. This would be as irrational as a gardener planting good seed in order not to grow plants. We know that cause and effect are interdependent because it is evident in the way things work – we see that phenomena do change. This interdependence lies behind the karmic patterns that cause and effect produce. Without cause and effect there would be no cause for the production of any new phenomenon. There would be only space. It would also be feasible to have a live horned rabbit calved by a barren woman's son.

One second of time and infinite time are taking place in the same moment. The space occupied by one louse egg and universal space both occupy the same spot. Infinite time and universal space are as interdependent as one millionth of a second in the existence of the space occupied by a tiny louse egg. People are not aware of the cause of karma (dependent arising) because our minds are too slow to catch this natural process; this is the power of dependent arising.

If you sit in the sun on flat ground early in the morning or late in the day, you will cast a shadow that is a hundred times taller than you are. However, at mid-day, when the sun is high overhead, there is no shadow. In this analogy mid-day represents enlightenment where reality is unobscured. Just as light and shadow are related to one another, so ultimate reality (shunyata) and the appearances of dependent arising are interdependent. As with the notions of yin and yang, the 'female' emptiness is related to the 'male' dependent arising. Great emptiness produces tremendous dependent arising. The tremendous depth of understanding of emptiness attained at the moment of enlightenment, the realization of Great Emptiness, is called the 'Mother of the Buddhas'.

This means that each time you go to emptiness, apply emptiness again, and continue to do so, again and again, then finally, you go beyond, to luminous mind – the luminosity of primordial interdependent origination.

It does not matter whether Buddha is explained or not, whether Buddha is enlightened or not, whether Buddha is deluded or not, whether Buddha is samsaric or enlightened – the primordial natural state is perfect freedom. Nothing else is necessary. This is so pure that from a butcher to a Buddha all is 'sameness'. Really, there is no time or space for anything new to be caused. Accordingly, Dzogchen, or Ati-yoga, primordially embodies, in itself, the six perfections. In this sense it may be referred to as a tigle (single dot without physical dimension), majestic, constantly radiating its glory, and remaining as its own tsultrim (perfection of morality), its own measure of itself. Similarly, this tigle being like a trillionth of a tip of a single hair, unchanging, one pointed, present, being without time and encompassing all of time, remains as its samten (perfection of meditation).

So, from this perspective, the paramitas are the transcendent true nature of all states of interdependent origination (samsara), from the hell realms to the heavenly realms. For example, the true nature of a phenomenon such as DNA actually transcends notions such as 'primordial' and 'eternal'. The primordial Buddha (Tib. Kuntuzangpo) sees his own face (realizes the true nature of mind) and in the same instant arises his own purity, Samantabhadri (Tib. Kuntuzangmo). This unity of the two is sherab (the sixth paramita, the perfection of wisdom). The cause is so deep that Kuntuzangpo is the blue-black colour of deepest space, and she, Kuntuzangmo, is the white of the brightest explosion of energy. Their sound is A HAM, and the seed syllable of the All-Good is BRUM.

This reality Saraha expressed as Mahamudra ('maha' meaning great, and 'mudra' meaning seal), indicating the luminosity and emptiness of mind. Garab Dorje expressed it as Dzogchen ('dzog' meaning complete, and 'chen' meaning great), as nothing can transcend this completeness. Both of these have the same meaning. Mahamudra expresses the greatness of the profundity of emptiness, and Dzogchen, the greatness of the nakedness of the true nature. The inseparability of these two is the Madhyamaka – Nagarjuna's expression of the Middle Way.

Whoever grasps at this meaning perceives something different. This is like the story of the blind men feeling an elephant: as each man felt a different part of this huge animal each was left with a different impression as to the appearance of the beast. However, all the descriptions were incorrect, the true description eluded them all. One may grasp at a part, but it is really something else. Even if one just watches without grasping, it is still something else. Through repeated meditation one gets closer and closer to the goal. This is called 'trying to reach Lhasa', because by merely saying 'Lhasa' one gets no closer. The mind is the goal, and with each sitting one's journey evolves. Whoever comes to realize dependent origination – realizes everything.

20
MANDALA OFFERING

MANDALA OFFERING IS IMPORTANT for the Vajrayana practitioner because body, speech and mental visualization are all involved. When doing this practice one should use mandala disks of the highest quality possible. Gold is the best, however stone or wooden disks can be used if you have nothing else. Quality offerings are gems, semi-precious stones, corn, or other grains. Grains should be coated using saffron water. If you have no equipment at all, offer the objects of your five senses with your hands in the mandala offering mudra. The quality of the disks and offerings is an omen of the strength of your merit. The speech involved is the mandala prayer. Mentally visualize that the forms of the ordinary world around you are the manifestation of the essence of your body, wealth, virtue and merit. The form, structure and shape of the mandala offering itself varies according to different traditions or to whatever conceptual framework of the world you believe in. The fourth and fifth levels of personal involvement are one's qualities, which include one's virtue and merit, and one's activity, which is the union of emptiness and great bliss.

The mandala offering is widely used: every time one sees one's guru, when requesting a teaching and in appreciation after a teaching, when one sees a temple or a stupa, at holy places of pilgrimage, in the presence of relics, at times of purification, and during the recitation of the Seven Branch Prayer.[1] The Vajrayana foundation practices include the recitation of one hundred thousand mandala offerings. The most important point of all to remember is that mandala offering is the key to limitless merit.

Chogyal Phakpa wrote the *Thirty-Seven Point Mandala Offering* that is common to all the Tibetan traditions. Besides this, there are also nirmanakaya and sambhogakaya mandala offerings. I myself have composed a sambhogakaya mandala offering that is quite long. I think of this as a great universal offering and am very pleased that some of my students have begun the hundred thousand repetitions because so much merit is accumulated.

In his practice Lama Tsong Khapa wore through many stone mandala disks. He realized that mandala offering was the most important practice that could be performed on one's meditation seat. Milarepa's non-dual mandala offering was non-dual meditation. To his heart student Gampopa, Milarepa taught the complete yogas and Mahamudra, but reserved his most precious teaching for the last moment of their last meeting. After thirteen months of practice Gampopa displayed amazing accomplishment, but when Milarepa praised him, he expressed only his wish for that 'most precious teaching' that Milarepa had promised. Later, when taking leave of his teacher, Gampopa reminded him again of his promise. At the very last moment Milarepa lifted his cotton clothing and showed his buttocks, thickly calloused, and said, 'I meditated this long and finally achieved enlightenment, this is the only way to full enlightenment.' Milarepa accumulated merit in this way – thus it was his secret mandala offering.

Mandala offering has four aspects that must be understood: external, inner, secret, and suchness. The external aspect refers to ordinary concept or belief about the universe, be that an ancient, modern, or scientific view. The inner aspect is the physical structure of the body – from the head and spinal cord (Mount Meru) to the three divisions of each of the four limbs (the four continents and eight subcontinents), to the two sense organs of sight and hearing and the other senses, to the seven important internal organs, to the bodily fluids, down to the millions of pores and hairs – adorned with the marks of physical beauty (teeth, nails, nice skin, and pleasant complexion). The secret mandala of accomplishment is the five chakras and three channels (lalana, rasana and avadhuti channels of sun, moon, and space energies) which comprise the structure of the subtle body. The suchness aspect of the mandala offering is meditating according to the way of the Five Paths and Ten Bhumis, and is the realization of the 'union of the base and the result'. Thus Lama Phakpa's Thirty-Seven Point Mandala is symbolic of the Thirty-Seven Limbs of Enlightenment, which constitute the Mahayana path from the first bodhisattva vow to full and complete enlightenment.

The Thirty-Seven Limbs are as follows:

The Four Close Contemplations:
of body
of feelings
of mind
of external phenomena

The Four Perfect Abandonments:
abandonment of non-virtue that has been produced
non-generation of non-virtues that have not been produced
increasing the virtues that have been produced
making efforts to generate virtues that have not yet been produced

The Four Feet of the Miraculous:
aspiration
perseverance

thought
analysis

The Five Faculties (Causal):
faith
effort
mindfulness
concentration
wisdom

The Five Powers:
faith
effort
mindfulness
concentration
wisdom

The Seven Factors of Enlightenment:
mindfulness
wisdom
effort
joy
suppleness
concentration
equanimity

The Eightfold Noble Path:
right view
right thought
right speech
right effort
right livelihood
right mindfulness
right concentration
right action

The notion of Mount Meru at the centre of the six realms of sentient beings is derived from the ancient Indian view of the world; some western mythologies might place the Tree of Life here. However, in the Buddhist view the real centre of the structure of the universe is the mind. The primordial base at the centre is the intrinsic subtle mind. Mind is the originator of all phenomena, the clear nature of mind is the basis of appearance. The equanimity, non-duality, or 'sameness-ness' of buddha nature is the non-production of duality. The arising of the duality of cognizer and cognized that is termed the manas or 'egoic consciousness' produce the all-base consciousness (Skt. alaya vijnana); this is the explosion of the original base through eight gates or exits, the point of departure, of division, into either enlightenment or cyclic existence. The base is the primordial 'state' and the all-base consciousness produces the six sense consciousnesses. The all-base consciousness carries habitual tendencies that produce the karma of the inner and external elements that in turn project the world. There is not a single existent without mind.

In full and complete enlightenment, the very root of duality is gone. Enlightenment completely transforms the six senses and their objects into jnana (primordial wisdom – which is purified ignorance). Thus, to talk of the description of the mandala of the world as if Buddha had a dualistic view is profoundly erroneous. But if enlightenment is awakening from the ignorance of duality and thus where concepts disappear, why did Lord Buddha mention Mount Meru as recorded in the sutras?

Enlightenment and unenlightenment are different ways of perceiving and understanding. The six realms of sentient beings, the unenlightened, have ordinary perception understanding through the five sensations and elements of existence formed by the atoms and energies created by ordinary karma. All the knowledge of beings in the six realms belongs to this type of understanding. Their perceptions are led by duality – ego and karma dealing with external realities. Ordinary beings can communicate their knowledge of the senses without recourse to meditation or Vajrasattva purification, by using the five elements and scientific and technological equipment that provides extensions of the senses for discerning subtler phenomena. However, the 'perceivers' themselves are limited because they are composed of the same five elements. They cannot detect beyond the elements. They cannot see beyond dualistic time and space. This is the limit of scientific investigation, and scientists as such are spiritually unenlightened.

The perception of enlightened ones is different from that of ordinary beings. By 'enlightened ones' I am referring now to those who have gone beyond the first bhumi - who have penetrated to emptiness and are beyond ordinary perceptions, understanding, knowledge, and views. Enlightened perception is divided into three, the dharmakaya, the sambhogakaya, and the nirmanakaya, all of which are enlightened views and completely 'gone beyond' the ordinary. Just as the butterfly stays around the flower while a supersonic jet such as Concorde passes over the clouds, or a spacecraft passes by space dust, so the two ways of understanding are quite different. Ordinary understanding cannot detect enlightenment just as the butterfly cannot see where the jet has gone when it passes above the clouds. Buddhism is like the supersonic jet or spacecraft, while scientific knowledge is like the butterfly. The butterfly cannot judge the others from its vantage point, and in the same way enlightenment cannot be detected by science.

Buddha dharmakaya view is beyond the reach of the tenth bhumi bodhisattvas, and the sambhogakaya manifestation of enlightened power is beyond even the first bhumi. However the very purpose of the nirmanakaya is to benefit and guide ordinary sentient beings, and it is manifested by the dharmakaya and sambhogakaya in order to be perceived by sentient beings. Since it has form, it can be born of parents, and show the Twelve Nirmanakaya Deeds[2] as Buddha Shakyamuni did. It can use human languages, wear clothes, eat food, manifest either a male or female figure, and have an ordinary name. But at the same time, the nirmanakaya is the manifestation of the dharmakaya and sambhogakaya, which means that it is equal to and the same as the dharmakaya and sambhogakaya. That is, totally 'gone beyond'. The nirmanakaya's knowledge is beyond ordinary knowledge and has nothing to do with the five elements or the activities of the sciences, and does not depend upon ordinary energy, time, or space.

The ancient Indian view of Mount Meru as the centre of the world did not originate in ordinary geography, but in the subtle body ('channels and winds') visions of the yogis. As it was part the culture at the time of Buddha Shakyamuni, this central mountain was considered measurable in worldly terms. However, even though the nirmanakaya Buddha taught this ordinary geography his knowledge was beyond that of ordinary existence. His speech was used solely for our benefit with the goal of leading us to enlightenment by teaching the paths of purification and accumulation of merit. A drumbeat presupposes an instrument to produce the sound, and the drum itself requires a certain structure of specific materials and drumsticks, but this does not mean that the musician who beats the drum has to be put together in the same way and be made of the same skin and wood in order to play the drum. Just so, the nirmanakaya conspires to spread the sound of the holy dharma. The beater of a drum is not the same as the drum, but he can still use it to produce the sound of the drumbeat. However, unlike the nirmanakaya, he cannot beat the drum now and emit the sound much later.

When describing the geography of Mount Meru with the surrounding continents and sub-continents the Buddha wove in teachings on ethics and morals, virtue and sin, and their effects. The top of Mount Meru was a heavenly realm, the dwelling place of beings of good worldly karma and great merit. Here, there were no volcanic eruptions, no hurricanes, no snow and freezing cold, nor any deserts and burning heat, and this part of the mountain was composed of precious gems. This method of teaching uses a familiar geographical feature but reveals it is a home of extraordinary quality – that of the gods, and thereby teaches the value of virtuous living. A mountain is a worldly, perceivable, measurable thing, but with this teaching it becomes something almost beyond what is ordinary and knowable because of the quality of its structure. Mount Meru becomes a manifestation of the result of virtue. In this way, the nirmanakaya explains what is important for sentient beings by using their own experience, concepts, and language. What is meaningful to ordinary vessel-beings, what suits their minds, dissolving like honey in warm water, will change with time over the ages.

How can science test the truth of the enlightened view; what measurable evidence can there be? Why did the Buddha not teach the sutras with explanations that accord with modern science? Above, I explained that even when in nirmanakaya form the enlightened one does not return to samsaric views. He has gone beyond ordinary views that are based on the ignorance of duality and the senses. If the Buddha had taught about the globe, the atmosphere, and what happens within the earth and beyond, it would only create more ordinary thought and distractions and actually lead away from the path of virtue. If this were the case, enlightenment would be impossible for other beings to achieve, because both the Buddha and the students would be caught in the web of worldly games of time, space, and energy. When the worldly body is full of worldly thoughts there is no room for the path to enlightenment. The Buddha himself would then appear to be an ordinary science professor or researcher in need of instruments for observations. And even though he would most surely have been a genius surpassing even a Galileo, what would have become of the three yanas path to enlightenment? If he had followed that course, perhaps the earth would have already been destroyed by nuclear weapons, because there would not have been the example and teachings of Nagarjuna, Garab Dorje, Shri Singha, Padma Sambhava, Bodhidharma, and Milarepa. Even as a teenager, Siddhartha had more power and acuity than Galileo or Einstein. The arrow he drew penetrated nine layers of iron where his closest rival could barely penetrate one layer. In competitions he could throw an elephant with one hand. Resting beside a tree he cast no shadow, and shade never bothered him because sunshine followed him everywhere. Even though we might think that Lord Buddha's scientific knowledge was less than our own, in actuality he must have been genius enough to teach what we know now, and much more.

Sakya Pandita explained that the Buddha guided beings through the conventional (relative) truth of the times to lead them to ultimate truth, whereas others guided their followers with the truth but it ultimately led them to failure. Rising up amidst the flames of his funeral pyre to address his last words to Rechungpa, who had arrived too late, Milarepa said:

> In the invisible realm of the heavens,
> There is a Buddha who skillfully uses falsehoods,
> Guiding sentient beings toward relative truth.
> Little time have they to realize ultimate truth.
> O Rechung, abandon concepts.

Taken together, the lines of this quote mean that Lord Buddha's teachings are 'jik ten tun jok' (they accord with worldly beliefs, or the views of the worldly). Buddha said that while the worldly dispute with him, he never disputed with them. He followed what they believed in order to lead them to the truth. Besides, meditation achievement is beyond the three realms: the kamadhatu (sphere of desire), the rupadhatu (sphere of form) and the arupadhatu (sphere beyond form). A great Indian mahapandita said that the highest point of enlightenment that non-believers can attain is the pinnacle of the dhatus (spheres of existence) – the highest god realm. This is because they have not realized shunyata, and will therefore fall back again into the lower realms. On the other hand, even if the Buddha had not achieved the arupadhatu level of samadhi he would still be beyond the pinnacle of existence, having risen to full and complete enlightenment.

The point is that relative views of the world do change, so tremendous faith in the sutras is essential. Therefore, even if something of a relative nature in a sutra contradicts your view of things, your modern sensibility, don't let this destroy your faith and create doubt – as that only damages you. We must recognize that worldly views are limited, even the views of a top scientist like Einstein, or Stephen Hawking in our modern time. Samsaric views are limited views. However much we are able to explain, we still cannot explain Lord Buddha's view. He is called omniscient, but he is beyond ordinary views. When we insert our own views into reading the sutras it is like a mosquito analyzing the eagle's view. Not comprehending the eagle's view, the mosquito won't believe it, and so rejects it. There are different truths, different perceptions, and different levels of realization. Both the eagle and the mosquito have their own relative truth. Our views cannot contain the Buddha's omniscience. I've read that some people try to use the sciences to validate the teachings of Buddha and other religions. To me, that is wrong. I think we should try to use Buddhist teachings to validate scientific views. Anyway, we don't need to look to the sciences to provide proof for the sutras, because science (i.e., knowledge through the senses and the extensions of the senses) is not the correct validator of the dharma. One does not need the evidence of science for the Buddha's truth. Buddha used eighty-four thousand different ways to explain his teachings, because his purpose was to help sentient beings of differing disposition understand the Four Noble Truths and lead them to liberation. Whether the medicine the teachings utilise is absolute truth or relative truth, the goal of all the teachings is to end the suffering of sentient beings by preventing the negative emotions. In your home you may have the full set of the Scriptures (Skt. Tripitaka) or you may have a few sutras on your shrine; in either case, if you have tremendous devotion, faith, and confidence, the blessings will abound.

Arya Asanga made the general point that in order to study the sutras one must first learn the 'keys of correct understanding', which are the keys of learning. To measure the ingredients of the Three Baskets of the Dharma one must use the graduated measuring cup that discerns relative truth and absolute truth methods. So here in seven sections (A-G) I will outline these methods for making this important distinction between statements made by the Buddha in different sutras and tantras.

A. THE FOUR KINDS OF INTERPRETIVE SUTRAS

1. Interpretative sutras primarily stressing the intention of the Buddha to encourage conversion from non-virtue to virtue, and ignorance to knowledge.

    These are not teachings of absolute truth, but as they lead to the dharma like one might hook fish from the ocean of suffering, they are beneficial. As some students are frightened by the truth of emptiness and would reject absolute truth teaching, in some sources the Buddha taught that five skandhas exist and that there is a truly existing external world. By using this method of presentation, the listener is less threatened and willing to learn more. The Buddha has realized emptiness but expresses a view that things are like an illusion or dreamlike, and so leads a narrow-minded student into the profound teachings through the presentation in the abhidharma and the vinaya.

2. Interpretative sutras stressing the teaching of absolute emptiness.

    In these sutras the Buddha taught that all conditioned phenomena are essenceless and naturally empty. However, Buddha actually taught both existence and non-existence:

    (2a) He taught the labelling nature (Tib. kuntak) in which phenomena do not exist independently and are without essence, since they only appear through labelling or designation.

    (2b) Then he taught that the perfectly accomplished nature (Tib. yongdrup) or ultimate reality is existent because it is not dependently arising.

    These two terms appear contradictory, but there is no confusion. The Yogachara (Chittamatra or 'Mind Only' School) used them to lead to a correct interpretation of emptiness. Although the 'perfectly accomplished nature" was criticized by some as being merely a reworking of the Hindu philosophical concept of atman, and undermining belief in karma, the Yogacharins claimed that their system corrected the leaning towards the extreme of nihilism in the Madhyamaka schools.

3. Interpretative sutras concerned with antidotes.

   One must consider the purpose of certain things that Buddha said. For example, when people wondered why Shakyamuni Buddha had a stature and a lifespan they considered unworthy of a Buddha, he told them that in a certain era of the past he was Vairochana Buddha. These people were then satisfied that he was not different from the great ones, that he was equal to the Jina buddhas. Whether he was or was not Vairochana (he was neither lying nor not lying) was immaterial, because he was equal to all the buddhas of the three times in possessing dharmakaya and in his activity. Those who came to him were satisfied that he was as great as Vairochana Buddha. They were happy and respected him. His answer to them was based upon the equality of all buddhas.

4. The Fourth category of interpretative sutras is two-fold:

   (4a) Interpretative sutras that primarily stress the Buddha's intent to encourage those of weak aptitude, teaching that enlightenment can be achieved through striving through the two accumulations.

   (4b) Interpretative sutras where the meaning of words is hidden.

Some philosophers and religious people considered the Buddha's teaching easy to understand and therefore inferior to other more sophisticated systems. Hence for them, the Buddha made his teachings more esoteric and difficult to understand.

Thus, in the *Udanavarga*, he taught:

> Father and mother are to be killed,
> King and country are to be destroyed,
> Take out the hearts of the pure caste and their followers,
> Whoever does this will be perfectly purified.

This teaching refers to breaking the Twelve Links of Dependent Origination.[3] The 'father' is craving and the 'mother' is grasping. The 'king' is the all-base consciousness of all who possess habitual tendencies and karma, and is also an indictment of the sense consciousnesses that follow. Lastly, 'hearts of the clean caste' refers both to the view of atman maintained by the brahmin caste, the emphasis of some monks on rules and outward appearances, and is even a reference to the custom of animal sacrifice. The highest morality is to destroy these. Here the truth of the Buddha's words is not as they appear. Another example of this would be Mount Meru and its true referent (e.g., spinal column and head in the inner aspect of mandala).

B. THE FOUR CONSIDERATIONS

Each of these topics possess three characteristics:

    a) what is considered;
    b) what is its purpose;
    c) what is the contradiction.

1. The Consideration where the teachings appear contrary but the meaning is the same.

    (a) The sameness of the dharmakaya of all Buddhas is indicated in a statement such as, "Previously I was Vairochana."

    (b) This statement was neither a complete lie nor the complete truth but helped his followers to have greater faith, and to thus accumulate greater merit.

    (c) If he was Vairochana before, then why did he appear in a seemingly lesser form as Shakyamuni Buddha?

2. The Consideration of determining another meaning.

    (I)

    (a) The causes of cyclic existence must be severed.

    (b) For those who needed a more esoteric, difficult style of teaching, those who thought the Buddha's teaching was too simple for them.

    (c) The words: "Kill one's father and mother and you are purified," are completely different from: "Kill ignorance (father) and negative action (mother), the causes of cyclic existence must be severed."

(II)

(a) All dharmas are without essence.

(b) The view of phenomena in the Mind Only School:

- (i) The labelling nature signifies that phenomena are empty and delusory since they are merely conceptual labelling.

- (ii) The 'dependent' (Tib. zhenwang) nature is divided into two types:

    1. The pure dependent nature of phenomena is the mutual dependence, and hence emptiness, of subject and object.

    2. The impure dependent nature comprises all samsaric phenomena – all dependently arising. As they are free from the four extremes of being produced by self, by other, by both, or neither, they are not truly existent.

- (iii) The 'perfectly accomplished' nature is the lack of essence of the extremes of purity and impurity. This is the way things really are.

3. The Consideration of 'other time' indicates that the time involved is other than stated but neither is it a lie.

   (a) Buddha describing the benefits of a mantra, says that one becomes enlightened if one does this mantra. If one recites the Sukhavati prayer, one will be immediately reborn in Sukhavati.

   (b) The results are true but one must accumulate enough merit first, so unless one's merit is sufficient one must practice a long time for the result.

   (c) Doing a mantra one time, does result in immediate enlightenment.

4. The Consideration of the mentality of the person.

    (a) Praising generosity as superior to moral conduct.

    (b) Some are very attached to the value of moral conduct so the Buddha persuades them to consider the practice of generosity by placing its value above moral training. The Buddha's intention is to teach the equal importance of all the Six Perfections.

    (c) Morality is one of the perfections, the same as generosity.

C. THE FOUR CORRECT RELIANCES (I)

All highly developed Buddhist practitioners must follow these.

1. Relying on the meaning and not on the expression. Don't judge the truth of a teaching based on its style, on how well structured the grammar, how beautiful the poetry, or how scholarly the treatise.
2. Relying on the teachings and not upon the teacher or the person who wrote them. One should not reject a teaching because the teacher is a little ugly, or not very skillful.
3. Relying on primordial wisdom and not upon ordinary mind or ordinary knowledge.
4. Relying on the definitive or absolute teachings and not upon the interpretative or relative teachings.

D. THE FOUR CORRECT RELIANCES (II)

1. Rely on the transcendental dharma, that is the Thirty-Seven Limbs of Enlightenment representing the path and the Prajnaparamita representing the ultimate. Both of these are more important than the language of texts and the five sciences because they lead directly to enlightenment.
2. Rely on a person who has the correct view and correct morals, especially the correct view of the Mahayana. It doesn't matter whether he or she is a noble or not, a tulku or not, has a famous name as a scholar or not, or has many followers or not, and so on.
3. Rely on primordial wisdom. What is important in a teacher is that they have realized the true egolessness that is emptiness and the luminous nature of mind. That what he says is true or the most

erudite from a worldly point of view, is unimportant.
4. Rely on the definitive rather than on the provisional teaching.
The definitive (Skt. nitartha; Tib. ngedon) teaching is beyond the renunciate mind of the shravaka and the inherent nihilism or eternalism of provisional (Skt. neyartha; Tib. drang don) views.

E. THE FOUR APPROPRIATE REASONINGS

Using Suitable Reasoning or Logic to Validate.

1. Reasoning from functionality.
   A fruit depends originally on the seed, for example, the rest of the links of the chain of dependant origination arise from the seed of ignorance. If an eye has no retina, the eye consciousness cannot work.
2. Reasoning from causation.
   The appropriate activity of the eye consciousness is seeing not hearing. Barley comes from barley grains not from rice grains.
3. Reasoning from inference.
   If there is smoke, there is fire. If there are waterfowl in the sky, there is water nearby.
4. Reasoning from nature.
   All phenomena have their own nature. Phenomena are validated by their own nature: fire is hot, liquid flows downwards, the sun radiates.

The above keys are essential for studying the Three Baskets of vinaya, sutras, and abhidharma. The following keys are applied to all categories of Lord Buddha's teachings.

F. THE SIX KEYS OF UNDERSTANDING THE TANTRIC DOCTRINE OF THE VAJRAYANA

1. Provisional Meaning.
   The relative methods that aid in approaching the ultimate truth, such as making a shrine, making offerings, mudras, sadhanas – especially the development stage, and the texts explaining the relative meaning.
2. Definitive Meaning.
   Completion stage teachings, especially Mahamudra and Ati, and Inseparability of Samsara and Nirvana.

3. Teaching with Intent.
   One vajra word has two meanings. There are three categories or considerations:

   (a) Consideration of Time.
       'If one does this mantra then on one's very seat one will be instantly enlightened.' This refers to the future when enough merit has been accumulated but some students need to hear this.

   (b) Consideration of Meaning.
       For instance, when it is said that one must take the consort from the Victorious One, it means that one must always practice the transcendental prajnaparamita, emptiness, which is known as the Queen Mother of the buddhas and bodhisattvas. Ordinary people might think that this means that they need to take a consort to become enlightened.

   (c) Consideration of Personal Way of Thinking.
       When the tantras say to sleep with the wife of another, take what is not given, lie, and kill, the great meaning is secret. The real meaning signified here is the great union of emptiness and compassion. This would be taught in consideration of those who consider the esoteric alone to hold great meaning.

       (i) 'Taking the wife of another' means taking and practicing the great qualities that belong to enlightenment alone.

       (ii) 'Taking what is not given' signifies that in practising chandali and karmamudra one 'takes the red and white drops that are the source of bliss'. However, one already possesses these oneself so one is 'taking what is not given'.

       (iii) 'To lie' refers to the fact that many teachings are of provisional meaning. Hence, they may look like lies when contrasted with the ultimate; however, the ultimate is beyond words and explanations.

(iv) In prana practice 'one has to kill', but it is self-clinging which is to be slain. The wisdom wind eliminates the karmic winds which are the basis for creating samsaric delusion and ego-clinging.

4. Consideration of the Direct Procedure (Tib. Gongmin; 'Without intention').

In such passages there is no concealed meaning; the words are to be directly understood and clearly indicate the practice of virtue, the general Buddhist view.

5. Literal Meaning (Tib. Dra ji zhinpa).

Again, the meaning and the words correspond clearly, but this case refers to words that are common to all or most religions. Religions have common teachings. For instance, Hinduism has yogas, mandalas, meditation, fire ceremonies, and rituals in common with Buddhism – the words are similar and without hidden meaning.

6. Non-literal Meaning.

The Vajrayana teaches through secret symbols such as hand symbols and technical language where the meaning is hidden (the dakini language), where the ten winds are 'gotracha', and the tsok meat and beer are 'mamsa' and 'madana'.

G. FOUR TYPES OF MEANING

1. Same Meaning.

Where words associated with the five sciences or general Vajrayana have the same meaning as the Sanskrit or logical terms of Buddhism.

2. General Meaning.

(i) A practitioner hears that anuttarayoga is the fastest way to enlightenment and then worries that he has wasted time studying the sutrayana and practicing kriya yoga. The Vajrayana says there's no need for regret because these practices form part of the stage-by-stage preparation for the highest practice.

(ii) Someone who does Vajrayana practice comes to regret it when he hears that "clean and dirty are the same" and "one must kill to be purified," and then thinks Vajrayana is no better than shamanism which practices sacrificing animals, that is, harming and acting with great desire. However, the Vajrayana shares the general teachings on moral discipline and generating bodhichitta with common teachings.

(iii) The practice of visualisation is common or general as well in that the deity of the development stage visualization is also associated with the completion stage.

3. Hidden Meaning (Tib. be don).
   The completion stage techniques of the winds and channels, karma mudra and so on, are examples of teachings that can be given only to very special students, because the bliss-desire phenomena are hidden (first example). Furthermore, absolute truth is hidden.

4. The Highest Teachings all have a Common Goal.
   Ultimate clear light, the completion stage of clear light, khorde yerme and atiyoga achieve the union of luminous and illusory body or the Seven Qualities of Buddha Vajradhara.[4]

Highly intelligent, middling and slow students need different teachings in the same way that an adult, a teenager or a child would. If you do not have all these keys, no matter how much you study the sutrayana and shastras, all your study will fail. To correctly follow the teachings of the three yanas, first study these keys.

21
PILGRIMAGE

THE LOCATION OF ONE'S PRACTICE IS VERY IMPORTANT. Before entering parinirvana, Lord Shakyamuni said that a person must make one pilgrimage in his or her lifetime to the four holy places. These are the Buddha's birthplace in Lumbini, his place of enlightenment in Bodhgaya, the place where he first turned the wheel of the Dharma in Sarnath, and the place of his passing in Kushinagara. Furthermore, Padma Sambhava said that because practicing for one week in a holy place equals a year of practice elsewhere, his followers must visit the three principal caves where he stayed, and they will never again fall to the lower realms.

Pilgrimage (Tib. nekor) is very important for purification, for accumulation of merit, and for improving realization, as well as being a travelling meditation and an experience of homelessness. It is more important to relax by staying for a time in these places than to engage in endless travelling. There are many holy places of pilgrimage in India. The foremost of these is Bodhgaya, in Bihar, the centre of the Dharma, where, as mentioned above, Lord Buddha attained full enlightenment. It is the chief of all the holy places of pilgrimage. The construction of the great stupa at Bodhgaya is said to have been initiated and sponsored by King Ashoka (273–236 BCE). At the top is a second small stupa made by Nagarjuna that houses Buddha relics. Around the stupa are stone pillars also made by Nagarjuna, which have carvings of eight Mahakala and eight Tara faces. It is said that whoever sees the great stupa receives some blessing, as it was here that Buddha sat beneath the Bodhi tree and attained full enlightenment. During the week that followed he remained seated facing the Bodhi tree. During the second week he arose for the first time, leaving a footprint embedded in the rock. He then took five more steps before standing still, at each step he left another footprint in the rock, totalling seven. So, this is an extremely holy place. Nearby flows the Nairanjana River, beside which Buddha had meditated for six years prior to enlightenment. During the first two of those years, he would partake of a little food each day, during the second two years he took only a little rice each day, and during the final two years his practice was so ascetic that he no longer needed oxygen and did not even breathe. At this time, he achieved the highest realization of worldly meditation. A short distance from this place of meditation a farm woman offered Buddha some boiled milk. This was the first time he took food again – and, consequently, the one hundred and twelve marks of the nirmanakaya appeared on his body. It was after this that he went to sit beneath the Bodhi tree.

Seven miles south-east of Bodhgaya is the famous cemetery of Dorgasherai (known in Tibetan as Selwatsal, meaning 'cool forest') where many great yogis have practiced. On a rocky hill nearby is the cave of Mahasiddha Shavaripa and a sandalwood tree sacred to the six-armed Mahakala. Many people believe that, on a hill near the city of Gaya, Buddha was offered honey by a monkey. This hill is also a place of pilgrimage. Not far away is the area of Rajgir that was famous as the capital of King Bimbisara's kingdom. There are five mountains nearby and it was in a cave there that Buddha's regent, Arhat Mahakashyapa, as well as arhats Ananda and Upali and the other 500 arhats assembled for the first Buddhist Council. This was held under the royal patronage of King Ajatasratu of Magadha, in the same summer as Lord Buddha's passing into parinirvana. Here Ananda recited the collection of the Sutra teachings, Upali recited the Vinaya teachings, and Mahakashyapa recited the Abhidharma. These three teachings make up the present-day Tripitaka (the Three Baskets).

In Rajgir is a hill called Gridhrakuta (Vulture Peak) where Buddha turned the second wheel of the doctrine, giving the Perfection of Wisdom teachings that are the source of the Madhyamaka school, and thus one of the two principal sources of the Mahayana tradition. At that time all the gods, goddesses, nagas, naginis and bodhisattvas assembled there to listen. It is thus a very important place of pilgrimage for Mahayana practitioners. When visiting here one should be especially sure to read the *Heart Sutra* and the *Diamond Sutra*. Also near Rajgir are the hot springs where Buddha and his disciples bathed, referred to in the Tripitaka as the 'Hot Spring Temple'. This is a healing spring, and it is also very beneficial to bathe in the waters of the small river nearby, the Saraswati, whose waters bring healing and blessings. This is especially beneficial for arthritis and other diseases of old age and is also said to improve one's capacity for wisdom. There is no longer a Buddhist temple here and the hot springs belong mainly to Hindu temples used by the local people. Here one should imagine oneself to be in Lord Buddha's time and not focus on the present situation. Nearby is a small hill in a forest of bamboo shrubs called Belubana where Buddha stayed for several years.

One can then go on to visit Nalanda – the site of the most famous Buddhist University in Asia. Aryadeva, Shantarakshita, Padma Sambhava, Chandrakirti, and all the famous Mahapanditas were educated at Nalanda. The late Khunu Rinpoche (d. 1976) said that Nalanda covered twelve square miles at the time it was destroyed, over eight hundred years ago. The ruins of the famous shrine and stupa of Shariputra can still be seen.

It is said that on the way from Gaya to Kolkata (Calcutta), in Bihar, is a branch of the river Ganges where there is a Hindu shrine situated on top of a big rock. On the opposite bank of the river is a small rocky hill where Vikramashila, a famous Vajrayana university and monastery, is said to have stood. There are also caves once used by Naropa at Pullahari, Vikramashila and Odantapuri. Odantapuri monastery was very famous; in fact, Guru Padma Sambhava modelled the monastery of Samye in Tibet after it. The original site is forgotten now, however, although it would be very good if it were to be rediscovered.

Pataliputra, nowadays the town of Patna, in Bihar, was the capital of the Dharmaraja Ashoka. Here one can also visit the Ashoka Museum and see many blessing relics, and a very special statue of Ashoka's queen. Forty-nine days after his enlightenment Lord Buddha traveled to Varanasi, and the holy place known as Sarnath that lies just to the north. Here he met his first five disciples to whom he gave his first teaching of the Four Noble Truths and the Eightfold Noble Path, which brought them all to full enlightenment. Including Buddha himself, these were the first six enlightened human beings of the current Buddhist era on Earth. This teaching was given in the place known as the Deer Park, at Sarnath, where there are holy ruins of a monastery and stupa. There is also a stone pillar from Ashoka's time bearing a local script of 2,000 years ago. The inscription tells us that the pillar marks the place where the Victorious One turned the wheel of the Dharma. During one special ceremony every November on the full moon, one can view the Buddha's bones and relics displayed at the Dharmapala temple.

The Buddha spent many rainy seasons in the area of Shravasti that was the capital of the ancient kingdom of Kosala. This was the longest period that he stayed in any one place. Here, the six highest Hindu philosophers and yogins of the day challenged Buddha to a contest of miracles. He accepted, and defeated them in a tremendous fifteen-day demonstration of miracles between the new and full moon. In the Tibetan lunar calendar, this is the first new moon of the year, and also marks the New Year (Tib. Losar). When this competition was held, it was witnessed by the people of four kingdoms:

> On the first day of the month King Prasenajit made offerings to Lord Buddha. When the Buddha put his toothpick into the soil there immediately grew up a forest of large trees that covered an area extending for five hundred yojana[1] in all directions. The trees were laden with fruit and were emitting fragrances. Everybody received the taste and scent of these trees.
>
> On the second day, when King Udrayana offered him food, the water with which Lord Buddha washed his mouth turned into a beautiful pool, the colour of gems. From this pool appeared many colours and lotus flowers, and from these flowers people received beautiful fragrances.
>
> On the third day, when Shun-tsin made offerings, to the left and right of Lord Buddha there appeared two mountains of gems. On top of these were grasses and fruit, of which all the people and animals ate their fill.
>
> On the fourth day, when Indravarma made offerings to Lord Buddha, four fresh-water springs appeared, one in each of the four directions. From the water came the sound of the four limitless teachings.

On the fifth day, when Brahmadatta made offerings to him, many illuminations of lights issued from Lord Buddha's mouth. Wherever these lights touched all the pleasures of body and mind were felt.

On the sixth day, when noble families from Magadha made offerings to Lord Buddha, all the people became very happy and relaxed, and each made wishing prayers and praised the enlightenment quality of Lord Buddha.

On the seventh day, when the Shakya people made offerings to Lord Buddha, he blessed all the people, whereupon each became a king with the seven royal possessions of a Chakravartin and experienced great pleasure and happiness.

On the eighth day, when Indra made offerings to Lord Buddha, the sound of elephants issued from the lion throne. Five Vajrapanis appeared, and the non-Buddhist teachers became frightened.

On the ninth day, when Brahmaraja made offerings to him, everyone could see Lord Buddha's body appearing as large as the expanse of the Brahma heaven, and radiating great lights.

On the tenth day, when the four great kings of the four directions made offerings to Lord Buddha, his body covered the whole expanse of samsara and everyone could see many lights and hear the sound of his teaching.

On the eleventh day, when the merchant Anathapindika made offerings to him, although Lord Buddha stayed seated on the lion throne, his body disappeared and transformed into lights, and the sound of his voice teaching Dharma could be heard by all.

On the twelfth day, when the householder Tse-ta made offerings to him, lights issued from Lord Buddha's body and radiated to the three-thousand-fold universes. Countless Buddhas seated on lotuses, each radiating light to a further three-thousand-fold universes, endlessly, could be seen by all.

On the thirteenth day, when King Shun-tsin made offerings to him, great lights radiated from Lord Buddha's navel illuminating the three thousand universes. Wherever these lights touched sentient beings all their negative karma and defilements were removed, and everyone received fruit and nectars.

On the fourteenth day, when King Udrayana threw flowers while making offerings to Lord Buddha, all the flowers multiplied to cover the universe and were seen by everyone.

On the fifteenth day, when King Bimbisara made offerings, food with one hundred delicious qualities of taste filled all empty vessels, and when

Lord Buddha beat his palm on the ground all the limitless sentient beings of the hell realms were liberated.[2]

It was while staying in Shravasti that Buddha instituted the Vinaya rules. Four special shrines were kept and the eighty chief arhats resided here. As this was the chief residence of Lord Buddha it is a very important place to see, although it is now just ruins. Buddha resided here for twenty-five summer rainy season retreats, together with all the arhats and noble bhikshus and bhikshunis. The title of arhat is given to a monk who has reached full enlightenment according to the Shravakayana tradition. The title means 'one who has subdued all enemies,' i.e., one who has destroyed the inner negative emotions and achieved an egoless state.

There are also many different places of pilgrimage in southern India such as Nagarjunakonda – the place where Nagarjuna lived in Mysore. Near Bombay are the Ajanta and Ellora caves where temples are carved into the rock and have escaped undamaged through the ages. These are the best examples of the Buddhist art of cave-carving and are also places of great blessing. One should pay homage here and if possible, pray and meditate for a while also. The Sanchi stupa made by Dharmaraja Ashoka, and many other general holy sites can also be visited in the area.

In Himachal Pradesh is Rewalsar, known in Tibetan as Tso Pema (Lotus Lake). This was once part of the ancient kingdom of Zahor. The king of Zahor had a beautiful daughter named Mandarava who constantly refused to wed, despite the requests of many kings from other districts, because she wished to remain celibate and practice the Dharma. Guru Rinpoche descended to her retreat centre from the sky riding on the rays of the sun, and he became her Dharma guide. A poor cowherd, who bore the nine marks of ugliness on his body, often saw Guru Rinpoche arriving and he spread rumours about this until, eventually, news of his daughter's bad reputation reached the king. In anger over a man visiting her, the king imprisoned Mandarava in a pit in the present-day town of Mandi and had Guru Rinpoche burned in a fire. However, within a week all the oil from the pyre had transformed into a lake, and all the wood had transformed into a lotus upon which Guru Rinpoche in deity form was seated, unharmed, worshipped by many dakas and dakinis who surrounded him. The king was very sorry for what he had done, and asking for forgiveness he offered his traditional king's costume to Guru Rinpoche and released Mandarava. The pit where she was kept can still be seen in Mandi. Tso Pema is very holy to pilgrims who respect Guru Rinpoche, and particularly so on the tenth day of each Tibetan lunar month. On this day – it is especially meritorious to circumambulate the lake at sunrise, midday, sunset and late at night reciting the Guru Rinpoche mantra in song, to hold a ganachakra puja, and also to do some Guru Rinpoche retreat practice. On top of the mountain above Tso Pema is the cave of Mandarava and Guru Rinpoche.

There are many other famous sites in the same area. On the way to Rewalsar from Patankot is Telokpur. The 16th Gyalwang Karmapa (1924–1981) told me that this is the place where the great siddha Tilopa, the lineage guru of the Kagyu sect, was eating fish when his student Naropa first met him. At that meeting, Naropa had some doubts in his mind. Tilopa realized this and vomited the fish he had eaten back into the running water, alive and well. This miracle cleared away Naropa's doubts. Sister Palmo and I therefore founded the Karma Drubgyud Dhargyay Ling[3] nunnery there. From this nunnery another has since been established near the main seat of the Gyalwang Karmapa at Rumtek, in Sikkim. There is also a three-year retreat nunnery in Sherab Ling near T'ai Situ Rinpoche's monastery.[4] Near Telokpur are two other Vajrayana holy places called Kangra and Jolamukhai ('fire-mouth') where natural fire comes from the ground.

In southern India near Bangalore, which was previously the capital of the kingdom of Bangala, is the birthplace of Shantarakshita, the famous abbot of Samye. Nearby is Tsampaka, once the city of Tsampa, which was one of the six famous cities in the time of Lord Buddha. East of Kolkata (Calcutta), in present-day Bangladesh, is Chittagong. Here there is a Mahamuni temple where the Shravakayana lineage has remained unbroken from the Buddha's time to the present. Orissa, once in the ancient country of Kalinga, was the site of King Ashoka's biggest battle and was a most important centre of the Vajrayana. It is rumoured that Vajrayana is still practiced here today in secret by some ostensibly Hindu yogins.

Far to the south of Orissa near Guntur, in Andra Pradesh, is Sri Dhamakatyaka. According to the Tibetan scholar Gendun Chopel, this is where King Chandra received the first Kalachakra teaching from Lord Shakyamuni. However, some people have recently claimed that this actually took place in Malaysia, and others claim that it was in Indonesia. Also in this area is Shri Parvata where Nagarjuna and his chief disciple Aryadeva had their permanent residence. It is very important to pay homage in this area and to recite the *Prajnaparamita Sutra*, Madhyamaka texts and the *Manjusrinamasamgiti*.

Regarding Sri Lanka, Tibetan legend recounts:

> Its girls are dakinis,
> its rivers are pearls,
> and its land is jewels.

Sri Lanka is the oldest continuously Buddhist country and many people who live there believe that the Buddha visited it on numerous occasions. King Ashoka sent his son Mahinda and his daughter Sanghamitta there to establish a monastery and a nunnery. The only direct descendant of the original Bodhi tree under which Buddha attained enlightenment exists in Sri Lanka. This is now one of the oldest trees in existence as it is more than 2,000 years old. King Ashoka sent the bodhi seed from which it grew to Sri Lanka with his son and daughter. A special Wesak festival is held here on Buddha's Birthday each May; a celebration that is equivalent to Christmas in the West. Buddha relics there include a tooth and a footprint. At one point, Guru Rinpoche left Tibet to go to Sri Lanka. Hindus also regard this as an historically important place because of its connection with the battle related in the epic story of the Ramayana. Because of Sri Lanka's great importance, and because it is the home of very ancient Buddhist relics, it is necessary to make a visit there to pay one's respects.

Nepal is a very important country of pilgrimage for Buddhists as there are many places there that have great blessing. Unlike many sites in India, these locations have not been disturbed through the centuries and so this blessing has never been lost. Lumbini is the birthplace of Lord Buddha, as we noted previously. Shakyamuni Buddha was the fourth of the 1,000 Buddhas of this aeon. Through his bodhisattva activity practicing the six perfections over countless lifetimes of self-sacrifice for sentient beings he finally, through his wisdom and compassion, took the nirmanakaya form of Shakyamuni. Reincarnating for sentient beings as prince of the Shakya clan of Kapilavastu in Nepal, he was born in Lumbini in the Shakya kingdom. His father was King Shuddhodhana and his mother Queen Mahamaya. He was born miraculously, and immediately took seven steps in each of the four directions. White lotus flowers appeared at each step and he pointed his finger to the sky saying, "I am the Enlightened One." A pillar marking this as the birthplace of Buddha dates from the time of King Ashoka. At Kushinagara, when Lord Buddha reached his eighty-first year, he lay down on his right side by two Sala trees, and after saying that everything is impermanent and that this would be the last time anyone would see him in his nirmanakaya body, he passed away at last into Mahaparinirvana.

Nepal is especially important for Vajrayana pilgrimage as many Buddhist yogins went there, such as Nagarjuna, Naropa, and other siddhas. The Swayambhu stupa is of special importance as this is believed to be the reliquary of an earlier Buddha known in Tibetan as Tsuktorchen. The name Swayambhu means 'naturally appearing' and derives from the following legend: The Kathmandu valley was once covered by a huge lake. From this lake a thousand-petalled lotus flower made of five jewels appeared, holding at its centre a crystal stupa the same height as the length of a man's forearm and hand. This was called the Swayambhu stupa. Later, Lord Buddha, Protector of All Sentient Beings, appeared in the world, and from Wutaishan (Five Peak Mountain) in China the Bodhisattva Manjushri incarnated as Vajra Acharya Manjudeva. He made a pilgrimage to the Swayambhu stupa, flying miraculously over the lake. As only those with miracle powers could possibly visit this remarkable shrine, he decided to dry up the lake so that everyone could pay homage. With his sword he cut through the southern range of the hills surrounding the valley and after a full day and night the lake drained dry, leaving the stupa protected on a hill. Later, to protect the stupa still further, the Vajra Acharya Shantishri covered both it and the hill and built a big stupa. Around this stupa he built five towns, each with a shrine to one of the elemental gods of earth, water, wind, jewel and fire. Because of the blessings brought by these shrines, Nepal became very prosperous in every way. This is a very holy stupa, principal of the three most famous stupas in Nepal.

There is also a Vulture Peak Mountain in Nepal, called Kimdol Bahl where Buddha is said to have taught the Perfection of Wisdom. The blessing power of this place is said to equal that of the real Vulture Peak Mountain in India. Kimdol Bahl means 'Pile of Rice'. There is a very ancient Bodhi tree growing there, and many of the Mahasiddhas and Mahapanditas of ancient times stayed here. Near Swayambhu there is the Manjushri asana (throne), and a stupa of Mahakashyapa, the Buddha preceding Shakyamuni. There is also a stupa that is a reliquary and monument to Vasubandhu, who came from India with one thousand arhats and established many Dharma centres in Nepal. When he finally passed away, his students built this stupa.

Near Kathmandu is the Boudhanath stupa. According to legend, a local girl who was an incarnation of Avalokiteshvara lived here at one time. After she passed away, her emanation returned as a lady called Shamvara, who kept pigs. This lady and her sons built the stupa at Boudhanath[5] many hundreds of years ago. The stupa has a long history and very great blessing, and houses many of Lord Buddha's relics. A little further from Kathmandu is Namo Buddha. The Jataka[6] tales tell that in an earlier incarnation Lord Buddha was once a greatly compassionate prince who gave his body to a starving tigress and her cubs to eat. His bones lie in the stupa at Namo Buddha. Also in Nepal is a cave called Nyishang Gurta, where Milarepa stayed, and this is where the famous incident of the huntsman and the deer occurred, which is recounted in *The One Hundred Thousand Songs of Mila* (Tib. *Mila Gurbum*). At Pharping there is a Vajrayogini shrine that carries great blessings; this stands in a cave where Marpa Lotsawa stayed for a long time. Also here, are the Asura and Yanglaysho caves, where the Precious Guru, Padma Sambhava, meditated on Vajrakilaya and subdued all evils through his enlightened wrathful activity.[7]

There are some other places of pilgrimage that are of special importance to those who practice Vajrayana – the yogis and yoginis who have received Vajrayana initiation. Many of these holy sites are seldom visited nowadays and the locations of some are no longer known. The pilgrim would need reliable help to find the exact spots, and some of the areas can be dangerous to visit. Many of these are also Hindu tantric holy places, which might make them easier to locate. Those Vajrayana practitioners who have achieved some siddhi should go to these twenty-four Vajrayana energy places, that are divided into three levels corresponding to the chakras of mind, speech and body. These places are associated with all the deities of Anuttara yoga, such as Chakrasamvara, Guhyasamaja and Hevajra, because these places are where they subdued the twenty-four

Maras. In ancient times, these sites were of profound importance to the Eighty-Four Mahasiddhas and others who practiced there, because they are centres of tantric energy, just as acupuncture points are energy centres of the body.

These places are actually primordial energy centres, naturally established at the time the Earth itself was formed. It is said that Maharudra[8] recognized this, and so he and his consort came to the chief centre at Bodhgaya and his twenty-four ministers went to the other twenty-four places so as to take control of them. They engaged in extremely negative activities such as eating human flesh, drinking blood, wearing ornaments made of human bones, clothes of human, elephant and tiger skins, and garlands of skulls. Later, the five Jina Buddhas emanated from the buddha realms in wrathful form. Hayagriva and Vajra Yogini, or, according to the Chakrasamvara tantra, Heruka and Vajrayogini, subdued Maharudra and his consort, and the forty-eight dakas and dakinis, subdued the other twenty-four evil couples. The costume of Maharudra and his followers came to symbolize the various aspects of enlightenment. The tiger skin symbolizes that which is beyond thought, the wings became vajra wings symbolizing all-pervading compassion, and so on. Thus, their body, speech and mind were taken over by the body, speech and mind of the Herukas, and their old bodies were left behind like old snake skins. This Vajrayana history is, of course, to be read as a symbolic account.

Bodhgaya is the centre, and the other twenty-four Vajrayana energy places are divided up into three mind, speech and body groups of eight places each, they are as follows:

1. Purnagiri (or Puliramalaya) in the region of Karnataka in South India. Some people say that this is Patna, the capital of King Ashoka's kingdom.
2. Oddiyana in the Swat valley in Northern Pakistan, the most treasured place and source of the Vajrayana teachings.
3. Jalandhara in the Upper Kangra Valley in Himachal Pradesh.
4. Kamarupa in Assam.
5. Arbuta Mount Abu in Rajasthan.
6. Godavari at the source of the Deccan River.
7. Ramesvaran in Tamil Nadu.
8. Devikota in West Bengal. The other name for this is Tsarita, and there are many mountains of this name with blessings similar to this one, such as Tsarita in Southern Tibet.
9. Malaya in Madhya Pradesh.
10. Odra in North Orissa.
11. Trisakune – the Sita River.
12. Kosala.
13. Kalinga in South Orissa.

14. Lampaka near Mardan.
15. Kanchi southwest of Madras.
16. Mount Kailasha in the Himalayas in Tibet.
17. Pretapuri.
18. Grhadeva near Kathmandu.
19. Surastra in south west India.
20. Suvarnadvipa, possibly to be identified with Sumatra.
21. Nagara near Jalandhara.
22. Sindhu, the Indus River north of Karachi in Pakistan.
23. Maru near Lahore in Pakistan.
24. Kuluta, not far from Tso Pema in Mandi on top of the mountain.

The Vajrayana practitioner, in particular, should make a pilgrimage to Oddiyana. This is in the northwestern region of present-day Pakistan, in the Swat valley. In this region there are the remains of a Buddhist monastery at Butkara, and a carving of Buddha in the rock at Jehanabad. There is a Buddhist legend that tells how Lord Buddha, in one of his previous lives as a bodhisattva, sacrificed his life in order to receive just one verse of holy teachings here. This region is the birthplace of Guru Rinpoche. Furthermore, in this region Saraha, Tilopa and others of the Eighty-Four Mahasiddhas achieved great and profound powers. They also found all the Vajrayana doctrine here. One part of the mountains of this area is reputed to be a secret treasury of the whole Vajrayana library of teachings. Someone who is fully enlightened can receive transmission of these teachings there. However, it remains simply a rocky mountain for ordinary people. Vajrayogini came from the country of Oddiyana, and during the time of the Eighty-Four Mahasiddhas the women in the local villages were said to be her emanations. When the Tibetan Mahasiddha Orgyenpa (1230–1309 CE)[9] went to Oddiyana on a pilgrimage, a local lady cooked him a bowl of soup, and on drinking this he realized enlightenment. The great Tibetan scholar Gendun Chopel[10] later visited the region. He said that although he did not see or receive blessings from any dakinis, he did meet very pretty girls who were the great-grand nieces of Vajrayogini. He claimed he was sure that the Swat valley was ancient Oddiyana as he could find no other place that could have been. He also wrote many geographical accounts of holy Buddhist places. Therefore, Oddiyana is a very important place as it is the Vajrayana equivalent to Sarnath.

Great experiences such as these have only happened to those who have achieved enlightenment, however, it is very good for ordinary Vajrayana practitioners to make this pilgrimage. Whilst there, I think that they should perform large rituals such as those of Chakrasamvara, Guhyasamaja or Vajrayogini, with extensive ganachakra offerings, and thus receive strong purification and blessings for quick improvements in their Vajrayana practice. Gendun Chopel warned pilgrims to this area to be careful of the tribal people as they may throw stones or try to kill people. Therefore, one needs not only to have a valid visa but also to travel in a group when visiting the Swat valley. It is very sad that great Vajrayana masters no longer visit Oddiyana, home of the Vajrayana; therefore, I am making special mention of it here.

In the thirteenth century, Sakya Pandita and some Kagyupa scholars had differing views about the benefits to ordinary people of visiting these places. Sakya Pandita[11] said that those who have achieved a certain level of realization in Vajrayana practice have to visit them, but that ordinary practitioners will only meet with hindrances, for example local demons and hardships, or at best gain nothing from their visit. He said that those who go to a holy place for the purpose of practice receive more blessing than other visitors, and that if one's purpose is not spiritual there is no receipt of blessings no matter where one goes. For example, the many herdsmen living in the area surrounding Mount Kailasha receive no particular blessing. It is very important for those who are training in Vajrayana practice to perform the mandala ceremony of deities such as Hevajra, Kalachakra, Chakrasamvara, and Yamantaka when visiting these places, as well as ganachakra pujas and meditation.

The twenty-four holy places correspond to the inner twenty-four chakras of the Vajrayana subtle-body; for example, Jalandhara relates to the crown of the head, and Oddiyana to the left ear. When seeking to liberate each chakra point one must go to the corresponding holy place and make contact with all the dakas and dakinis who can help lead one to enlightenment quickly, in this very lifetime.

In Sikkim, famous for its many secret Guru Rinpoche and dakini caves, there is one place that is particularly special. In Bhutan, there is Guru Rinpoche's Dorje Drollo cave, called the 'Tiger's Nest' (Tib. Paro Taktsang), and near Bhumtang there is an imprint of his body in the rock of a cave. Also in Bhutan are the monasteries of the great Nyingma masters Longchenpa and Pema Lingpa. Bhutan and Thailand are the only two remaining countries in the world that are actually Buddhist royal kingdoms.

In Tibet is the famous Mount Kailasha that is important to both Hinduism and Vajrayana Buddhism. Here Lord Buddha miraculously left a footprint in rock at each of the four corners of this mountain, and it was here also that Milarepa performed many miracles. Nearby is lake Manasarowara and the Jambu tree from which the archaic name for India, Jambudvipa, is derived. Mount Kailasha was regarded as the centre of the universe in ancient mythology. Also known in ancient times as Mount Meru, it is 'Holder of Heaven' for Buddhists. Chakrasamvara, and the Hindu god Shiva and his consort Umadevi, are said to reside here. When Atisha came to Tibet, he could see five hundred arhats residing at Mount Kailasha.

Mount Tsarita in southern Tibet is the holy mountain of Chakrasamvara. These mountains are special for the Kagyupas because this is where Kagyu yogins and yoginis practiced and attained enlightenment in ancient times. There are also many secret places in Tibet that are holy to Padma Sambhava and Milarepa. If one travels in the Kham region of eastern Tibet it would be very beneficial to see some of these holy places. They are important because they are the sites of many events associated with gaining enlightenment, such as enlightened beings performing special ceremonies, or people actually attaining enlightenment, and these activities have imbued the land with blessings. If siddhas have visited there, then others who have high realization and pure vision can contact deities, dakas and dakinis, and receive blessings in these holy places. In this case, ordinary rock, snow and elements disappear, like opening the gate of a temple. Sakya Pandita said that for ordinary practitioners nothing like this happens and they simply see ordinary mountains, rivers and lakes, and feel the cold.

Nearly two thousand years ago two arhats, with white horses carrying the sutras, came to Lo Yung in China. This event marked the beginning of Buddhism in China, and a monastery known as Bai Ma Si (White Horse Monastery) was established here between 58–75 CE. There are four famous sacred Buddhist mountains of China, which are known as The Four Mountains of Great Renown. They are believed to be the dwelling places of the four Bodhisattvas – Avalokiteshvara, Manjushri, Samantabhadra and Kshitigarbha. Putoshan, the first of these, is sacred to Kuan Yin (Skt. Avalokitesvara). It lies in the east on the island of Putuo just to the south of Shanghai. (Putuo is an abbreviation of Potalaka – the Sanskrit name for Avalokiteshvara/Kuan Yin's dwelling place). To the north, near Beijing in Shanxi province, Wutaishan rises to over three thousand metres above sea level. This is the dwelling place of Wenshu (Manjushri). In Tibetan it is known as Riwo Tsenga, or Five Peak Mountain. Omeishan is the third sacred mountain and lies to the west in Szechuan province. This is the dwelling place of Puhien (Samantabhadra). In Tibetan it is known as Langchen Jingri ('Elephant in Standing Posture'). The fourth mountain, Kuhuashan, lies to the southwest of Shanghai in Anhwei province, and is the dwelling place of Titsang (Kshitigarbha).

There are many other Buddhist holy places in China. One of these is the Cave of the Sixteen Arhats – the meditation place of Bodhidharma. One should attempt to locate and visit China's holy places so as to pay homage and receive blessing. In 1987, archaeologists discovered Buddha relics – finger bones of Lord Buddha – dating from the Tang Dynasty. One should try to see and pay homage to these. In Myanmar (Burma), the great golden Shwedagon pagoda in Yangon (Rangoon) is said to contain eight strands of Lord Buddha's hair and some of his nails. It is reputed to have been built during Buddha's lifetime by a Burmese merchant to whom he gave the hairs, and to whom he first taught the Mangalam Sutra. There are also four other important holy Buddhist sites in Myanmar, and, like India, there are many other holy places where Buddha taught. As in other Buddhist countries of pilgrimage, one should visit and pay homage in the holy places, go to special monasteries to make an offering to the sangha, and feed the poor and the sick. These activities establish an energy connection for the pilgrim.

In Indonesia (Skt. Suvarnadvipa) is the very famous Borobudur stupa where Atisha stayed for many years studying the Mahayana doctrine from his teacher Jowo

Serlingpa. Indonesia was a great Mahayana country at that time. It is referred to in ancient history as Grain Island, one of the many islands around Jambudvipa. The Tibetan scholar and Dzogchen master Melong Guru thought this is where Lord Buddha first taught the Kalachakra.

Thailand is another Buddhist country. In the capital city of Krung Thep (Bangkok) is the main temple of the king that houses the Emerald Buddha, said to have been made by the god Indra and to equal the value of the whole of Jambudvipa. If Buddhists visit, they should pay homage. Old Nihon (now Japan) and Cauli (now Korea) also have holy temples and stupas. Tibetan histories say that after the two arhats brought the sutras out of India to China, one of them flew miraculously through the air to Cauli, an event that was a blessing omen for the establishment of Buddhism in Korea. Also, at Bamiyan in Afghanistan there was a giant standing Buddha carved into the sandstone cliffs that was the tallest Buddha image in existence. All the old Buddhist kingdoms have historical relics that carry great blessings, and so whoever wants to make a long pilgrimage to pay homage and accumulate blessing, should travel around to these places.

I have mentioned the important places for pilgrimage here, but if one wishes to make a more extensive pilgrimage, more detailed information can be found about individual countries. It would be beneficial for future generations if someone would one day compile a detailed written record of all the Buddhist holy places, including their locations and good directions for travelling to them. One should try to go on a pilgrimage and practice in each place for at least some hours or days. It is especially good to pray for peace and the increase of happiness and prosperity for all sentient beings. Also, to collect a little dust or stones from each site brings numerous blessings. This collection should be brought back to one's own monastery, Dharma centre, or home and put into stupas and statues. This brings together the blessing energy of all the holy places visited and also blesses the place to which it has been brought, so that it too becomes a holy place. All prayers of dedication are very important. One should share all the merit of one's individual good deeds and those of all sentient beings, for the benefit of all beings. Mahayana practitioners especially should make as many wishing prayers for the benefit of all beings as possible, such as *The King of Aspiration Prayers*, the *Bhadracharya Pranidhana*. It is especially important to meditate on the Four Limitless Thoughts for all sentient beings to be free from suffering and hindrances, to quickly become enlightened, and for all to have happiness, health, and the causes of happiness. As the power of prayers made by ordinary people cannot compare with that of enlightened beings it is best to pray,

> "Just as for all the buddhas and bodhisattvas of the past, present and future, the seed of bodhichitta was first established, and then the long duration of their practice of the six perfections for sentient beings led to their achievement of full enlightenment, may I myself, in the same way, lead

all sentient beings, not a single one excluded, to enjoy both temporary happiness and the permanent experience of enlightenment."

One should also pray for the blessing of each of these holy places to help bring one's wishing prayers to fulfillment. With this as the main prayer, one should then do as many wishing prayers as possible. It is very important when one visits these holy places to refrain from doing, or even entertaining the thought of doing, any of the ten negative actions. One should make an offering to the local main temple and to the monks and nuns, and give to beggars wherever one goes even if one can give only a tiny amount such as a dime. One should prepare ahead of time by keeping plenty of small change on hand. It is difficult for people who come from lucky and wealthy countries to really know the suffering of people who are starving, because they have no experience of real suffering themselves. When one has no possessions left and no food, each day brings so much worry. There is no choice of diet; if one is lucky one eats, and therefore becomes very unhealthy and endures great mental suffering. One also has to live in the worst places because one is homeless. This is created basically by the individual's previous bad karma (actions) such as having been greedy, covetous, or having despised others. It is a life of constant suffering, where even if one is able to find some food for oneself and one's family for today, one must then worry about tomorrow. Because of this even a mere five cents bring happiness equal to that of a rich person being given one hundred dollars. When I was young, I went on pilgrimage in Tibet and I was sometimes hungry on the long journey along very difficult roads. The weather was very bad. I had to beg at the doors of strangers for a little tsampa or tea when I was hungry and thirsty, and dogs were very aggressive. I was very happy if someone would give a little tsampa or tea, it would taste quite delicious! If no one gave anything I would feel very upset. Therefore, I have experience of these feelings myself.

If one has been left very sick and in pain from an accident, and someone is kind enough to administer medicine or bandages, or to take one to the doctor or to hospital, then a deep feeling of gratitude arises and one feels the need to thank one's benefactor many times over. Similarly, if one does not know the language of a country and has to deal with difficult situations, such as officials in a visa office who have rude facial expressions and do not want to listen, it makes one feel very happy if someone helps, and, again, one repeatedly expresses thanks. When you have had some experience of the needs of others then it becomes easy to give. Even if you do not want to give something, it is important not to be rude. Beggars are human beings and are not our enemies, so why should we be rude to them?

The histories of the Mahayana saints of ancient times tell how even though they had no worldly possessions and were very poor, if they met someone in need, they would willingly give even their own flesh and blood to help. Nowadays we may not be able to practice to this extent but one should always give something. Always try to be more generous in attitude and be careful not to allow one's helpful inclinations to diminish. If someone requests medicine, one should help. If people are begging for money, one should try to overcome any reluctance or negativity. Some people do not like to give money to young beggars as they feel that these people should be able to work. This may be somewhat true in affluent countries where, in general, everyone has a better chance to work hard and become successful. However, for those living in developing countries, especially when the country itself is basically very poor and has a weak economy, it is very hard to improve one's lot. Many people lose all hope in the face of their difficulties. The result of this is that apathy increases, they become poorer, and eventually they become beggars. The combination of this unavailability of work, loss of drive, and mental and physical sickness results in tremendous suffering, and so one should be generous. The Mahayana doctrine says that one should give even to the rich and comfortable if they beg.

Lama Kalu Rinpoche[12] gave food to beggars in Bodhgaya, for example, and many wealthy Dharma people also do this. I rejoice very much in this compassionate activity. I pray that I too will be able to do this in the future, and further "May I be able to stop all begging and feed all the other beings in the universe who suffer in this way, may I give organs and blood to all who need them, and may I be able to turn all my energy of body, speech and mind into beneficial things for all sentient beings," just as is described in the Bodhicharyavatara. In this Mahayana practice the bodhisattva's wishing prayers create all the benefits needed by sentient beings, such as doctors and medicine for the sick, food and water for the hungry and thirsty, fire and warmth for the cold, houses or caves for the homeless, cooling winds for the hot, light to dispel darkness, friends for the lonely, gems for ornaments, and so on. The arising of these things is the ripening fruit of the wishing prayers of past Buddhas and Bodhisattvas, and if we also make such wishing prayers, we are providing these benefits for the future.

NOTES

INTRODUCTION

1. Shravakayana includes all the early (non-Mahayana) schools of Buddhism, that separated into eighteen sects. In the Tibetan Buddhist tradition, the Theravada is characterised as one of the four principal of these Shravaka systems alongside Mahasamghika, Sarvastivada, and Sammatiya. Of all these, the only one that has continued to the present day is the Theravada (Eng. 'The Doctrine of the Elders'). The elements of the Shravaka system present in Tibetan Buddhism are predominantly derived from Sarvastivada as in its Vinaya ordination lineage and half of its Abhidharma.

2. The Four Noble Truths are: the truth of suffering, the truth of the causes of suffering, the truth of the cessation of suffering, and the truth of the path.

3. The Eightfold Noble Path comprises: right view, right thought, right speech, right effort, right livelihood, right mindfulness, right concentration, and right action.

4. Samsara (Tib. khorwa) may be translated into English as 'cyclic existence.' This is the vicious cycle of the continual rebirth of beings into the six realms of existence, wherein individual beings are led by their previous karma (action, cause and effect). The wheel of existence is frightful and fraught with the sufferings of birth, sickness, old age, and death. It arises from a state of ignorance, in contrast to the state of liberation. The basis of samsara is the five skandhas (aggregates) of form, feeling, perception, formations and consciousness. The essential characteristic of samsara is pain and suffering. It is beginningless and endless. It cannot liberate itself by itself, as the night cannot dispel the night but applying the antidote to samsara reveals the possibility of liberation. In the moment of liberation there is no more samsara; it has disappeared.

    Such is the basic view. The subtle view is that the basis of samsara is luminosity. Samsara is therefore like a dream state; neither is there an intrinsically existent nirvana.

5. Karma means action. This includes every action of body, speech, or mind, performed by people or other sentient beings. While these actions may be positive

or negative, or done consciously or unconsciously, all of them continually create positive or negative results according to the condition of each action. Karma is thus like the 'genetic code' of samsara and the 'illustrator' of the samsaric world.

6. Arhat means 'foe destroyer'. This refers to one who has liberated himself from the cycle of birth, aging, sickness and death, and attained the state of liberation through the elimination of the obstruction to liberation inherent in the disturbing emotions and primitive beliefs about reality.

7. The notion that the perceiving subject and the perceived objects have true existence when, in fact, they are devoid of such a reality.

8. The four kayas are otherwise known as the four bodies of Buddha:
    1. Svabhavikakaya – the intrinsic body
    2. Jnanadharmakaya – wisdom truth body
    3. Sambhogakaya – complete enjoyment body
    4. Nirmanakaya – emanation enjoyment body

(Tsepak Rigzin, *Tibetan-English Dictionary of Buddhist Terminology*, Library of Tibetan Works and Archives, 1986)

A BRIEF BIOGRAPHY OF KARMA THINLEY RINPOCHE

1. Trizin: 'Tri' has two meanings: holder of the Sakya Dharma throne and therefore the head of all the Sakya; and holder of the temporal throne, the erstwhile political ruler of Tibet, a position made as an offering to Sakya Trizin Chogyal Phakpa (1235–1280) by his student, the Emperor Kublai Khan.

Chapter 1
NON-SECTARIANISM

1. Nagarjuna, who was born in southern India around the first century of the Common Era, was the greatest of all Buddhist philosophers. Early in his career, having received the transmission of the *Perfection of Wisdom Sutra*, he established the Madhyamaka philosophical school in which the definitive meaning of Lord Buddha's teaching was explained as the exposition of the true nature of reality beyond all extremes of one-sided views. His numerous works include such texts as the *Mulamadhyamakakarika*, the *Ratnavali* and the *Suhrlekha*. His major disciple was the scholar Aryadeva, who did much to further the Madhyamaka school.

NOTES

2. Shes rab snying po'i mdo in *Wa na dpal sa skya'i zhal don* (Central Institute of Tibetan Higher Studies: Varanasi, 2001), 164.

Chapter 2
MILAREPA

1. In the 'new tantra' tradition of Tibetan Buddhism, adhered to by the Sakya, Kagyu and Gelug schools, the sambhogakaya buddha Vajradhara is regarded as the primordial buddha (Tib. Sangjay dangpo; Skt. Adi-Buddha), who is responsible for the initial promulgation of the tantric transmissions.

2. 'Full enlightenment', as used in a Buddhist sense, means full buddhahood, beyond worldly being. The term enlightenment applies to those who have attained the first bhumi and beyond, where Mahamudra and Dzogchen are completely realized; beyond any worldly stage of mind. It cannot be applied to (the experience) of ordinary practitioners because 'ordinary' means that they are not yet purified of defilements and have not yet accumulated enough merit. In contrast, 'Sangyay' (Tibetan for Buddha), indicates full purification and accumulation of merit.

3. G.C. Chang, *The Hundred Thousand Songs of Milarepa*, Shambhala, 1977, Vol. 1, p. 25.

4. Samaya (Tib. damtsik) is the sacred bond or commitment established at the time of receiving Vajrayana empowerment, transmission and teaching. Although the samaya commitment is wide-ranging, covering the yoga and anuttara-tantra fourteen root and eight minor, downfalls, its principal focus is the relationship between guru and disciple. Thus, the disciple maintains his or her connection to, and reverence for, the sacredness of the teaching through unswerving devotion to the guru.

5. Padma Sambhava, also known as Guru Rinpoche, was the Indian Dharma master of primary importance in the introduction of Buddhism to Tibet during the so-called 'Early Diffusion' of Buddhism, that took place in the eighth century CE. His transmission of various cycles of tantric instruction subsequently became the core teachings of the Nyingma ('ancient') tradition of Tibetan Buddhism. According to Nyingma doctrine, Padma Sambhava is the embodiment of the Buddhas of the past, present and future, and specifically the emanation-body (Tib. Tulku) of Buddha Amitabha.

6. Dakini (Tib. khandroma; Eng. sky-goer). A class of female mystic beings who may be divided into three principal categories: (a) the 'simultaneously-born' da-

kinis who are manifestations of the sambhogakaya; (b) the 'realm-born' dakinis who dwell in sacred places located in India; and (c) 'mantra-born' dakinis who are spiritually realized female tantric practitioners.

7. Tathagatas – literally 'those who have gone to suchness' – an epithet of a fully-enlightened Buddha.

8. Drogon Rechen (1148–1218) was the great disciple of Karmapa Dusum Khyenpa (1110–1193), who held the lineage of Mahamudra after his master's passing. He subsequently passed it to his disciple Pomdrakpa, who in turn transmitted it to the second Karmapa lama, Karma Pakshi (1206–1283). See Karma Thinley, *The History of the Sixteen Karmapas of Tibet*, Prajna Press, Boulder, 1980, p. 45.

9. Jambuling, literally 'Rose Apple Island', the southern continent in each of the one billion worlds comprising the 'Endurance' world system and equated to India in our world.

Chapter 3
REFUGE

1. The six realms of cyclic existence are those of the gods, asuras (jealous gods), humans, animals, pretas (hungry ghosts), and the hells. See Mipham Rinpoche, *Gateway to Knowledge*, Rangjung Yeshe, 2001.

2. Asanga, the third/fourth century Kashmiri Mahayana philosopher was, along with his brother Vasubandhu, the founder of the Yogachara school of tenets. His major works, based on Lord Buddha's 'third turning of the Wheel of Dharma', include the *Abhidharmasamuccaya* and the *Mahayanasamgraha*. In addition, Asanga received five profound teachings such as the *Uttaratantrashastra* from bodhisattva Maitreya in Tushita. These five texts are known collectively as 'The Five Dharmas of Maitreya'.

3. The five negative emotions (Tib. nyonmong; Skt. klesa) are ignorance or delusion (Tib. timuk; Skt. moha), passion (Tib. dochag; Skt. raga), aggression (Tib. zhedang; Skt. dvesa), pride (Tib. ngagyal; Skt. mana) and envy (Tib. tragdog; Skt. irsya).

4. Kadam. The Kadam tradition originated in the eleventh century CE from the teachings of the Indian master Atisha (979–1054) and his main Tibetan disciple Dromtonpa (1005–1064). Atisha emphasized the practice of sutra and tantra in a

'graded path' and also transmitted a series of instructions for meditation on bodhichitta known as 'mind-training.' Although to all intents and purposes the Kadam sect ceased to exist after the fourteenth century, its teachings have been preserved by the Kagyu and Gelug schools.

5. Drakpa Gyaltsen (1147–1216) was the third of the five founding patriarchs of the Sakya tradition. Son and disciple of Sachen Kunga Nyingpo, he was of great importance in spreading the teaching of 'The Path and its Fruit'. Drakpa Gyaltsen's mastery of the tantras led to his being recognised as Vajradhara by his contemporaries.

6. The fourth century philosopher Dignaga was the greatest master of logic and epistemology in Buddhist history. Originally from a brahmin family in southern India, Dignaga studied the Sautrantika and Chittamatra tenet-systems with such masters as Vasubandhu. Having established his reputation as a master of debate at Nalanda University, Dignaga composed a number of works setting out his revolutionary system of logic, a system which was later extended by Dharmakirti.

7. The bodhisattva Maitreya is the next Buddha and thus the fifth of the one thousand Buddhas to appear in the fortunate aeon. At present he dwells as regent of Sakyamuni Buddha in the heaven of Tushita, where he teaches the gods of that realm.

8. Maitreya, *Mahayanottaratantrashastra*, Rumtek, Sikkim, India, n.d. 4A-4B.

9. The ten perfections (Skt. paramitas) are: generosity, morality, patience, diligence, meditation, wisdom (Tib. sherab), skillful means, wishing-prayer (Tib. monlam), power, and primordial wisdom (Tib. yeshe).

10. The bhumis are the ten successive spiritual levels traversed by bodhisattvas on the path to Buddhahood once they have transcended worldliness. Lord Buddha explained the qualities and practices inherent to each level in such discourses as the Dashabhumika. Later, Candrakirti gave a detailed analysis of the bhumis in his Madhyamakavatara.

11. Siddhis: Mundane and transcendental accomplishments achieved through Vajrayana practice. See Lama Jampa Thaye, *Diamond Sky*, Rabsel Publications, 2023.

12. See Lama Jampa Thaye, *Garland of Gold*, Rabsel Publications, 2022, pp.10-12.

13. Maha Sandhi (equivalent to the Tibetan term Dzogpa chenpo) is the most important doctrine of the Nyingma tradition. According to Atiyoga teaching, all dharmas of cyclical existence and nirvana are fundamentally empty. Since everything is therefore perfect as it is, liberation arises naturally, without need for acceptance or rejection.

14. Saraha was one of the greatest of the Mahasiddhas (Tib. drupthop; Eng. 'perfected one'), the Buddhist tantric saints, traditionally eighty-four in number, who flourished during the medieval period in India. Saraha received the transmission of Mahamudra (Tib. Chagja chenpo; Eng. 'Great Seal') directly from the bodhisattva Ratnamati and was thus the first human guru in the lineage. Amongst his numerous works, the *Doha Trilogy*, a cycle of songs directly pointing out the nature of mind, has been especially vital in the on-going transmission of Mahamudra.

15. Saraha, *Doha mDzod kyi gLu* in 'byams-mgon Kong-sprul, ed. *gDams-ngag mDzod*, pub. Dingo Chentze, Delhi, 1979, Vol. 7, p. 12.

16. Maitreya, *op. cit.*, p. 17A.

17. Maitreya, *op. cit.*, p. 4A

18. sGam-po-pa, *Dam-chos Yid-bzhin gyi Nor-bu Thar-pa Rin-po-che'i rGyan*, Rumtek, Sikkim, India, n.d., p. 172A.

19. The Chakravartin (Tib. Khorlo gyurwa) king is a universal monarch whose activity is dedicated to the maintenance and propagation of the Dharma. Whilst such rulers as Dawa Zangpo, the king of Shambhala, and Gesar, the king of Ling, may be regarded as prototypes of the Chakravartin king. Historical figures such as Ashoka in India and Trisong Detsen in Tibet may also be said to have displayed some of the characteristics of such a monarch, in that their reigns saw the establishment of great civilizations based on the Dharma.

20. Atisha (979–1053) was the great Bengali Dharma-master who taught in Tibet during the period known as the 'Later Diffusion' of the Dharma. As a scholar and master of all aspects of Buddhist practice, who had studied with innumerable gurus in India and elsewhere, Atisha was uniquely qualified to inspire clarity, stability and order within the Buddhist culture of Tibet, where he was subsequently revered as an emanation of the bodhisattva Manjushri. Through the endeavours of Atisha's chief Tibetan disciple, the layman Dromton (1005–1064), the Kadam sect later crystallized out of the transmission of Atisha's core teachings.

21. Hevajra (Tib. Gye Dorje) is a deity belonging to the anuttara-tantra class and is the principal meditation practice of the Sakya tradition of Tibetan Buddhism.

22. Sakya Pandita (1182–1251) was one of the founding masters of the Sakya tradition and one of the greatest philosophers to appear in the history of Buddhism in Tibet.

23. Sakya Pandita, *Legs-par bShad-pa Rin-po-che'i gTer*, pub. Ngor Phende Rinpoche, New Delhi, 1965, p. 4.

24. Nyingma. The Nyingmas comprise the oldest tradition of Tibetan Buddhism, having their origin in the teachings of the eighth century masters Guru Padma Sambhava and Shantarakshita. Other great masters who contributed to the development of the tradition include the 'omniscient' Longchen Rabjampa (1308–1364) and Jigme Lingpa (1729–1798). The school consists of both ordained and lay practitioners who follow both the unbroken oral-transmission lineages and the teachings in the 'treasures', composed and concealed most usually by Padma Sambhava, and subsequently rediscovered and propagated by predicted 'treasure-finders' (Tib. terton). The principal teaching in the tradition is Atiyoga which represents the pinnacle of the nine-vehicle spiritual path.

25. Gelug. The Gelug tradition of Tibetan Buddhism was founded by the great scholar Tsong Khapa Lobzang Dragpa (1357–1419). In early life Tsong Khapa studied with masters of all the major Tibetan lineages, and received extensive training in philosophical and meditational teachings. Subsequently he attracted many disciples and founded the monastery of Ganden, which became one of the three principal seats of the Gelug tradition. The tradition places emphasis on the 'graded path' to enlightenment (Tib. Lam rim) which was inherited from the Kadam school, and on the importance of careful upholding of the vinaya rules for monastics. In philosophy the Gelug have upheld the viewpoint of the Prasangika Madhyamika as interpreted by Tsong Khapa.

Chapter 4
GENERAL POINTS

1. Tenzing Norgay (1914–1986).

2. The 'four thoughts that turn the mind' (Tib. lodog namzhi) are the contemplation of the preciousness of human birth, impermanence, karma (action, cause and effect), and the defects of samsara.

3. On Lojong (Eng. mind training), see relevant chapter below. Also see, Karma Thinley, *Dispelling the Darkness of Suffering*, Rabsel Publications, 2023.

4. 'Sending and taking' (Tib. tonglen) is the main relative-view meditation technique used in Lojong. Lojong practice also includes ultimate-view meditation, and between-sessions bodhichitta practice supported by pithy reminders, or 'slogans'. The goal is to develop and perfect bodhichitta. Lojong requires lineage transmission (Tib. lung) and explanation from an experienced Buddhist teacher.

5. Dewachen (Skt. Sukhavati) is the 'pure land' or 'buddha-field' of the western direction, wherein dwells the Buddha Amitabha. In the sutras, Buddha explained how the pure land was produced as the actualisation of Amitabha's vows, made while he was a trainee bodhisattva named Dharmakara, to establish a realm wherein beings could without any delay or difficulty achieve Buddhahood. Thus Dewachen (literally 'possessing bliss') is a spiritual environment of the highest felicity. It is the aspiration of numerous Mahayana practitioners to achieve rebirth in this realm at the time of death, either through the tantric practice of consciousness transference (phowa) or through the power of devotion to Amitabha.

6. On Shamatha and Vipashyana see the relevant chapters below.

7. See Chandrakirti, *bpdbU-ma-la-'jug.pa*, Gangtok, 1979. The sixteen emptinesses are: outer emptiness, inner emptiness, emptiness of both outer and inner, great emptiness, emptiness of the beginningless and endless, emptiness of the conditioned, emptiness of the unconditioned, emptiness of emptiness, emptiness beyond extremes, intrinsic emptiness, emptiness of the characterless, emptiness of essence, emptiness of the indispensable, emptiness of the essence of non-entities, emptiness of phenomena, emptiness of specific characteristics.

Chapter 6
LOVING-KINDNESS

1. On The Four Limitless Thoughts see the relevant chapter below.

2. Shantideva, eighth-century poet and Prasangika Madhyamaka philosopher from Nalanda University in India, was one of the greatest figures in Mahayana Buddhist history. His works, particularly his masterpiece, *Adopting the Conduct of a Bodhisattva*, (*Bodhisattvacharyavatara*) serve as a profound guide to the sublime path of a bodhisattva, a path based on the complete blending of compassion and wisdom.

NOTES

3. Shantideva, *Bodhisattvacaryavatara*, Rumtek, Sikkim, India, n.d. p.19B.

Chapter 7
MAHAYANA

1. Nagas (Tib. klu) are snake-like spirits with human torsos and snake-like lower bodies. Typically, they inhabit watery environments and are often associated with treasure, an association which can extend to spiritual treasure, as in the case of the *Prajnaparamita* sutras which they guarded prior to Nagarjuna's making them public.

2. Chandrakirti was the greatest thinker of the Prasangika ('Consequentialist') branch of the Madhyamaka school of tenets. He lived in the seventh century CE. Author of the *Madhyamakavatara* and the *Prasannapada*, Chandrakirti's importance in regard to Madhyamaka is second only to that of Nagarjuna, since through his countering of the Svatantrika syllogistic method of establishing emptiness upheld by Bhavya and other thinkers, he ensured that the Prasangika would be of unparalleled influence in subsequent Buddhist philosophical developments.

3. Chandrakirti, *dbU-ma la-'jugs-pa*, Gangtok, 1979, p. 5.

4. *op cit.*, p. 9.

Chapter 8
MEAT-EATING

1. Quoted in Karma Thinley Rinpoche, *The Telescope of Wisdom*, Ganesha Press, 2009, p.129.

2. A mara is an evil tempter, or demon.

3. The term Bon is often, though not entirely accurately, used to characterize the pre-Buddhist religion of Tibet. Over the last millennium a form of Bon that appears to have been modified by its encounter with Buddhism has developed in Tibetan-speaking regions.

Chapter 9
LOJONG

1. The so-called 'four Kadam deities' are Shakyamuni, Green Tara, Achala and Avalokiteshvara. They were the patron deities most emphasized in the early Kadam tradition.

2. The ancient sciences included five major and five minor fields of study. These cover the following eighteen fields: music, amorous skills, housekeeping, mathematics, grammar, medicine, religious tradition, painting and handcrafts, archery, logic, pharmacology, discipline, reflection on study, astronomy, astrology, magic, history, and storytelling.

3. Bhaisajyaguru is the Buddha manifesting as a teacher of healing in order to bestow medical teachings. In the Vajrayana, the sadhana of Bhaisajyaguru is a widely practiced meditation, bestowing many benefits such as healing, strength and purification upon the practitioner.

4. Mipham Rinpoche (1846–1912) was a great Nyingma master who played an important role in the Rime movement that revitalised Tibetan Buddhism in the last century. Born in eastern Tibet, he studied with such gurus as Patrul Rinpoche (1808–1887) and Jamyang Khyentse Wangpo (1820–1892). Mipham Rinpoche was both a versatile scholar of the sutras and tantras and a creative researcher in such fields as poetics, mythology, alchemy, and medicine. Perhaps his greatest contribution was his systematisation of Dharma teachings into a single coherent structure, a feat evidenced in such works as his celebrated *Gateway to Knowledge*.

5. Dharmakirti was the great Indian philosopher responsible for spreading the tradition of logic established by Dignaga some two generations earlier, a tradition which he had himself received from Dignaga's disciple, Isvarasena. Dharmakirti authored seven renowned treatises on logic, the chief of which is the *Pramanavartika*.

6. Sakya Pandita (1182–1251), the fourth of the five founding patriarchs of the Sakya tradition and recognised by his contemporaries as an incarnation of Manjushri, is one of the greatest figures in the history of Tibetan Buddhism. In his youth he received the essential Vajrayana instructions from his uncle and guru Drakpa Gyaltsen. Subsequently, Sakya Pandita went on to acquire mastery over all extant fields of knowledge, both spiritual and secular, a mastery reflected not only in his spiritual attainments but also in his introduction to a Tibetan audience

of such disciplines as logic, poetics and lexicography. His numerous works, such as the *sDom.gsum Rab.dbye* (*Discriminating the Three Vows*) and *Tshad.ma'i Rig-pa'i gTer* (*A Treasure of Reasoning*), still exert a major influence on Tibetan Buddhist thought and practice.

7. Sakya Pandita, *Legs-bshad Rin-po-che'i gTer*, pub. Ngor Phende Rinpoche, New Delhi, 1965, p. 4.

8. Shantideva, *Bodhisattvacaryavatara*, Rumtek, n.d. pp. 3B-4A.

Chapter 10
THE FOUR LIMITLESS THOUGHTS

1. Chandrakirti, *op. cit.*, p.5.

Chapter 11
CALM MIND

1. See Chapter 4, Note 2.

Chapter 12
SHAMATHA

1. Shantideva, *op. cit.*, p. 45A.

2. For details of the seven-point position of Vairochana Buddha, see Karmapa Rangjung Dorje, *Phyag-chen Ma-rig Mun-sel*.

Chapter 14
THE POWER OF EMPTINESS

1. The five Jina Buddhas embody the five wisdoms (Tib. yeshe; Skt. jnana) of Buddhahood, which manifest in samsara as the five negative emotions. Each represents the transformation of one of the five psycho-physical constituents (Tib. phungpo; Skt. skandha) into an aspect of enlightened energy. Furthermore, each of the five Buddhas belongs to a specific family (Tib. rigs; Skt. kula) of Buddhahood. Each possesses a specific colour reflecting the quality of their form of spiritual energy and a particular realm or spiritual environment. These correspondences are as follows:

BUDDHA	Vairochana	Akshobya	Ratnasambhava	Amitabha	Amoghasiddhi
FAMILY	Tathagata	Vajra	Ratna	Padma	Karma
WISDOM	dharmadhatu	mirror-like	equality	discriminating	all-fulfilling
AGGREGATE	form	consciousness	feeling	perception	concepts
DEFILEMENT	ignorance	anger	pride	desire	jealousy
COLOUR	white	blue	yellow	red	green
REALM	'og-min	mNgon.dga'	dPal.ldan	Padma brTsegs	Las.rab

Chapter 17
VAJRAYANA

1. Whilst there have been a number of figures named Indrabhuti in Buddhist history, the one alluded to here is the great king to whom Lord Buddha gave the *Guhyasamajatantra*, a teaching specifically designed for lay practitioners, since it represents a skillful technique by which Buddhahood can be attained without the abandonment of worldly responsibilities and desires.

2. The deity Hevajra is the principal meditational deity of the Sakya tradition. The methods for meditation upon this deity originally derive from the *Hevajratantra*, which was revealed by Lord Buddha in the blissful form of Heruka. According to the classification of the tantras followed in the Sakyapa school, Hevajra is a non-dual tantra of the anuttara-tantra ('peerless') class.

3. Chogyal Phakpa (1235–1280) was the fifth of the five founding patriarchs of the Sakya tradition. His principal guru was his uncle, Sakya Pandita, in whose party he had travelled as a child to the Mongol court. After the passing of Sakya Pandita, Phakpa assumed the role of guru to Kublai Khan, leader of the Mongols, whose devotion had been awakened by Phakpa's earlier spiritual attainments. It is said that in return for the bestowal of the great empowerment of Hevajra, Kublai Khan gave his guru temporal power over Tibet. Thus, Phakpa became, in effect, *dharma-raja* and seventy-five years of Sakya rule followed in Tibet.

4. Chandrakirti, *op. cit.*, pp. 4-7.

Chapter 18
THE THREE YANAS

1. The nine principal yanas are: Shravakayana, Pratyekabuddhayana, Bodhisattvayana, Kriyayoga, Upayoga, Yoga, Mahayoga, Anuyoga and Atiyoga, in that order.

NOTES

2. Machig Labkyi Dronma (1055–1149) the peerless yogini who spread the contemplative system of Chod in its sutra, tantra and mahamudra transmissions.

3. The ten wrong actions are: taking life, stealing, sexual misconduct, lying, slander, harsh speech, frivolous speech, covetousness, malevolence and wrong views.

4. See Keith Dowman, *The Divine Madman*, Rider, London, 1980.

5. See Dhongthog Rinpoche, *The Sakya School of Tibetan Buddhism*, Wisdom Publications, 2016.

6. Vidyadhara means holder of the wisdom of the sambhogakaya form of the Buddha, which includes the five kayas and the five jnanas.

Chapter 20
MANDALA

1. The Seven-Fold Prayer, or Seven Limb Payer, comprising prostrations, offering, confession, rejoicing, requesting the turning of the Wheel of Dharma, supplicating the Buddhas not to pass into cessation (parinirvana) and dedication of merit, serves as the preliminary section of many prayers, such as the famed King of Aspiration Prayers.

2. See Lama Jampa Thaye, *Diamond Sky*, Rabsel Publications, 2023, pp 10-11.

3. On this topic see Lama Jampa Thaye, *Patterns in Emptiness*, Rabsel Publications, 2018.

4. The seven qualities of Vajradhara are: devoid of intrinsic nature, great bliss, in union, endowed with the sambhogakaya ('body of enjoyment'), unceasing, compassionate and unobstructed.

Chapter 21
PILGRIMAGE

1. A yojana is equal to 2,500 feet.

2. This account of the fifteen days of miracles was spread in Tibet by the Kashmiri scholar Sakyasri (1127–1225). For a slightly more detailed account see Geshe Wangyal, *The Door of Liberation*, Maurice Girodias, 1973, pp. 78-96.

3. In early 1984, four Tibetan nuns from the Telokpur nunnery took bhikshuni ordination in Hong Kong. It is commonly believed that the bhikshuni lineage never came to Tibet. If this is so, these four were the first Tibetan ladies to receive this ordination.

4. The Situpa line has been one of the senior incarnation lines in the Karma Kagyu tradition. Along with the Shamar and Gyaltsab incarnations, they have acted as regents during the infancy of the Karmapas, the supreme leaders of the school. In addition, the Situpas have been remarkable scholarly and meditational masters in their own rights — most notably the eighth of the line, Situ Chokyi Jungnay (1700–1774), who established the monastery of Palpung.

5. See Keith Dowman, *The Legend of the Great Stupa*, Dharma Publishing, 1973.

6. The Jataka Tales are stories of Buddha's lives previous to his manifestation of Buddhahood. See Aryasura, *The Marvellous Companion*, Dharma Publishing, 1983.

7. See Keith Dowman, *op. cit.*

8. Maharudra: a form of Shiva, here utilised as a symbol of fundamental egotism.

9. On Orgyenpa see G. Tucci, *Travels of Tibetan Pilgrims in the Swat Valley*, Calcutta, 1940.

10. Gendun Chopel was one of the outstanding Tibetan scholars of the modern period. An ex-Gelugpa monk, he authored an important history entitled *The White Annals*.

11. On this see Sakya Pandita, *sDom-gsum Rab-dbye*, pub. Ngawang Topgyal, New Delhi, 1987.

12. The late Kalu Rinpoche (1905–1989) was one of the leading Tibetan meditation teachers of the 20th century. A disciple of the siddha Norbu Dondrup and recognised as an emanation of Jamgon Kongtrul the Great, he was a consummate master of the Karma and Shangpa Kagyu transmissions.

GLOSSARY

B

Baram	'ba.ram
Bardo	bar.do
Be don	sbas don

C

Chaypa dang chayti jugpa	chad.pa.dang.bcas.tu.'jug.pa
Chaypa mepar jugpa	chad.par.med.par.'jug.pa
Chenno	mkhyen.no
Chigcharwa	gcig.char.ba
Chodrak Gyamtso	Chos.grags rGya.mtsho

D

Damngag jedpa	gdams.ngag.brjed.pa
Damtsik	dam.tshig
Dangpo	dang.po
Dawa	zla.ba
Daypa	dad.pa
Dewachen	bde.ba.can
Dochag	dod.chags
Dod kham	'dod khams
Doha	do.ha
Dorje	rdo.rje
Drakpa Gyaltsen	Grags.pa rGyal.mtshan
Drangdon	drang.don
Drebu'i tegpa	'bras.bu'i.theg.pa
Drenpa	dran.pa
Drenpay tob	dran.pa'i.stobs
Drigung Kyopa	Bri.gung sKyob.pa
Drimtu jugpa	bsgrims.tu.'jug.pa
Drolma	sGrol.ma
Drogon Rechen	Dro.mgon Ras.chen
Dromton	'brom.ston
Drukpa	'brugs.pa

Drupthop	grub.thob
Dujay	'du.byed
Dujeypa	'du.byed.pa
Dulwar jaypa	'dul.bar.byed.pa
Dunpa	'dun.pa
Dusum Khyenpa	Dus.gsum mKhyen.pa
Dzogpa chenpo	rdzogs.pa.chen.po
Dzogchen	rdzogs.chen

G

Gampopa	sGam.po.pa
Gelugpa	dGe.lugs.pa
Gendun	dge 'un
Gendun Chopel	dGe.'dun Cho.'phel
Geshe	dge.shes
Gewa'i Shenye	dge.ba'i.bshes.gnyen
Gom rim	sgom.rim
Gompay tob	goms pa'i.stobs
Gopa	rgod.pa
Gye Dorje	kye.rdo.rje
Gyingwa mugpa	'bying.ba.rmugs.pa
Gyingwa gopa	'bying.ba.rgod.pa
Gyopa	'gyod.pa
Gyu'i tegpa	rgyu'i.theg.pa
Gyud	rgyud
Gyundu jogpa	rgyun.du.'jog.pa

J

Jago pung ri	bya.rgod.phung.ri
Jamgon Kongtrul	'Jams.mgon Kong.sprul
Jamyang	'Jams.dbyangs
Jedpa	brjed.pa
Jigten Sumgon	'Jigs-rten gSum.mgon

K

Kachupa	Ka.'bcu.pa
Kadampa	bKa.'gdams.pa
Kagyu	bKa.'brgyud
Kampo Nenang	Kam.po gNas.nang
Karma Chagme	Karma Chags.med

Karma Pakshi	Karma Pak.shi
Karma Thinley	Karma 'phrin.las
Karmapa	Karma.pa
Kazhipa	bKa'.bzhi.pa
Khamtsang	Kham.tshang
Khenpo	mkhan.po
Khorlo	'khor.lo
Khorlo gyurwa	'khor.lo.bsgyur.ba
Khyentse	mKhyen.brtse
Konchog	dKon.mchog
Konchog sum	dKon.mchog.gsum
Kunga Nyingpo	Kun.dga' sNying.po
Kuntak	kun brtags

L

Lam rim	lam.rim
Lama	bla.ma
Lama kadrin chen chenno	bLa.ma.bka.drin.chen.mkhyen.no
Langchen Jingri	glang.chen.'gying.ri
Lantu jogpa	glan.tu.'jog.pa
Legpay Karma	Legs.pa'i sKar.ma
Leylo	le.lo
Lha thong	lhag.mthong
Lobsang	bLo.bzang
Longchen Rabjam	kLong-chen Rab.'byams
Lotsawa	Lo.tsa.ba

M

Marpa	Mar.pa
Martshang	sMar.tshang
Mikyo Dorje	Mi.bskyod rDo.rje
Milarepa	Mi.la.ras.pa
Mipham	Mi.pham
Mogu	mos.gus
Monlam	smon.lam

N

Nampar zhiwar jaypa	rnam.par.zhi.par.byed.pa
Nang jog	nang.'jog
Nekor	gnas skor

Nendo	gNas.mdo
Ngagyal	nga.rgyal
Ngedon	nges.don
Nyampar jogpa	mnyam.par.'jog.pa
Nyewar jogpa	nye.bar.'jog.pa
Nyepa nga	nyes.pa.lnga
Nyingma	rNying.ma
Nyenpo ngon par du gyipa	gnyen.po.mngon.par.du.byed.pa
Nyenpo ngon par du mi gyipa	gnyen.po.mngon.par.du.mi.byed.pa
Nyishang Gurta	sNyi.shang Gur.rta
Nyonmong	nyon.mongs

O

Ogmin	'Og.min

P

Padma Karpo	Padma dKar.po
Patrul	dPa'.sprul
Palpung	Pal.spungs
Phagmo Drupa	Phag.mo.gru.pa
Phakpa	'phags.pa
Phowa	'pho.ba
Phungpo	phung.po
Pomdrakpa	sPom.brag.pa

R

Rabjampa	Rab.'byams.pa
Rechen	Ras.chen
Rechungpa	Ras.chung.pa
Rig	rigs
Rangjung Rigpe Dorje	Rang.'byung Rig.pa'i rDo.rje
Rime	Ris.med
Rimgyipa	rim.gyis.pa
Rinpoche	rin.po.che

S

Sachen	Sa.chen
Sakya	Sa.skya
Sampay tob	bsam.pa'i.stobs
Samten bol chung	bsam.gtan.'bol.chung

Sangjay	sangs.rgyas
Sempa	sems.pa
Shedra	bshad.grwa
Sherab	shes.rab
Shezhin	shes.bzhin
Shezhin gyi top	shes.bzhin gyi.stobs
Shinay	zhi.gnas
Shin jang	shin.sbyangs
Shugseb	Shug.seb
Situ Chokyi Jungnay	Situ Chos.kyi 'Byung.gnas
Surmang	Zur.mang

T

Taklung	sTag.lung
Tang nyom	btang.snyom
Ter	gTer
Terton	gter ston
Thogalwa	thod.rgal.ba
Thopay tob	thos.pa'i.stobs
Tunshi	thun.bzhi
Timuk	gti.mug
Tonglen	gtong.len
Tongnyi nyingjay nyingpo chan	sTong.nyid.snying.rje'i.snying.po.can
Tongdang nyingjay zungjug	stong.dang.snying.rje.zung.'jug
Tragdog	phrag.dog
Trisong Detsen	Khri.srong lDe.brtsan
Trophu	Khro.phu
Trungmase	Trung.ma.se
Tsalpa	Tshal.pa
Tsawa sum	rtsa.ba.gsum
Tsawai lama	rtsa.ba'i.bla.ma
Tsechigtu jaypa	rtse.gcig.tu.byed.pa
Tseme	Tshad.ma'i
Tsolwa mepar jugpa	rtsol.ba.med.par.'jug.pa
Tsondru chyitob	brtson.'grus.kyi.stob
Tsong Khapa	Tsong.kha.pa
Tulku	sprul.sku

W

Wangpo	dWang.po

Y

Yamzang	gYa'.zang
Yelpa	gYel.pa
Yeshe	ye.shes
Yongdrup	yong su grub pa

Z

Zangpo	bzang.po
Zhenwang	gzhan gyi dbang
Zhedang	zhe.dang
Zhiwar jaypa	zhi.bar.byed.pa

EDITORS' BIOGRAPHIES

LAMA JAMPA THAYE is an Englishman who has studied for over five decades under Karma Thinley Rinpoche and other Tibetan masters. Appointed as his dharma-regent by Karma Thinley Rinpoche, he is well-known for his teachings and writings on Buddhism. He holds a Ph.D. in Buddhist Studies and is one of the few Westerners traditionally authorized to teach the Vajrayana.

KARMA NALJORMA (Maggie Fruitman) has studied under Karma Thinley Rinpoche since 1977. Born and raised in England, she lives in Toronto, Canada, with her husband and their family. In this city where Rinpoche resided for over fifty years, they continue to help at Kampo Gangra Drubgyudling, the Tibetan Vajrayana meditation centre founded by Rinpoche in 1973. Karma Naljorma is a graduate of Durham University in the U.K. and the University of Toronto.

ACKNOWLEDGMENTS

Lama Kadrin Chen Chenno!
Thank you Rinpoche for your endless kindness and patience

With gratitude to everyone who helped prepare this book for publication: Lama Jampa Thaye for his careful editing; Ani Tsultrim Zangmo for help transcribing; Soepa Tulku, Ngakpa Senge Dorje, Jetsunma Rigdzin Khandro and Dawa Urgyen for their support; and Benjamin Lister and Dan Hore of Ganesha Press for their additional assistance. Thank you also to John Negru of Sumeru Books for his active focus on Buddhist publication in Canada, as well as his publishing expertise.

Special appreciation and thanks to Namkha Tashi (Christopher Banigan) for the lovely line drawings and cover design.

Thanks also to Kirsty Chakravarty for the cover photograph, taken while Rinpoche was giving the transmission (lung) for Khunu Rinpoche's famous *Verses in Praise of Bodhichitta*.

May whatever merit has been gained in making these teachings available
become the source of enlightenment for all sentient beings,
and serve to spread calm, peace and happiness in all directions.

May all Bodhisattva wishing prayers
made for the benefit of sentient beings
be fulfilled.

www.ingramcontent.com/pod-product-compliance
Lightning Source LLC
Chambersburg PA
CBHW021855230426
43671CB00006B/398